THE SPIRIT OF A MAN

THE SPIRIT
OF A MAN

A VISION OF TRANSFORMATION
FOR BLACK MEN
AND THE WOMEN
WHO LOVE THEM

IYANLA VANZANT

HarperOne
An Imprint of HarperCollinsPublishers

HarperOne

HarperCollins books may be purchased for educational, business, or sales promotional use. For information, please e-mail the Special Markets Department at SPsales@harpercollins.com.

HarperCollins Web site: http://www.harpercollins.com

HarperCollins®, ■®, and HarperOne™ are trademarks of HarperCollins Publishers.

FIRST HARPERCOLLINS PAPERBACK EDITION PUBLISHED IN 1997

Library of Congress Cataloging-in-Publication Data
Vanzant, Iyanla.
The spirit of a man : a vision of transformation for Black men and the women who love them / Iyanla Vanzant. — 1st ed.
Includes bibliographical references.
ISBN: 978–0–06–251239–0
1. Afro-American women—Religious life. 2. Afro-American men—Religious life. 3. Vanzant, Iyanla. 4. Kunle, Awo Oshun. 5. Spiritual biography. 6. Yoruba (African people)—Religion. I. Title.
BV4468.2.A34V36   1996
305.38'896073—dc20   96–12258

23 24 25 26 27 LBC 50 49 48 47 46

In Memory of

Medgar Wiley Evers

who gave his life in the quest of Freedom
and whose Spirit continues to educate and empower
African men and women.

And
My Daddy,

Horace Lester Harris

If I could look you in the eye
I would tell you for the first time in my life, I love you.
Instead, I say it to you in spirit.

This book is also dedicated to Osun.

Osun is a deity in the Yoruba pantheon. She is the consciousness of beauty, laughter, wealth, creativity, and sensuality. In Yoruba belief, the energy of life called Osun is the needle that was used to weave together the fibers of the world. Osun represents unity. The presence of Osun is represented by unity of the mind, body, and spirit, the unity of people, and the uniform process of life. Osun is the presence of love.

In Yoruba culture, women pay homage to Osun when they are ready to receive a husband or to conceive a child, or when their physical health is failing. It is believed that Osun is the energy that travels through the blood. She is the foundation ingredient in all medicine and the energy that promotes internal healing. Yoruba men pay homage to Osun before they go to hunt or to war; they believe that asking her blessings will ensure their success. When men are in difficulty with authorities or their wives, they beg for Osun's pardon. She is the energy of the river, sweet water. Her presence is the sweetness that warms the heart. When men need money or business to provide for their families, they make offerings to Oṣun. She is the matron of the family, the one who brings and keeps the bloodline together.

Oṣun's favorite food offering is honey. Her color is yellow. She is the matron of the metal gold. Her number is five, representing change, emotions, fertility, and expansion. She is the source of the feminine energy that guides me. I am certain that she is the force that has guided me in preparing these words to share with you. She has taught me the power of unity within myself and among people.

> *A'dupe Iya Mi!* (I salute you, my mother!)
> *Okan Tutu.* (We are one heart.)
> I love you, *Iya Mi.*
> I thank you, Oṣun.
> May your divine energy come alive in the consciousness
>   of all whose eyes scan these words.
> And So It Is.
> *Ache! Ache! Ache!*

This book is also dedicated to all the men who loved me without question, without condition, and without expectations, demonstrating what the love of a "good man" can really do for you:

Awo Oṣun Kunle, my godfather, brother, friend;
Adeyemi Bandele, the first man to hold my hand;
Nana Ayibanwaah Bambara-Abban VII, my long-distance brother;
George Brown, my wise old uncle;
Alex Morgan, who just showed up one day and stayed;
Ron Norwood, who always knew and never said a word;
Ralph Lewis Stevenson, who knew and talked about it;
George "Hakim" Anderson, who guessed;
Bobbie Stevens, who accepted;
Michael Cornelius, who pulled it from the inside;
Louis (Sky Man) Morris, who taught me what to do with it;
Henry "Hank" Rucker, who adopted me;
Cody Anderson, who saw it in me and taught me how to use it;
Rev. Michael Beckwith, who said it louder;
Basil Farrington, who knew just how to say it;
Richard Whiten, who knew just what to say;

Damon Keith Vanzant, who didn't have to say it;
Lumumba and Kobi Bandele, who didn't know how to say it;
Heshimu Jaramogi, who said it once and never said anything else;
Oluwalomoju Adeyemi Vanzant, my biggest, brightest, and
best grandson;
and
Yusef Harris, my other half, who didn't know what to say.
All of you have taught me I Am Love!

CONTENTS

births. Black men are a continuation of the lives of those who lived in another time and place. The cellular memory of the ancestors guides Black men today.

Atonement is often referred to as "at-oneness." At one with God. At one with the spirit within. At one with all others. At-oneness is a function of living life from a foundation of a spiritual identity, grounded in spiritual principles, in pursuit of a spiritual purpose. The result is a being at one with universal power.

ACKNOWLEDGMENTS

In writing this book I would like to acknowledge Dr. Edison O. Jackson, president of Medgar Evers College of the City University of New York, for your support and encouragement and the "divinity" you have brought to the institution; Mrs. Myrlie Evers-Williams for your tenacity in keeping the spirit of Medgar alive; my friend and good conscience Mrs. Marjorie Battle, who never allows me the luxury of whining or complaining; Rev. Willie Wilson of Union Temple Baptist Church, Washington, D.C., for reminding me to "Keep the Fire Burning"; Rev. Frank Reid, pastor, Bethel A.M.E. Church, Baltimore, MD, who taught me to put on the whole armor of God; Denise Stinson, my agent, for her unwavering support of this project; Kandace Hawkinson and Barbara Moulton, my editors, for their patience with my process, and Dawn Daniels, my editor in spirit; Damon Keith Vanzant, my son, for being mᵛ spiritual guinea pig" and providing me with such valuable research information; my team of sister-friends at Inner Visions Spiritual Life Maintenance, Gemmia Vanzant, Ebun Adelona, Mama "Muhsinah" Berry Dawan, Adara Walton, Amalsi Zulu, Judith Hakimah, Janet Barber, and Lucille Gambrell, who continue to hold me up; Joia "Louise" Jefferson of In the Public Eye, my publicist, my friend, and my mirror, I truly could not have completed this without you; Ken Kizer, my rebirther, who kept me sane throughout this process, and his wife, Rene Kizer, who keeps him sane; and God the Father/Mother for continually reminding me to get out of the way, because "I of myself can do nothing."

Mighty Stream
(for Priestess Vanzant)

The truth pours from your lips
with a clear and certain sound;
pure as sparkling water
when you taste it;
breathtaking as real beauty
when you face it; Or,
hear it in your heart.
As raindrops
force the river to rise,
you speak to potentials asleep inside
with power that inspires
and invigorates
as it shakes awake
what is Black and Great,
Glorious and Bold,
in my Soul.
I hear echoes
of my Ancestors speaking
of pyramids,
Ashanti gold
and Yoruba rituals of old
and new;
I hear all things precious
and beautiful
flowing from you.

—Michael Green
January 1, 1994, A.M.

(This poem was written by a brother while he was incarcerated. He heard me speak during a radio interview. I received his letter and this poem several days before I completed this manuscript.)
Thank you, Michael.

MY BROTHER'S KEEPER

The gift of life is God's gift to you.
What you do with your life is
your gift to God.

Awo Oṣun Kunle is my godfather. His back is the ladder upon which I ascended in my spiritual growth and development. For twenty-five years he has been a servant of Orisa, a priest in the Yoruba tradition, dedicated to the service of the deity Oṣun. Six years ago, he was initiated, ordained as a high priest, a *Babalawo*, which means "Father of Mystery." Today, as an adviser to many junior priests and a counselor to thousands of nonpriests, Oṣun Kunle is the walking embodiment of the Yoruba proverb "No one knows the mysteries that lie at the bottom of the ocean." My godfather recognizes that he is a spiritual being. He has dedicated most of his life to identifying, understanding, and making peace with the mysteries of life and spirit. He is at one with his spiritual self. He has been able to integrate his spiritual understanding into a practical concept through which he addresses the day-to-day issues of living. By watching him and being guided by him, I too have come to understand the mystery and conflicts that African American men face and live to heal.

I met my godfather when I was eleven years old. His sister and I were best friends. I spent so much time at their home, his parents practically raised me and he became my older brother. When I had a performance in school, he was there. When I had problems in school or at home, he was there. When I needed advice, guidance, or straightening out, he gave it to me, openly, honestly, and lovingly. When I got pregnant at age sixteen, Oṣun Kunle stopped being my brother. He became my father—the father I needed and never had as an active participant in my life. He taught me that my body could fail but my spirit could not. He examined, and in some cases denounced, my behavior but left me, my spirit, intact. He let me know that no matter what I did or did not do, he loved me because I was his spiritual child, and that he would always be there for me, spirit to spirit.

I was separated from my godfather for many years. When I saw him again, he had been initiated into the priesthood. I noticed the change. It was subtle, almost unidentifiable—but you know when there is something different about your "father." Years later, I realized those changes were the manifestations of a cultural identity. The initiation, his training in the priesthood, his exposure to a culturally philosophical construct had transformed him from a Black man in America to a spiritually astute cultural custodian for the descendants of Africans in America. He was no longer concerned with the constructs and limitations of the society. He was standing on the backs of the ancestors. He was taller. He was stronger. I was not ready, nor did I understand the change.

Another separation followed this brief reunion with my godfather. This time, it was by my own design. I was not ready to surrender, to give up my materialistic, ego-centered lifestyle to embrace a life philosophy of spiritual constructs and principles. I was very busy struggling, suffering, trying to make it as a Black woman. I did not want anyone to tell me what to do or how to do it. I had no concept of what being a spiritual being or a being of African descent had to do with my day-to-day living. I was looking for personal freedom, political equality, and a good man, things I thought were being taken away or in some way denied. My godfather was talking culture, discipline, and spiritual evolution. I thought he had lost his mind.

By the time we saw each other again, I had been initiated into the priesthood. Without skipping a beat or asking any questions, he took me into his tutelage. He began to teach me the mysteries and protocols of being a priest. A master herbalist, a well-grounded student of astrology, a keeper of the culture, and a spiritually sensitive master, Oṣun Kunle guided me through the most difficult transformation of my life: from a physical being to a spiritual being. It was indeed a difficult process. I was not always obedient to the things my godfather said and taught me. I did not understand the Yoruba proverb "Old eyes have wider vision." I had my own way of seeing things. I had good reasons for hanging on to mental restrictions, emotional limitations, and frailties of humanness.

My godfather never argued with me. He was neither aggressive nor demanding. He never pushed or prodded me to accept "his way." Nor did he ever insist that I do anything because he said to do it. He always gave me the opportunity to choose. When I made poor choices, he instructed me on how to bring myself back into balance. He gave me the truth in such a simple and concise way. It cut through my flesh and bones into my soul. When I disobeyed his gentle advice, he would simply "nut up," thereby allowing me the opportunity to see the error of my ways and learn from my own mistakes. Inevitably, every time I messed up, it would be something he had told me, taught me, or given to me that would bring me back to my senses.

Today, when people say I am a powerful orator, I say, "No, I am a student of Oṣun Kunle." When I am told how simple and clear my writing is, I say, "Don't thank me, thank my godfather." When people meet me, having heard my tapes or read my work, they always remark, "I thought you were much older." I respond, "I am an old student of Oṣun Kunle." I love my godfather in a way that is indescribable by words. It is an honest love. It is an open love. It is the love between a man and a woman that has opened my eyes to the divine unity of life. This love has brought balance and clarity into my life. It is a divine love inspired and maintained by God. It is the foundation from which I move and breathe every day of my life.

It is not what my godfather has done for me that I love. It is what he has given to me: a philosophy, a concept, a framework for spiritual evolution and living. It is not the way he does things that has given me a concept of manhood. It is what he has been able not to do: he has not become a pawn in life or a victim of the world. Many people, including my own father, did not and do not understand the relationship I have with my godfather. Of course, we have been accused of being lovers. I suspect that is because so many people do not understand how to express love without a physical act. My godfather and I make love in our hearts and minds. Anything else would be incestuous.

I do not like to "share" him with anyone. I know that is a vestige of human-ness I still cling to. I realize he must be shared with the world. He has taught me the true meaning of living as a feminine energy by being a healthy and complete expression of masculine energy. I hope that my words infused with the wisdom of his words will be as healing for you as they have been for me.

INTRODUCTION

*Most people think they know the
answer. I am willing to admit, I don't
even know what the question is.*
                    Arsenio Hall

Thursday, November 25, 1993,
Thanksgiving morning, 6:20
A.M., I was awakened with a
jolt. It was the kind of spiritual experience to which I had become accustomed during the twenty-three years of my journey. I still had a lot
of cooking to do, but this jolt was not about turkey and dressing. I sat
straight up, threw my legs over the side of the bed, and had begun my
usual morning prayer of thanksgiving when it hit me like a thunder-
bolt: *write a book for the spiritual empowerment of Black men.* This
was not the first time the thought had occurred to me. Today, however, my usual arguments of why I could not, would not attempt to do
it were not working. The spirit in me was raging. It would not take no
for an answer this morning. The book would be written. And I would
write it, period. The other part of the message was that if I did not
write it, I would have a very difficult time trying to write anything else.
Why me? That is my usual question when I am prompted by Spirit to
do what I humanly think is impossible to do. The answer was very

clear. Balance. "Everything in life must be balanced. What you do for and give to women, you must do for and give to men."

We, Black men and women, have fallen out of balance. Men have fallen *out* of their hearts into their heads. Women have fallen *over* their hearts into their heads. We have both fallen out of the grace of spirit. We have been conditioned to honor a system of values built on contempt and disrespect for who we are as a community of people. This conditioning has taken us away from certain basic principles that are living memories in our DNA. These principles, which I believe are etched into our subconscious memory, are the keys to our basic nature. As a result of our fall, we are in conflict with both the value system of the society in which we live and our own basic nature. Black men, who instinctually want to stand among the leaders and direct the tides of the living world, often sit in fear of being annihilated, eliminated, or, worse, hung out or left hanging. Black women, who want to stand by or stand up for their male counterparts, have been stepped on or stepped over, accused by the very ones they desire to support of being out of "their place" in an attempt to take over. Although our basic nature is to embrace and support each other while taking the necessary steps toward a collective goal, we have been conditioned to compete with and against each other. We now treat each other as adversaries rather than allies. In all honesty, I for one have been able to identify the very ways and the number of times I have been guilty of this very divisive behavior.

Black men and women struggle to understand and balance our gender roles at home, at work, and within a context of social responsibilities while many of us are at a total loss as to how to balance our individual physical, emotional, and spiritual needs and responsibilities. The instinctual nature of the woman is to give and share, yet our conditioning encourages us to see usury and manipulation around every corner. While men love to be cared for and nurtured by a woman, foreign programming makes Black men suspicious that we are trying to take over, take control. The basic human instinct to be loving and caring is often overshadowed by ego needs, image building, and peer pressure. While Mama and Daddy preach "Do unto others . . ." and "Love thy neighbor . . . ," the world teaches us, "Everyone for himself when we hit the beach!" Fear of losing ground has replaced faith. The urge to give unselfishly is overshadowed by the compulsion to get. Rather than using things to help and serve people, we are taught to use people to get things. In the process, we lose a vital piece of our cultural and spiritual soul. Restoration of what we have lost, which I am calling an imbalance, is critical for Black men because they are the foundation of the Black community.

According to Yoruba culture, an ancient African belief system by which I live, the Father is the sun and the Mother is the moon. While both have an equal share of responsibility in the natural flow and order of life, there is generally greater recognition of the sun. This does not mean that the sun is more important or more powerful. It suggests that there is a conscious level of recognition of the sun's presence, energy, and role. We can see and feel the sun's rays. We are generally asleep when the moon is active. We look up to the sun. Our eyes are most probably closed when the moon rises to its fullest form. Still, these two dynamic powers, the masculine energy of the sun and the feminine energy of the moon, occupy the same space, harmoniously, each performing its function without conflict or competition. If the African American community is to reestablish a sense of peaceful balance, Black men and women must once again learn how to live in harmony. Harmony is a spiritual concept, not a political, economic, or social construct.

The average person notices when the sun is not present in the sky. There is no such acknowledgment when the moon is absent. While the moon controls the tides of the ocean, which comprises 97 percent of the water of the planet, no one notices its absence. It is just taken for granted that the moon is doing "its thing." This society monitors Black men to determine what is and is not happening for them. Black women have been more or less left to their own devices of survival. The monitoring of Black men, and lack of acknowledgment of Black women, is the essence of how we are treated in this society, and is also reflected in the way we treat each other in our interpersonal relationships. In response to conditioning in a society foreign to our basic nature, we have forgotten who we are, altered our roles, and lost our purpose.

In the spiritual universe, we have approached a critical time. This is a time when the spiritual energy and role of the male are quickly changing, desperately needed, and, as in the case of Black men, sorely missed. Black men must shine again. Be warm again. Stand in the face of the woman without fear, anger, or the need to hold on to a competitive edge. The woman must take her place, sometimes silently, doing what she knows she is capable of doing. What she knows she must do and can do whether or not the world cares to notice. The role, energy, and presence of the Black male spirit must be recognized, re-aligned, and honored. Only then can the world community in general, and the African American community specifically, regain balance and order. The major goal of this work is to begin the process of recognition, alignment, and honor of Black men among yourselves.

I began this project by having to admit to myself how frightening it was for me, a woman, to write a book for men. My experience has been that men do not like being told what to do. They are particularly not fond of being told how to be better men. I am willing to admit that I have no conscious memory of what it means to be a man. In meditation, prayer, and other, shall I say, spiritual experiences, I have seen myself as a man. I have been both a Black man and a white man. Today, however, I have no conscious memory of those experiences. What I do have is a great love for, respect for, and intuitive understanding of spirit and spiritual law. This book is a reflection of just that.

I know a great deal about transformation. I have been blessed with the knowledge and ability to transform myself from an ugly, orphaned, abused child into a spiritually conscious Black woman. Then, from being a Black woman into being a child of God. The prefix *trans-* means "beyond" or "over." The core *form* means "body" or "structure." The suffix *-ation* means "action." It is my hope that this book will be embraced as a guide in support of Black men taking action to move and live "beyond their bodies and structures."

This book is about healing. I have studied *A Course in Miracles,* which is a psychological paradigm for facilitating a shift in perception. *The Course* states, "Healing is to make happy." The history and experience of Black men in this country have fostered the belief that Black men cannot, will not, and do not deserve to be happy. The time has come to heal that belief. It is my goal that this book be used as a tool by which Black men heal their relationships: the relationship with their Creator, their inner self; the relationships they have with one another; and the relationship they have with women. Perhaps this is a selfish goal, but I would surely like to have a better relationship with all Black men. In my heart of hearts, I long to see us "at one" again.

I am a priestess, a minister, in the Yoruba tradition. My training in that culture has given me an insight into the spiritual mandates of an ancient civilization. In this book, I will share those mandates. I am a metaphysician. I have studied and understand the principles/energies beyond the physical plane that govern and influence the human/physical experience. This work is an attempt to help others tap into those energies and principles. I am an alchemist, trained in the arts and sciences of transforming energy, the life force. As people change their minds, their energy and lives will change. I will share how to begin that process in the pages of this work.

As a result of my experiences and training as a priestess, metaphysician, and alchemist, I have been able to support and assist individuals in developing their spiritual identity, in understanding their cultural foundation, and in transforming (changing) their consciousness and physical energy as it relates to both of these areas. While the information is readily available to all, African Americans have little experience in working through the spiritual transformation process. This facet of our culture has not been readily available. This part of our identity is rarely explored. It is an identity that we were once forbidden to acknowledge, and now we are not sure of the purpose for acknowledging it or the reason that we must do so.

It seems to me that not enough is being done to provide the Black community with the truth about our spiritual identity. I do not mean religious identity. This we have all been taught and use to keep ourselves separate. I mean spiritual identity, the truth of who we are at the core of our being. Spirituality is the consciously active means by which we can recognize, activate, and live the impartial, nonjudgmental, consistent truth of who we are. This may require that we alter or eliminate some long-held beliefs we now hold dear. For some, this will be too difficult. Some people need to believe that what they believe is right, even at the expense of knowing the truth. This conditioned response allows us to stay limited to what is comfortable and what we have been conditioned to believe. In this way, we are able to mold the truth to match our human concepts and ideals. Spiritually, it is impossible to change the truth. In fact, the foundation of spirituality is *surrender*. To be able to let go and let God do the work through you. If Black men and women are to survive, evolve, and flourish, we must relearn how to surrender to God. We must be willing to examine and question every spiritual value we now hold to be true and affirm, "Let there be light!"

Like Black women, Black men today are the children of those who chose to survive the horrors of history. It was our ancestors' conscious choice not to give in and not to die. As descendants of the parent race, we are genetically coded for genius. More important, we are spiritually encoded for divine evolution. It is not a matter of education, economics, or politics. It is a simple fact of life. At the core of every Black man is a power so awesome it literally boggles the mind. There is a cellular memory of greatness that the Black man cannot allow to lie dormant. Our collective history and current political condition would lead one to believe that this power has been lost. Nothing is ever lost in spirit! The power of spirit never dies! The power cannot be altered. The power is divine. It is the power, the force, the magnificence of the Creator. I cannot for the life of me figure out why no one is telling Black men how to pull up the power of their spirit and put it to work. I guess that is what this book is about.

As a woman dedicated to evolution and the empowerment of women, I am often accused of "tearing down" Black men. Some men have refused to read my work or attend my lectures, which they presume will be male-bashing sessions. Often this misunderstanding is the result of our conditioning to compete with each other. Sometimes, however, it is a reflection of the ego. Too often, men believe that everything women do and think centers around them. Sometime this is true. We do wait to exhale. Some men believe that women should take all their direction from men. As a cultural custodian, I know that this line of thinking is the result of colonization.

African culture mandates that women must be prepared to serve God and live with men. The training I provide for women has very little to do with men, what they think, or what they want. My purpose is to teach women how to use their God-given powers to ensure the survival of the people. My objective is to assist in the development of culturally and spiritually conscious women, who will ultimately unite with culturally and spiritually conscious men to produce children of the same nature. There are times and instances when women must receive their womanhood training in the absence of men. It is secret. It is sacred. The same is true for men. There are also those beautiful instances of sharing, when we come together to grow collectively. We love and trust each other enough to take what we need, to bring ourselves into alignment with one another and shine in the world. Like the sun and the moon, we do our thing individually in order to give collectively.

I guess what this work is really about is my love for Black men. My father, brother, son, grandsons, and soul mate are all Black men. I have been blessed to share moments of my life with them and some other courageous, loving, and generous Black men who will not make the history books. It is because of them, sometimes in spite of them, that I am who I am today. I believe it is my turn to share the knowledge I have received from the masculine energy in my body and the men in my life. It is for that reason alone that I choose to follow the urging of my spirit to produce this work. It is an act of courage for me. Courage most people assume women do not have or should not display. It is the way I believe I can best serve the universe at this time, by sharing what I have learned with others. It is an act of love. As I give love, I will receive it. It is an act of spirit sharing a vital part of itself.

Most important, I write this book for my son, Damon Keith Vanzant, with the hope that I can convey to him all the things I learned after he needed them. I write this book for my grandsons, Oluwalomoju Adeyemi and Adesola, because they will not be more statistics about Black men. I write this book because it is the woman's duty to nurture seeds. I am nurturing the divine seeds in the minds of Black men because I know they must grow. When these seeds grow, the world will be blessed with a powerful cadre of loving, peace-filled, wise Black men who will walk the path of their ancestors. I write because I know the path leads back to God.

I write this book to say simply and plainly what people have been unable or afraid to say. That is, God loves you Black men. He loves you not because you are Black, not because you are men. He loves you because you are made in his image and likeness. You are a part of God. Because you do not realize this, you are dying. As you die, you take a vital piece of God's love and beauty with you. The world needs your light. It needs your love. Every Black woman and child needs you also. I write this book because I am a mother. According to African culture, the mother is the first and most vital teacher. Etched into the memory of my soul are the secrets of the universe, passed on to me from the first mother. My duty as a woman is to pass that information on to the daughters, and to teach it to the sons. This book is my humble contribution to the education of the African sons.

The Beginning

I was telling a sister-friend something a male friend of mine had recently experienced. Driving home at 1:00 a.m., after a few hours with the boys and a few beers at a local bar, he pulled behind a jeep in which three young "brothers" were riding. He started daydreaming while waiting for the light to change, and his car rolled into the back of the jeep. Thinking he had only tapped the jeep, causing no damage, my friend waved apologetically to the men in the jeep. The "brothers" in the jeep jumped out, ran to peer at the rear bumper, and began hysterically cursing because my friend had hit their brand-new jeep with his MG midget.

My friend got out of his car. Seeing there was no damage, he sincerely, meekly, apologized. The "brothers" in the jeep would not hear of it. My friend

1

became a stupid so-and-so, a crazy mf, on and on. "You hit my jeep, man!" My friend explained it was an accident. "No, it wasn't!" My friend hadn't caused any damage. "Yes, you did!" Eventually there was a screaming match. The three young brothers circled around my friend making threatening gestures. Three against one, on a hot summer night, in an urban ghetto, when a status symbol has been encroached, can be a very dangerous situation. My friend, who had been really cool up to that point, now had to prove he wasn't a so-and-so, a punk, or an mf.

As the three stood threateningly around him, he reached into his pocket and produced an ancient phallic symbol, a rusty switchblade knife. He flicked the blade, challenging his opponents, asking, "What you gonna do, punks?" It was just about that time the police arrived. They found my forty-eight-year-old friend standing there with a knife in his hands, confronting three young men who now kept their most deadly weapon, their tongues, absolutely still. Needless to say, my very professional, very well educated friend got arrested. As my sister-friend and I reviewed the incident, we agreed it made absolutely no sense. How could a potty-trained, formally educated, housebroken adult do something so absolutely ridiculous? As I ended the story, I remember saying to my friend, "Men are so stupid!"

As it rolled off my tongue, something in me quickly and forcefully reminded me again, *Your father is a man. Your brother is a man.* My inner dialogue continued, *Well, they are stupid too! They too believe they have to prove how baaad they are!* The spirit within me was poised for the showdown: *Your grandsons are men. Your son is a man. So is your godfather!* That hit home. My father and my brother were one thing. My son, grandsons, and godfather were completely different stories. Yes, they are all males, but there is a difference—or at least I thought there was a difference. Older men should know better, I thought to myself. Then I realized, they do know better. In the hearts and minds of all Black men, you know you can do better and be better; perhaps you just haven't figured out how to get it done. Intuitively, you know you are not what you were divinely created to be.

IF YOU WANT TO
KNOW THE END, LOOK
AT THE BEGINNING

*The Negro race, like all races, is
going to be saved by its exceptional
men.*

                              W. E. B. Du Bois

Let me tell you what I know about Black men. In the beginning, Black men were created spiritually good. This goodness was buried in the core of their being. It was a divine right, not a social title bestowed by human judgments and perceptions. The goodness of Black men is an inborn, natural station, a gift from the Creator. Black men were so very good, all that they did was good. You built civilizations and institutions, and you made remarkable discoveries that continue to influence the world as we know it today. This goodness was passed on from father to son, from generation to generation. As a result, Black men are still good. Anyone who takes the time to make a close examination will discover that Black men are hardworking, family-conscious, loving individuals striving to reach a goal and realize a dream. Black men are well educated, socially and politically astute, good to their wives and mates, dedicated to their children and their communities.

These are average Black men. They are the ones seen daily and known intimately. Unfortunately, as a result of racially charged media stereotyping and social disenfranchisement, society forgets about the average Black man: the police officer, fireman, postal clerk, telephone installer, plumber, mail carrier, service station owner, sales clerk, accountant. In my experience, the average, often-forgotten Black man is not in jail, does not drink wine on the street corner, does not steal, rape old ladies, sire and then abandon his children. You are not dangerous, violent, lost, or in need of a social program to fulfill your basic human needs. You are a child of God, born to fulfill a divine mission. That mission is buried in your soul, the one you lost.

Black men who are good inside and out are concerned about the state of world affairs, the future of your communities, and your own physical and emotional well-being in a hostile society that stigmatizes you because your beginnings, in this part of the hemisphere, stem from an ancestral condition of servitude. The average Black man is not heard. Sometimes you are not heard because you choose not to speak. More often than not, you are not heard because, when you speak, no one takes the time to listen. When a person is not heard above the roar of others, he is not acknowledged. When a person is not acknowledged, he loses his spirit. Spirit in all of its definitions. Spirit meaning God, the all-powerful presence, the omnipotent being. Spirit meaning the sense of *Self* with a capital *S*, the "I Am" of who you are. And spirit defined as enthusiasm, excitement, zeal, fight, ingenuity, and all-encompassing love.

In the case of the average Black man, even when you are heard, people often walk away choosing to believe they heard something other than what you actually said. Then they say something is wrong with you. The impact of always being told something is wrong with you, of not being acknowledged and losing your spirit, has been the depletion of your will, desire, and ability to live fully and consciously according to the true nature of your soul, which is good. In the more severe cases, lack of acknowledgment and lack of spirit will manifest in Black men as confusion, hopelessness, and a disrespect for life and other living things.

On the day I was talking to my friend and heard myself say, "Black men are so stupid!" I was shocked. I have watched Black men all my life. I watched my father and his friends, my brother and his friends, my son and his friends. As a Black woman who has watched so many Black men, I thought I had the right to make that statement. Within moments, a deeper truth hit me. Black men have been at the center of my life. While I have watched them, I have also wanted them, waited for them, waited on them, because I have loved them. So why would I want and wait for someone I think is stupid? Most of the women I know who come together and sit around talking, talk about Black men. Whether we are talking about loving them or complaining about them, Black men always show up in our conversations. My father was a Black man. My husband was a Black man. My son, grandsons, and godsons are Black men. Was I raised by somebody stupid? Did I raise somebody stupid? Did I think my daughters would find good husbands in a pool of stupid people? Where did I get the notion that Black men are stupid?

Most of the women I know get dressed in the morning considering what "their man" or some man will say about their outfit. We cut our hair, buy our shoes, paint our faces as ways to attract the attention of Black men. So I asked myself, Why do women spend so much time focusing on people we believe are stupid? I am well aware that Black men are not stupid. But where did I get this notion? I did not dare open the matter up for debate among my friends. Instead, I took the matter within, into contemplation, meditation, if you will. What I realized was that Black men have lost their souls. In this instance, soul means the true essence of who you are. You have lost your soul to fear, anger, pain, and suffering. For many, you have lost it to the fear, anger, and pain of Black women. I also realized that the search for the soul lost by Black men is the responsibility of both Black men and Black women.

EVERY SHUT EYE AIN'T SLEEP

Throughout my life, I have watched the men around me strive to "make something of themselves." As I reflect on who these men were and what they did, it never seemed to be enough. I know hundreds of women who ask in their hearts, of God and the rest of the world, "What can I do to help this man, these men?" The answers, while we women profess to want them, need them, in order to save ourselves and the men we love, may in fact be something we are afraid of having. If our men, the fathers, brothers, lovers, husbands, and sons, were truly living up to their highest potential, what kind of new demands and expectations would that place on us? In the face of our inability to help you, it seems that we have accepted the fact that Black men behave stupidly, live in mediocrity, die early, leaving little or nothing behind for the women who loved them or for their children. Yet we push you, saying we want more, demanding more from you, almost expecting that our demands will go unfulfilled. In actuality, we need the piece of your soul that is missing, the energy of your spirit that has been killed off.

Black men are taught how to live, to get, to have, to do all the things that you were told represented what a *man* should be. The job. The house. The family. And let us not forget the car. All of these represent the things a man must have in order to be acknowledged. As a Black female, living in a white-male-dominated, class-oriented society, I know how striving to be and get what other people deemed right for me destroyed my inner voice, self-image, and Self. I can only imagine that the effects have been the same, if not greater, for Black men. As a woman, if I missed the mark, I could hope some man would come along and provide the things for me. But who wants to give anything to a man? More important, can a man still be a man if he accepts from a woman or the world at large that which he could not acquire for himself? I have always told my daughters to be sure to ask their suitors, "What are you bringing to the table?"

What does it mean to be a man? Depending on who is asked, the answer could be anything from a rich and powerful, influential leader of people to a gun-toting, foul-mouthed renegade. To a 90 percent certainty, most of the definitions will lean toward having or doing a particular thing. Rarely would a respondent allude to a *state of being*. Doing is physical. It is action. For men, *doing* is a function of masculine persona. *Being*, on the other hand, is spiritual. It is an inward movement, a consciousness of the natural essence. Few men are taught the true spiritual essence of their masculinity. The Black men I have watched were not taught how to *be* men. They were taught what men *do*. Because we live in a world where the physical and visible stimuli dominate, being and doing are often confused. As children, we are all taught if you *do* certain things, you will *be* a certain way. For men, the *doing*-to-*being* process is the path to power, honor, and acknowledgment. It is not, however, the path to finding the soul.

A VIEW FROM THE BRIDGE

My brother was taught to do. He was taught to compete. He had to walk tall, run fast, throw far, in order to outdo his competitors. My father taught him about doing. Yet, as far as he was concerned, my brother could never *do* enough. My grandmother would say, "Let the boy be!" My father's retort was, "If you had your way, he'd be a sissy!" Black men must *do* whatever is necessary not to *be* a sissy. Sissy as it relates to men is one who is quiet, meek, noncompetitive, nonaggressive; one whose masculinity is questionable and up for grabs. Spirit is quiet, noncompetitive, nonaggressive, and invisible. Spirit is also genderless and colorless because it represents all that God is. When I think about my brother and his peers, my father and his peers, being a man was not only what you did, it was the posture, the manner in which you moved. It was a physical or outer demonstration. I don't recall ever hearing anyone tell my brother he was good inside. I don't remember ever hearing about his mission, his purpose, or his everlasting connection to his Creator. What my brother was taught was bravado.

In light of all that you have been told, have seen, and have experienced it is understandable that you have developed some very bad habits. Those of us who watch you struggle with what you have been taught and cannot figure out know that old habits are hard to break. We know many of you think very poorly of yourselves. You expect very little for or from yourselves. We know many of you are totally unaware of the Spirit within you or its purpose in your life. We know a few of you recognize that there is *a Spirit* that contributes to your life, but we also know you cannot figure out what to do with it or about it. Still, we cheer you on and throw our hands up, helplessly disgusted when you don't make it, when you do not get the things you compete for. We, the onlookers, forget that we are the same ones who are not listening and not hearing what you striving Black men say. Through your competitive actions we, like you, fail to recognize that you have been taught what to *do* rather than how to *be*.

WHAT IS THE PROBLEM?

Most men are taught that they must be busy doing something. A busy man is an important man. He is needed. He is popular. A busy man lives on the edge of life, juggling many things, handling emergencies, responding to crises and being in control. A busy man is empowered, not by who he is but because of what he does. It is embarrassing for a man to say, "I don't have anything to do" because busyness is a kind of validation that is often translated to "I am somebody. I have important things to do." A man who is engaged in doing the urgent, empowering, and validating activities of life may miss his most important duty of all: righting the relationship in his soul with the Creator of his life.

You cannot expect to have a good relationship with anything or anyone God created if you do not have a good relationship with God. How many family or busines relationships do you know of that have been destroyed by dissention among the people involved? People sitting in the same room who dislike or distrust one another will not make a great deal of progress together. The same is true for people who do not trust the Spirit. The Spirit in your soul is the Spirit of life in every other soul. When you know, love, and trust that Spirit, being conscious of its presence, that knowledge takes precedence over doing. When you can be peaceful in the presence of Spirit, human urgency no longer rules your life and human acceptance is no longer a priority. A man who is at peace in the spiritual realm is not lured to do what he is taught men must do to be right in the world.

My father was dishonorably discharged from the army. Arrested for selling cigarettes on the black market, he served a few years in Fort Leavenworth before being promised freedom if he would agree to go to Germany on a suicide mission. I guess he figured he had nothing else to lose. He often said, "As a Black man you are in jail when you are not in jail." He went. He survived. When my father came back to the United States expecting to be freed, he was booted out of the United States Army dishonorably. Many years later, Hollywood made a movie about the mission on which he had served. My father never made a dime from that movie. All his life he had difficulty finding a job because of his discharge status.

I think my father was an angry Black man. I don't know whether he got angry before he stole and sold the cigarettes or after he was dishonorably discharged. In his anger, he decided that the system and the world were against him. He lived by that decision. My father was angry, but he knew how to "front." He knew all the things a man was expected to do, and he learned to do them to the best of his ability.

During the 1950s, it was difficult for an angry, frightened Black man to maneuver his way around society outside the system and still be "legal." It was not unheard of, however, for the angry, frightened, and unacknowledged to front well enough to find a way to make it outside the system. My father was a numbers runner and a gambler. He had many women and several children by a few of them. And he always had a car. By his standards and according to all his friends, he was "a good man." He did the best he could with what he had to work with.

Each time my father was arrested for running numbers, he got angrier. Whenever he was confronted, pushed to make a choice between my stepmother, who was his wife (and whom I think of as my mother), and his girlfriend, the mother of five of his children, he got even more angry. When his Cadillac was repossessed, or when my brother and I needed shoes, again, or when he could not get his clothes out of the cleaners, or when the landlord came to collect the rent, his anger turned to rage. In his rage, my father taught my brother to be angry at the system that had failed to acknowledge and then betrayed him. He taught my brother all about rage while my grandmother, mother, and I stood silently by believing we did not have a viable alternative. Who the hell wants to talk about spirit or things of a spiritual nature when the rent is due, all your good clothes are at the cleaners, and "the man" just repossessed your car?

I remember the stories my father told my brother and me about being a poor Black boy in rural Virginia. He talked about being hungry even though he worked twelve hours a day in "some white woman's kitchen" with his mother. He told us stories about being a shoe-shine boy and how many times he had been kicked in the face. I remember how he would scream and holler about the indignities he had experienced. He told my brother and, on very special occasions when I would be allowed to listen, I also heard how it was necessary to fight and claw your way through the world. He specifically told my brother never, never, to let anyone question his manhood. Never let them know you are afraid or how bad you might be doing. I don't think anyone ever taught my father he had a right to be angry about some things or how to channel the energy of those things he was angry about. I don't believe he thought he had a right ever to be afraid.

When he was eight, nine, or ten, I don't think my brother had any idea what manhood was. But I do believe that my father's anger, coupled with all the stories about scratching and clawing, scared the bejesus out of him. Of course, he could not mention it to anyone.

According to the neighborhood legends, the "men" who ran the world had "screwed" my father, but they could not stop him from being a man. In January 1984, on the same day that the African American community had the first opportunity to vote for the Reverend Jesse Jackson, a Black man, in the presidential primary, my father took his own life. He left a note to his mother and his wife saying he was sorry. He left nothing, absolutely nothing, for any of his children. Fear and anger had robbed his children of our inheritance. We pooled our money to have him cremated because that is what he said he wanted. It was our duty to him.

I believe my brother grew up to be a frightened and angry Black man. When the street gangs chased him home from school, he was frightened. When my father chastised him for not fighting back, he got angry. When he was bused to the lily-white junior high school, to face hostile white teachers, students, and community residents, he was frightened. When the teachers ignored him, he got angry. When his all-Black football team was not allowed to play in the league, or when they played and lost because the white referees made bad calls or no calls, he got angrier. When he shattered his knee and could not play football, the only thing he really wanted to do, he got downright scared. An unacknowledged man who cannot do what he desires to do to make his own way has a right to be frightened. My brother was taught he could not be frightened, so he got angry. After that, he got drunk. He got drunk to escape his fear. He stayed drunk because he was angry.

I have known and loved some scared, angry, drunk, hostile, even violent Black men. Like my friend who jumped out of his car, many fathers, brothers, uncles, cousins, and husbands have good reasons for being scared and angry. You know life is not fair, but you cannot accept being outright cheated. You know life offers many opportunities, but it seems you just cannot find them. As Black men, you know you are at war, even when you are not sure with whom or for what. For many, it may seem as though your enemy is an amorphous shadow that stalks and threatens you, and whose only intent is to destroy you because you are Black and male. The problem is, your enemy cannot be seen. If you had to describe what it *feels* like, I imagine you might say, It is a winged monster with poisonous fangs and an infinite number of tentacles and claws. This monster reaches into every aspect of life, waiting for you to show up. If you show your face anywhere, the monster attacks you, silently.

The monster, whether it is racism, injustice, poverty, lack of acknowledgment, fear, or anger, loves to twist Black men between its claws. It lives by draining your life's dreams, goals, and sometimes, your blood. I can imagine it is very difficult to fight the monster when people keep telling you it does not exist. *They* say the civil rights movement killed the monster, plucked its fangs out and cut off its wings. *They* say all men are equal, with equal opportunity. But we know better. Black men in America know that the sting of racist hate, injustice, and inequality is alive and well. How do you fight an invisible enemy? It is frightening. It makes you angry. What the men in my life and other Black men may want to consider is, the monster cannot alter who and what you are born to be. Just because it challenges you does not mean it will win. To fight back, however, you must have a soul. You must have the Spirit.

WHO CAN SAVE BLACK MEN?

A male friend of mine was walking in downtown Philadelphia when he was approached by a wide-eyed woman. "Are you saved? Are you saved?" she repeatedly demanded to know. He stopped walking as she circled him quoting Bible scriptures. When he could get a word in, he calmly asked her, "What do I have to be saved from?" She reminded him that he was born in sin and needed to be "washed in the blood." Unsuccessfully, he tried to get her to explain why his parents' act of love was a sin and why he needed to be saved from what they had done. She ignored his questions and continued to quote scriptures. When she had exhausted her efforts to get him to admit to and change his sinful ways, she began to pray for his salvation. "Dear Lord, save this sinning heathen!"

While she prayed, he asked her, "If your Lord were here talking to me, do you think he would be screaming and hollering in my face? If you are a representation of how your Lord behaves, I don't want anything to do with him!"

"That's why you need to be saved!" she screamed at him. "You don't know who you are! You need to be saved from yourself!"

What do Black men need to be saved from? Is it themselves? Is it the world? I believe Black men need to be saved from the bad thoughts you have about yourselves and the bad habits you have picked up. I believe you need to be saved from negative self-talk and negative self-images. More important, I know Black men need to be saved from ignorance. The ignorance about the power of the Spirit within you. The Spirit that sustains your life. The Spirit that breathes through you and controls your bodily functions. The spirit of God, of which you are a carbon copy walking upon the face of the earth. Ignorance of that spirit robs you of your divinity and your ability to stand in the face of the giant and cast your stone without fear. I also believe you need to be saved from the aggressiveness of *doing* so that you will know how to *be*.

As a Black woman, I often wonder if the salvation of men is for my own sake or in pursuit of an intangible experience neither of us is clear about. There is a psychological approach to shifting perceptions called *A Course in Miracles,* which states, "You cannot solve your problem because you do not know what your problem is." According to *The Course,* the only problem we have as human beings is the belief that we are separated from God. As a result of the perceived separation, we suffer and struggle with issues, searching for answers that are buried in our true nature. No matter how difficult the questions in life may be, we know the answer because God knows the answer. God is the inner goodness born within every person. There is nothing we must do to receive it. We must learn, however, to be in contact with that inner self. This contact, once it is made, results in a state of being that is good.

Like most Black women, I have often wondered what it is that Black men really want. Is it peace? Love? Is it self-actualization? Money? Do Black men really want forty acres of land and a mule? I also wonder how they know that what they want will give them the *experience* they are searching for? What if the thing Black men truly want is an intangible experience? What does freedom feel like? What does peace feel like? How will you know it when you experience it if you have never had it? As Black men search through and query life, what is it that you need, want, and expect from Black women? As you contemplate these things, I wonder if you realize that we are also trying to find answers to the same questions. In the process of loving, supporting, and reaching out to you, we too are searching for our goodness within and without.

THISAWAY, THATAWAY

I often think about the similarities and differences among the men I have known in my life. Why is it that some come through the maze with flying colors and others fumble around hopelessly? Using my father, brother, husband, son, grandsons, and godfather as examples, I found a few plausible explanations. My father had been hardened by his life experiences. He taught my brother to be hard. It was a father's attempt to save his son from suffering the indignities he had suffered. As Black men in America, with completely different experiences, they had both been made to feel so wrong, so inadequate, so often, they believed it was their duty to prove there was nothing *wrong* with them. They could not or dared not try to prove it to the world, so they laid the burdens of proof on their women, children, and each other.

My father and brother yelled, argued, sometimes fought to prove their point and hold their ground at home. They were each set in their ways, which they believed was the only way. The right way. They were attached to their opinions, which, of course, always served to prove that they were right. They were unwilling to change. Saw no need to change. They were right about the things they believed in and if you did not agree with them, you were wrong. Period. My father, brother, and husband seemed too scared, too skeptical, too disappointed by past failures or rejection to make new choices and take new steps to do the things they said they wanted to do. They lived in the pain of unfulfillment, and it was painful for me to live among them.

In response to the demands of capitalism and the American dream, my father, brother, and husband were among the Black men who were conditioned to believe that their value, self-worth, and most of the problems in life hinge on money: the lack of it; the devaluation of it; how people will use you to get it; what others will do to you to get the little bit that you have. Some Black men I have known believed that by obtaining the right job, or a car, which they often could not afford, they would immediately be elevated to a position of "all rightness." How can it be all right to ground your sense of self in something that can so easily be repossessed? A physical sense of security is the easiest to lose because it is determined by external factors. Those Black men who understand the tenuous nature of physical fulfillment often look to the intangible experiences such as justice, freedom, equality, and acceptance by other people. Black men and women believe these intangible experiences will solve all the challenges we face in life. Whom do we want to be equal to? Accepted by? More important, why? We have been taught to define ourselves, seek and limit ourselves within the confines of a physical realm that is ever changing.

My grandson, at age four, has not yet developed opinions he is willing to fight or die for. He is still eager to learn and is open to new experiences. He is still impressionable. He has not yet figured out who he is or what that means to the rest of the world. In fact, he does not care what the world thinks about him. As a result, my grandson Oluwa is free to explore and experience life as it happens, without set opinions and preconceived notions into which everything has to fit. He is more than willing to take risks. Oluwa believes in and has faith in the overall goodness of people. I know because I have had to explain to him at least a thousand times why he must not talk to strangers, who a stranger is, and how he can tell a good stranger from a not-good stranger. Even when things do not go the way he would like them to go, he is willing to dig in and try again. He has not yet figured out what was right and what or who was wrong. He doesn't *know* anything and is willing to admit that without fear of being judged or criticized. All of his *doing* is focused on his personal pleasure, not the demands of the world. Oluwa still trusts life, which is something that my father and brother stopped doing long ago.

LIVING IN THE GOODNESS

My godfather is a willing servant of God, spirit, and spiritual principles. This man lives, moves, breathes, and draws his total sense of being from the presence of spirit. As a Yoruba priest, a minister ordained in the ancient traditions of his ancestors, my godfather is a counselor. While most men I know aspire to achieve some degree of wealth, fame, acceptance, and influence, my godfather lives moment to moment in pursuit of peace, clarity, understanding, and the balancing of his head and heart. At fifty years old, he did not have a single gray hair on his head. He never worries about anything. Perhaps it is because he will not leave his house, implement a plan or goal, or respond to a question unless he is prompted and assured by his own inner voice. That voice, his spiritual guidance, is his sense of power. He says it brings him peace and assurance—what our ancestors called "blessed assurance." My godfather is not concerned with the ways of the world. He believes they are traps. Once you give yourself over to the demands of the world, you no longer have control over what you do and who you are; you are now subject to the changing demands of people and events with which you have no intimate contact. Losing your sense of self to the world is what he calls an "identity crisis."

Yoruba culture has supported my godfather in identifying himself as a Black man without crisis or struggle. African culture acknowledges Black men. Yoruba, the culture or way of life embraced by the people of southwestern Nigeria, gave my godfather a land of origin, a place to belong to. Understanding that more than 87 percent of the slaves transported to North America came from this region helped him to identify his ancestral and spiritual heritage. Once this was done, he had a foundation, a cultural foundation that provided him with a standard of behavior and a philosophy by which he could govern his life. All people need a place to which they belong. A place from which they can draw strength and a sense of self, no matter where they find themselves.

In my godfather's case, Yoruba culture prescribed a lifestyle and social mores, which he has followed as a meaningful process for structuring his life. For the descendants of Africans born in this foreign place, living in a foreign culture, it is important to embrace a philosophy that inspires and enhances our instinctual urges and innate characteristics. For my godfather, Yoruba culture provided mental, emotional, and spiritual constructs from which he could derive a balanced life. Not everyone, however, is a descendant of the Yoruba. According to my godfather, this does not matter. Being an African or anything else will not help you if you do not know where you come from. You come from God. Africa was just an important stop on the journey. In your quest to get back to the beginning of your existence, you must go all the way back to God. Being an African will provide you with a road map, not a guarantee that you will make it.

My godfather teaches other men and women how to get back to God as descendants of Africa. He also teaches them about power. According to Yoruba tradition, the lion is not the only representation of power in the universe. Yes, the roar of the lion subdues the will of others by striking fear in the heart. Yes, the lion's size, position, and reputation among other beasts is one of aggressive authority. Yes, the lion is powerful, but so are the sun and the moon. Bále (pronounced Balay), as I call my godfather, taught me about the power of silence: the power of peace, the power of obedience to your own head and inner voice. With a clear and peaceful mind comes power.

I remember once Bále asked me, "If you could be anything in the world, what would you choose to be?" I was young at the time; I didn't know any better. After what I considered to be deep reflection on what I knew about life, I responded that I would be a chicken. In my mind, everyone liked chickens. They were very useful, in high demand, and put to extremely versatile uses. He laughed and said, "Me, I want to be a cool, clear glass of water." You can see it and see through it. What you cannot see is the power in it. My godfather has taught me that it is not always wise to demonstrate your power. Once you understand what it is and how it operates, you must simply live in it and through it, not because of it.

My godfather was not always like this. In his wild youthful days, he was fast-talking, hot-tempered, and very busy *doing* to make his way in the world. He was a up-in-your-face kind of guy. Something—I am not really sure what—turned him around. He surrendered his mind, body, and most important, his ego to the goodness of spirit. Today he is the gentlest, most loving, compassionate, and wise man I know. These terms are not what we are taught to associate with the concepts of masculine power. The world expects men to be forceful, aggressive, and domineering. This boisterous demonstration of manhood is not an African concept; it is an outgrowth of the European conquest of the world. African culture stresses balance, harmony, peace, and being flexible enough to meet the ever-growing, ever-changing demands of life. These are not qualities one develops through aggression, domination, or the many other attributes we ascribe to men of power today.

THE POWER OF SILENCE

Wisdom is silent. Love is silent. Patience is silent. Life is actually silent. It is the silent merging of the sperm and the egg; a unity created in an orderly flow of events, a harmonious interaction that produces the thing we know as life. This order, flow, harmony, and balance of the unlike forces in life have absolutely nothing to do with how much money you have, how fast your car can go, where you live, or how many degrees you hold. The flow of life is the same for everyone. It is the degree of awareness, acknowledgment, acceptance, and understanding of how life flows that will determine how and where you live in the universal scheme of things. My godfather understands that quality of life is really what matters. What you are able to accomplish in life will be determined by your understanding of how life works. It is not how fast, how hard, or with how much bravado you live that matters.

There is no way I can say men are stupid and still honor what this man has taught me about men and about being a woman. He has taught me that it is my duty as a Black woman to recognize the fear in Black men, to acknowledge their anger, and to realize it is not my fault. He says it is of utmost importance to our collective survival that women look beyond the hostility men display in order to see the truth of who Black men are. Black men are our mirrors; they reflect a part of who and what we are. They were marinated in our wombs. Therefore, we must pray for the spirits of Black men because they reflect the angry, hostile part of ourselves. When we shift in our thoughts and feelings, the men in our lives will shift. Prayer and forgiveness are the responsible ways women can assist the men they love in finding their souls. It is also the only way to create the balance, harmony, love, and peace needed to overcome the challenges the total Self of the African American community confronts in the world.

When I think about my father and brother in light of what I know about my godfather, I see some very definite benefits in Black men living a spiritual life. The first benefit is that culture provides you with a philosophy and standards, a framework from which you can approach life. African cultures, for example, are "we" rather than "I" oriented frameworks. People are not isolated, left to fend on their own. Culture also provides traditions, rituals, and ceremonies that enliven the spirit and connect one person to another. When the spirit is alive, it is alert and focused. This gives you inner strength. Cultural constructs foster the development of character, a framework within which you are expected to function. The development of character shifts the focus from what you do to how you do it for the benefit of "we."

Character developed through adherence to African culture is inevitably grounded in a spiritual philosophy or spiritual principles. A spiritual philosophy takes the human guesswork out of living. It brings the mental, emotional, and physical being into alignment with the mandates of a higher order—a divine spiritual order. The natural order of God. Through a spiritual philosophy that encourages you to practice spiritual principles, your character is strengthened. Your mind is cleansed and focused through participation in spiritual ceremony and ritual. Your body, which has no mind of its own, ultimately becomes obedient to the focused mind of a spiritually grounded character.

Aside from culture, a spiritually grounded lifestyle provides a process for living. It prescribes routines, which foster the development of discipline. Process also evokes purposeful preparation, patience, persistence, and reliance upon the natural order of the divine rather than the random acts of people. Spiritual principles and practices encourage conscientious thought and action because they are grounded in a framework of accountability to a divine source. This accountability raises the consciousness from the limitation and restriction of being human to the unlimited resources of an omnipresent Creator. A spiritual consciousness reminds you of your connection to all and your oneness with God. Living from the sense of oneness, you become aware of your interdependence on others as the path to evolution for all. Competition is evolved to sharing. Anger is evolved to compassion. Fear is evolved to faith when men and women become reliant on divine rather than social intervention.

Because my godfather is a Black man grounded in a culturally based spiritual philosophy, the often expected and accepted tug-of-war does not exist between him and the women in his life. I find it easy to talk to him about things I would never have mentioned to my father. Where my father quickly became annoyed with my questions or opinions, Bále seems to be open to my feelings and thoughts. He does not live in fear of being challenged or proved wrong. He has nothing to prove to me, no need to be in control of me or what I think. This makes him less threatening and aggressive. I can share what I am thinking and feeling with him and he never tells me what I *should* or *should not* be feeling or doing. He supports me in interpreting my experiences from within myself.

Because my godfather has incorporated certain principles into his life and lives by them, he encourages me to do the same based on my experiences, not his. Bále starts every day with prayer. He is humble without feeling humiliated. He cherishes times of silence and solitude. He is realistic about what he can do, cannot do, will do, and will not do for himself and others. When he says he cannot do something for you or with you, you know it is a decision based on what he believes is good and right for everyone involved. As a result, he is always able to honor his word. You can always count on him to do what he says he will do without conflicting responsibilities or time constraints. He moves slowly, deliberately, and effectively. I have never seen him set out to do anything that does not get done. He knows success, not according to the standards of the world, but according to the standards he has set for himself. Lack of success and conflicting responsibilities convinced my father to believe he was a failure. He was enough of a failure to end his own life. Lack of success and disillusionment keep my brother in a state of fear and rage.

KNOWLEDGE EQUALS
THE FREEDOM TO CHOOSE

In his book *Visions for Black Men,* Dr. Na'im Akbar wrote:

> We are sophisticated enough to understand that the best wars are fought with knowledge. We understand that as soon as the African man stands up and declares himself to be a man, he has put himself in absolute and immediate opposition to the [system] which has defined him by [its] definition as less than a man or not a man.

I am quite sure the United States Army had a perfectly logical rationale for not honoring the promise made to my father. It appears as though there was a belief that he was less than a man who should have been grateful not to be rotting away in Leavenworth. The emasculation of my father did not begin when he went to prison or end when he was dishonorably discharged. Throughout his life he was rejected, denied, betrayed, and oppressed by a system that thrives on the diminished capacity of Black men. I now believe, however, that his biggest problem was that he accepted as true what other people thought, felt, and said about him.

Neither the army nor the society at large knew that my father, Horace Lester Harris, was a mathematical genius. He could add columns of numbers in his head—no pencil needed. My grandparents could not afford to send him to college, and with a dishonorable discharge, no bank or accounting firm would hire him. The fact that he was a Black man only exacerbated the issue. Still, he was able to put his skills to use running numbers. The work was steady. The money good. It was the best he could do and he hated it. He wanted to be a "real" man with a "real" job. My father often said it wasn't fair or just, the way he had been treated simply because he was a Black man. What he did to himself, my mother, and his children was just as unfair and unjust.

Where do Black men begin to redress the injustices they have experienced? By whose law do you want the crimes against you to be judged? If one hundred Black men were asked this question, there would be at least fifty different answers. If you asked another one hundred what they have *personally* experienced as a result of the social and political history of Black men in this country, you would probably get ninety-nine completely different responses. The experiences, perceptions, and judgments of every person will vary according to his needs and his individual experiences. In the case of Black men, however, we probably all agree that "something" needs to be done, even if we cannot agree on who needs to do it.

According to the laws of the land, when people are aggrieved, they have the right to petition an authority for redress of their grievance. In the case of Black men and women, the authority we have been taught to petition is the source of our grievances. As we begin to understand that our petitions to human authorities will not result in an adequate solution, perhaps we will take our petitions to a Higher Authority. An authority who "knows our needs even before we ask." An authority that we were given as a birthright. This authority is etched in our souls. It has not been beaten out, forced out, or changed at its most essential core. Neither fear nor anger has or can alter the true nature of the inner authority of Self. The authority of God. The "I Am" presence. Unfortunately, far too many Black men know nothing about this inner authority. Even far more have lost faith in it.

> *All power and effectiveness come*
> *from following the law of creation.*
> *There is no substitute for knowing*
> *how things happen and acting ac-*
> *cordingly.*   The Tao of Power

Life begins in the spirit. This is not something that I or any other living being has made up. The coming together of two lives to promote the silent, unaided development of a new life in the darkness of the womb is a spiritual as well as a physical phenomenon. It is a process that was not created in the minds of men. It is a process that can be altered only by the intentional interruption of the orderly flow of natural events. Life is a spiritual process where the unseen becomes seen, the unknown becomes known and tangible at just the right time. Timing leads to power. The creative force of life, the powerful vastness of Spirit that exists within our being, unfolds with time according to conscious acknowledgment of its presence. When Black men gain knowledge of and begin to understand the spiritual laws and principles that govern life and creation, you will shift into a conscious state of empowerment. You will have the ability to transform your reality from within yourself. You will no longer be totally reliant on the world.

A natural question would be, Where do we find it? Where do Black men gain knowledge and understanding about the spiritual realm and a spiritual approach to living? The first step is to be willing. You must be willing to change, give up, shift your perception from a physical to a spiritual way of living. Spirit meaning God. Living meaning the ability to manifest godliness. Your willingness cannot be based on a desire to escape where you are, to escape doing bad or feeling bad about what you are doing. It must be a willingness born of the desire to know the truth about God, spirit, in relation to who you are.

The knowledge of the truth about your identity will ultimately translate to inner or spiritual strength and external or physical ability to live in a divine state. To attain this knowledge, you must be willing to surrender everything you now believe about yourself and the world in order to recognize the truth that surrounds you. For some, this will involve reexamining your beliefs about God. It is your system of beliefs that hinders or enhances the ability to utilize the knowledge you gain in life. Life is a process. Spiritual reality is a process. The process begins with a willingness to clean out the heart and open the mind. The result is awareness, alignment, and harmony within the being. When there is alignment within the self, the mysteries of the spiritual realm and the wealth of life are at your disposal.

LOOKING AT THE MAN IN THE MIRROR

To understand spiritual principles in a spiritual process, you must be aware of your true nature and the presence of spirit as a function of who and what you are. Awareness requires openness. Black men must be open to the unknown, unproved, unseen influences of spirit. Grandma always knew when we were not telling the truth. She said she could feel it, *in her spirit*. She had premonitions about things and people. Grandma was aware that spirit moves within before you see it in the world. This faculty of spiritual intuition is not reserved solely for women. Black men who are open and willing to become aware of spirit become spiritually powerful.

Awareness is an essential phase of developing a spiritual reality, because what you are being asked to look to, rely on, may not make sense. It may not be logical in the physical world. You cannot see spiritual principles working. You cannot control how they work. In the absence of the willingness to surrender physical contact and control, you can never become intuitively aware of the unseen presence of spirit. Surrender, as it is used in a spiritual context, does not mean you become weak or passive. Surrender means you are willing to accept that the spirit of God is active in your life, whether or not you can see it working or understand how it works. Awareness of the invisible action of spirit makes surrender less challenging. Like the mighty oak that willingly surrenders to the changes of the seasons, yet never loses its position as the "mighty" oak, in moving from a human to a spiritual reality, Black men become mighty.

As you become aware of God as the omnipresent Spirit of life, you learn to accept God's presence in everything: the good and the bad. Acceptance of a Higher Power is not difficult. Accepting that this power can and does work in and through your life becomes a challenge. It is easy to say, "I believe in spirit or God." The issue becomes, Do you accept the energy of God in your life, no matter what it looks like? Your life may look pretty crappy right now. But can you accept that even now God is present? Even when it looks like the world is against you, even when it looks like the world is too big or too small for you, God is right where you are, working through you and waiting for you to acknowledge God's presence. Acceptance will mean giving up some of your old thoughts and beliefs in order to embrace a new way of thinking. Giving up means change. One of the biggest challenges we face in life is finding the willingness, strength, and discipline to change.

God is the energy force that sustains all life. The sustaining force of God is what we call spirit. This spirit moves according to the energy we give it in the form of conscious awareness. This awareness then motivates our behavior. If you are not aware of the presence of spirit in your being or your life, you remain limited to the frailties of being human. If you are not willing to become aware, your knowledge and beliefs are limited to human perceptions. Perceptions are formed in response to experiences and the assimilation of information, which is then clouded by emotions. Fear, anger, shame, guilt are toxic emotions that cloud the ability to perceive the truth. The experiences of Black men, and the tainted information you receive about who and what you are, hinder your ability to perceive the presence of spirit and to move from the human to the spiritual realm. As a result, Black men who believe they are broke remain broke. Black men who believe they are beaten are beaten. Black men who are aware of the power and the presence of God within their being stand as the mighty oak, wealthy and unbending in the changing winds of life.

Choice is an important aspect of the spiritual reality. The dictionary defines choice as "worthy of being chosen; selected with care; of high quality." If you were told that you chose to be broke and beaten, you would scream No! Few Black men understand that no matter what is going on in your life, you always have the ability to make choices. In fact, the outward conditions of your life reflect the choices you have made or failed to make. What have you chosen to believe about yourself? What choices have you made based on those beliefs? What have you chosen to believe about other people and what they can do to you or prevent you from doing? Through awareness and acceptance that the presence of God is active in your life, you become able to choose thoughts, words, and actions that reflect the belief that there is a power of good present in your soul.

How do you begin the process of moving from a human to a spiritual sense of being? You begin by walking into your bathroom and standing before the mirror. Looking yourself squarely in the eyes and saying, "I love you." You begin by having affection for yourself. Broke, unemployed, divorced, ex-con, ex-addict, or corporate executive fearful of the glass ceiling. You are more than that, more than just a Black man. You are a child of the Most High. You are an individually unique manifestation of God. In developing a spiritual approach to life, you must learn to be affectionate and loving toward yourself.

God is love. God always exudes loves toward its creations. God loves you in spite of the errors committed in ignorance of Self. Even in anger, frustration, depletion, and deflation, you must love yourself. No matter who your daddy was, or whether you knew him, love yourself. No matter who your mama was, what she did to you or did not do for you, you must learn to love yourself. If your brother is gay, or if your sister has had six children out of wedlock whom you have not seen in three years, love yourself. Look at you! Accept that the spirit of God lives in you. You are a wonderfully divine creation of God! When you can look at yourself, accept who and what you are, and love yourself unconditionally, your soul is saved. Your spirit is empowered. Your *Self*, with a capital S, comes alive.

Loving that Self in the mirror is the key not only to surviving but to flourishing in the midst of racism, social injustice, economic and political inequality. Once you fully love your Self, you cannot be depleted by the loss of a job. You instinctively know you are not defined by what you do. You work for God, Inc.; there is always something better for you to do. When you love your Self, you cannot walk out the door and kill your brother. You feel too good about yourself to soil your soul or risk going to jail. When you really love your Self, you cannot walk away from your children. You know they are a part of you, and you feel good about them. When you feel that good about yourself, you don't beat women, you don't do drugs, you don't even hate white people. You feel good, so you make good choices about what you do, what you say, and how you conduct your life and affairs. This Self-love, which is founded on the presence of God in your being and the spirit of God moving in your life, gives you the patience and ability to trust that there is a rainbow on the other side of the storm. In other words, you willingly surrender to the natural order and process of life.

How do you love yourself when you are a Black man who is unacknowledged, unappreciated, and angry at the world? How do you love yourself when you have been belittled and maligned? How do you love yourself when you know you've made mistakes, and have yet to admit them to yourself or anyone else? You may have left your wife for another woman. And now, you are about to leave her. You may have ignored your child's birthday because you didn't have the money for a gift. You may have ruined your credit buying things you really didn't need and knew you could not afford. You may drink a little, snort a little, and tell big lies to the people dearest to you. Then you come home with yourself, to your Self. How do you love the face you see in the mirror? The same way God does—totally, unconditionally, without reservation.

The spirit of God within you realizes that you are growing through your experiences to that point when you become willing to become aware and accept the presence of God in your soul as your source, your supply, your guidance, and your protection. When you accept this to be the truth about yourself, you will find your soul. When you know the truth, you make better choices. When you make better choices, you evolve from a limited human being to an enlightened spiritual being and an exceptional man.

CULTIVATING A SPIRITUAL GARDEN IN THE MINDS AND LIVES OF BLACK MEN

The ego opposes all appreciation, all
recognition, all sane perception and
knowledge. If you keep in mind
what the spirit offers you, you cannot
be vigilant for anything but God.   A Course in Miracles

Seeds must be planted in the garden. The planted seed must be nurtured with commitment and care. The care includes inspection for and elimination of destructive pests and the uprooting of weeds. Self-defeating thoughts and behaviors are destructive in the minds and lives of Black men. People who judge, criticize, blame, and find fault are pests. They cannot be ignored. They must be eliminated from your mind and heart, from your mental, emotional, and spiritual environment. Cultivating a garden is a time-consuming process. As it relates to spirituality, most of us can intellectually see the need to embrace certain spiritual practices. However, we are just as ready to admit, "I don't have time! I have too many other things to do!" In effect, we are saying that others things are more important than the cultivation and care of the source of our lives: the spirit. The intellect retorts, "No! That is not what I am saying!" However, the moment an opportunity to make overtime money presents itself, prayer and meditation go right out the window.

Spirituality is a lifetime commitment. It is a way of life that requires a consistent effort of daily practice or, at the very least, a daily consciousness of spiritual principles and values. For Black men who have been conditioned to make money, get things, be better, have more, spirituality may seem like a time-consuming luxury. For those of you with a decent job, a decent home, goals and dreams, who are living in a certain comfort zone, you may believe, "I don't need spiritual practices or teachings." If you go to church, if your children are fairly stable, if your health is good, you may question the practical benefits of looking for anything more than you have. For those of you who fit into this category, the issue is, How do you feel? Are you peaceful or stressed out? Are you open and forgiving or do you hold grudges and seek revenge? Are you an opinionated screamer who sees how ridiculously people behave? Or are you loving and accepting of everyone? Whether you have a BMW in the driveway or ride the iron horse, the question becomes, Can I feel better, be better, than I am now? Evolution of the consciousness and betterment of the being are the goal of a spiritual consciousness, which can only be cultivated in the garden of your heart and mind.

There are certain universal truths Black men will need to understand in order to free yourselves from the grips of the four-hundred-year-old lesson of oppression. You must cultivate your garden in order to have a good crop. The garden includes the mind, body, and spirit. If you continue to hate white men, be angry in response to injustice, and challenge systems and structures with hate or fear, you will in effect contribute to the already existing imbalances and spiritual weeds. If you continue to respond to physical domination with physical aggression, the cycle of fear, anger, hate, and greed will never end. If the Black man is in fact the father of all human civilizations, you then have the responsibility to do whatever is necessary to ensure the evolution and survival of the human family. Black men must therefore reestablish themselves as the spiritual foundation upon which the entire world community can stand.

That you are frightened, angry, and unstable is a difficult concept for anyone to accept. It defies the intellect. You have been taught that fear is indicative of weakness. Black men do not easily admit to weakness. The intellectual response is to lay blame and respond in defiance. The intellect says, If somebody hits you, hit back. It is, however, the intellect that ultimately becomes imbalanced. In response to unfulfilled desires, fear, and miseducation, the intellect will respond to fear with fear, to anger with anger. The intellect is polluted by the sights, sounds, and judgments of the physical world. The intellect cannot "see" spirit, so the intellect does not "know" spirit. The intellect does what it is programmed to do. The human experience provides motivation for intellectual decisions. The intellect is programmed to conquer and control. The intellect views forceful intimidation as a useful tool. The brain interprets fear as a useful tool for conquering the individual will, leading to submission. Consequently, all human beings are programmed to fear, resent, and seek selfish control of one another. We want to do to "them" what they did to "us." If you could do it to "them," you would have already done it.

Perhaps it is time for Black men to consider another approach to life and living. I believe it is time for them to retill the soil, plant new seeds, and harvest a different kind of crop. If you take the focus off having money and getting things, if you surrender anger to understanding, fear to acceptance, and hate to love, the universe will respond by bringing you more of what you focus on. The new seeds you plant will produce a way of life created in the silent power of spirit, a power that is unlimited and unhindered by human beings of any race. When Black men shift from the intellect to the spirit, you are bound to find a new way of life. This will be a life dedicated to peace, joy, and compassion. It is the kind of life that our earliest ancestors knew. A life centered on the omnipotent power and presence of God. From all that I have been taught, seen, and experienced in my own shift, God is good all the time, no matter what anyone else says or does. The payoff of unlimited goodness, for an indefinite period, sure sounds like something worth working toward.

The Process

The Parable of the Acorns

There was once a very large community of acorns living in a mighty oak tree.[1] From birth, the acorns had been taught that their ultimate purpose in life was to achieve the highest level of acornness, represented by a highly polished shell. To help them achieve this, the acorn leaders established acorn health clubs, acorn beauty parlors, and acorn shell–polishing institutions. All acorns

---

[1] This parable is adapted from the original version presented by John W. Aikens, *Explorations in Awareness* (Lakemont, GA: CSA Press, 1966).

were expected to master the ability to keep their shells polished and assist other acorns in developing their skills to do the same.

Some acorns were not satisfied. They did not believe that life should be limited to self-polishing and helping others learn how to polish. These acorns were resented and criticized by the majority. It is not nice to have your complacency disturbed, your comfort zone challenged. They would shout at the doubtful acorns, "Hey, this is the way it has always been! Why are you asking those stupid questions? Who are you to question anyway?" The doubtful acorns explained that they had noticed some things that the acorn leaders had not explained. They had become aware that no matter how highly polished an acorn was, there came a time when it would fall from the tree. The shell would crack. Moisture would seep in and cause what was known as acorn death. If all acorns had to die no matter how polished their shells were, why should they spend their lives polishing their shells?

These questions came to the attention of the acorn priests. They stepped forward to reassure all the acorns. It had been revealed to them, they said, that if an acorn obeyed all the commands of the priests and the leaders, kept its shell highly polished, paid its taxes and tithes, when the acorn died it would be transported to acorn heaven. Once there, no acorn ever had to worry about falling or losing its luster. There would be warm breezes forever, and every acorn would sit at the right hand of the acorn god and achieve acorn immortality. To assure the acorns of their rightful place in acorn heaven, there was a ritual the priests could do—for a small fee, of course. Whenever an acorn fell, the priests would perform special rites on the ground in the exact place the acorn had fallen. The following spring, if a plant grew in that spot, the remaining acorn family would know that the deceased acorn had made it to heaven. The acorns were once again reassured and went back to polishing their shells.

As time went on, there came to this acorn community a new acorn who described himself as an acorn prophet. The acorn prophet began to hold nightly meetings at which he told the acorns who gathered that they were being misled by the priests and leaders. The acorn prophet revealed that inside every acorn lived a mighty oak. According to the prophet, the purpose of acorn life was to grow into oakness. He further explained that falling to the ground was simply a step in the process. To become an oak, it would be necessary to stop being an acorn. The falling process actually was the beginning of a new life. The prophet said each acorn owed it to the world to develop itself through hard work, loving gestures, and deliberate concentration to become a mighty oak tree.

While many acorns thought the message was pretty far-fetched, they could not help but be drawn to the acorn prophet. His words were so loving, although it was evident from his lackluster appearance that he had not been to the acorn beauty parlor in a while. Still, he had a glow. More than a luster, his glow seemed to come from the inside. He explained it was his oakness and that every acorn had the same ability. All they had to do was believe, work on their purpose in life, and never fear the fall from the tree.

When the acorn priests heard of the tales being told by the acorn prophet, they were extremely upset. "He'll ruin our business! We had better do something quick!" They did. They called together a group of acorn scientists and ordered them to launch an immediate investigation to refute the acorn prophet's theory. The acorn scientists gathered many acorns upon which they conducted many experiments. When the experiments were complete, they prepared scholarly papers documenting the lack of evidence for oakness being present in any acorn. In all the specimens examined, there was nothing the scientists could see, hear, smell, touch, or taste to indicate that an acorn was anything other than an acorn.

When the acorn community heard this, they once again bowed to the priests and the scientists because they knew everything. The priests then sent for the acorn prophet and turned him over to the courts. He was found guilty of unlawful challenge of the acorn hierarchy and blasphemy against the acorn priesthood. He was sentenced to death. In a very pompous and elaborate event, the acorn prophet was pushed from the tree to his death. The acorn priests did not perform the sacred ritual, and the following spring no plant grew upon the spot where the prophet had fallen.

There were a few acorns who continued to question the teachings of the acorn priests, although they felt guilty doing so. In secret meetings, they would gather to discuss and examine the written teachings the acorn prophet had left behind. Without a plan, or even an intent, they began to work with the principles the prophet had spoken of. They began to tap into their oakness with silent and deliberate thought. They shifted their attention from polishing their shells to developing their oakness. Miraculously, with no special rites or ceremony, they began to feel like oaks, think like oaks, behave like oaks. In a very short time, they too began to glow. Although their luster was not as high as the priests told them it should be, they were peaceful, tranquil, loving, and seemingly wise in dealing with the pressures of acorn life. Their glow drew more and more acorns to the secret nightly meetings. Before long, there was a mighty oakness movement in the acorn community.

Once again, some leery acorn tipped off the priests. They came and seized the papers of the acorn prophet from the leaders of the oak movement. They reworded the papers to make them harmless and claimed to be the authors of the papers all along. The acorn priests were very careful to emphasize in the new oak document that oakness had only happened once, that the acorn prophet was the one and only example of oakness, and that all who aspired to be like him should keep their shells highly polished and pay their tithes and taxes.

Despite the various efforts on the part of the acorn priests and royalty to squelch the oak movement, the acorn community continued to question. Why did they live in an oak tree? If they lived in the body of the oak, did they not have the same qualities and attributes? These wayward acorns remained convinced that it was their purpose in life to make real, to realize, and to bring forth their oakness. The acorn priests monitored them very closely. Whenever one made too much sense or caused too much of a stirring in the community, they would pay the acorn thugs to come secretly in the night, capture the unorthodox acorn, and feed it to the squirrels. They had dispensed with the public ritual of throwing acorns to the ground because the surrounding community had become flooded, annoyingly so, with hundreds of oak trees.

2

A MILLION MEN
MARCHED

A person completely wrapped up in
himself makes a very small package.
                    Denzel Washington

I have often wondered what men talk about when they get together. I suspected that they talk about sports. They probably talk about work. I really believe they talk about women: what they want from us, do to us, think about us. But what do they talk about when there are a million of them who don't know each other? It never crossed my mind that they would talk about what they have done and no longer want to do. I never imagined they would explore the topics of fatherhood, husbandhood, manhood, and self-hood. My mama never told me that men talked like that. I never heard my daddy talk about anything like that. Surely it was unimaginable that one million Black men would come together to talk about righting themselves, getting closer to God, or being better men for the sake of the women and children. When I heard they were getting together, I wondered, What the hell are they going to talk about?

I watched them gather. It was a beautiful thing to see. I watched them laugh. From where I stood, it appeared as if they felt totally free to laugh, to just be happy, for the first time in a long while. I watched those who were a little late, running to catch up with the others. Some wore baseball caps backward. Many ran in groups. But for the first time in a long time, no one was suspicious when they ran by. No one wondered what they were up to or what they were running away from. In fact, as I saw it, they were running to each other to embrace. Some of them were running to cry, to heal, to atone. It was a beautiful thing to watch and to cry for: a million Black men gathering.

I really don't care how many were there or not there. I cried because so many showed up. Perhaps I had fewer reservations than some of my sisters because I was very conscious of the language they used to promote the march. *Atonement* is not the language used when malice or deception is intended. They could have called it a day of strength or a day of pride. They did not. Atonement is a spiritual concept indicating a conscious intent to seek redemption. They spoke about forgiveness. Forgiveness appeals to the heart, not the ego. Many Black women have had their hearts broken or abused and their egos damaged by Black men. Many of us have not forgiven them for it. In many instances, our egos are not ready to forgive.

What really caught my ear was *healing*. Healing is a term I rarely hear my brothers or lovers use. To hear them use that term was shocking. To ask for healing indicates that one recognizes that something is wrong. Most men I know are not willing to admit that anything is *wrong* with them. Perhaps it was easier for me to accept that the men needed to march, to gather, because I know in my own life that God has used the most unusual situations to create extraordinary results. The results remain to be seen, but I know God has a plan.

I saw my father out there on that mall, although he has been dead for eleven years. I saw my former husband out there. He too has been on the other side for quite some time. My brother was there. My son was there. In fact, all the men in my life I have ever told, "Do something! Just do something!" were out there, whether or not they were present. I saw them making an effort, taking a step to do something for themselves. It made me proud. It made me humble. It scared me half to death!

The gathering of a million Black men helped me realize how long I have been the man in my life. I have been doing all the things I wanted a man to do for me and with me. While doing is not an activity exclusively reserved for men, women have been doing their part and the man's part for so long, we leave little room for them to show up in our lives. That I had been asked to stay home and not *do* was frightening. It created conflict in my brain. My personal affirmation, "Can't no man tell me what to do!" pounded in my mind. How dare they! was my next thought. But then I remembered the language. *Atone,* become one with the concept. Unite with the God self in myself and with all the men who would gather. *Forgive,* give up judgment. Release fears, anger, resentment, to make way for a change. *Heal,* allow the pain, the infection to come to the surface in order to be restored to a state of wholeness and goodness. All of it defied my intellect. Good! It meant that Spirit was in charge. I was not.

There was a mysterious kind of peace in the air. I was more than fifteen miles away from the march site, but I could feel the peace. I watched them gather and I cried. Crying cleanses the spirit. It releases the poisonous toxins that build up in the heart and mind. I listened to them and I was proud. It felt good to be proud of my father, brother, husband, son, grandson, and the hard-hat-wearing brothers who sometimes whistle at me. I cooked for them and waited for them to come home—my mate, my son-in-law and his cousins and their friends, my longtime childhood friends and their friends and their children. My home was a "way station." I waited for my four-year-old grandson to come home and share his experiences. I was excited.

It was not the fact that they gathered that gave me hope. It was the process they were given that excited me. Life is a process. Within that process are principles and guidelines with which one must be aligned. Principles woven into a plan of action ultimately produce an evolutionary framework. I am not familiar with any process, principles, or guidelines to which Black men have collectively been exposed. Surely you all get the golden rule, table manners, and personal hygiene hints at home. But where in the Black community is there a process, plan, or principles to which we are exposed en masse and encouraged to employ for our collective well-being? I remember when my father was arrested for running numbers. When the police handcuffed him and escorted him away, he stood alone. He looked frightened. His eyes were downcast. His head hung shamefully as all the neighbors who placed bets with him peered through their curtains. When his buddies paid his bail and brought him home, he was alive again. He held his head high. His eyes were bright. The shame dissolved. There really is strength in numbers.

I often think about the many brothers I knew who were members of the Nation of Islam. When they were in the nation, they were sharp. They wore those impeccably pressed suits, sold those papers and pies, and drew their strength from the brigade of brothers and sisters who stood behind them. Seen and unseen. When the Honorable Elijah Mohammed passed, the nation separated. Many of the brothers were lost. In the group, it was easy to stay in step. When the group spirit and energy disbanded, the brothers forgot the principles. Theirs was a group process. Without the group, the individuals seemed unprepared, unsure. They became unstable. They reverted to what they had known before the nation. Some, including my husband and brother-in-law, went back to drugs, crime, and the streets. I do not mean to suggest that the principles or the process taught by the nation was faulty, or that it did not fill a desperate need in the Black community. I am, however, suggesting that it is crucial that every member of the group be empowered and enabled to practice every principle of the process in the absence of the group. For many brothers in the nation, that did not happen.

The process of atonement was the beauty of the march. Every individual present was given a tidy little package of mental notes to take home and work on. The group was not in existence long enough to make anyone dependent. The group generated individual responsibility. No longer can Black men say, "We don't know what to do to help ourselves." They are no longer held to foreign standards given to them by the "oppressor." Black women cannot claim not to know what to tell their sons in the absence of their fathers. Black boys no longer need to be confused about where to begin and what to do as they approach manhood. The Day of Atonement produced a process. If that process is employed in your individual and our collective lives, it will bring us to a state of oneness, rightness, abundance, and *God-ness*. The fact that the process came through a Black man is wonderful. The fact that it is grounded in spiritual principles is evolutionary.

THE PROCESS: BEGIN WITHIN

The inherent nature of men is to direct activity and energy outward. A man is the physical embodiment of the masculine nature and energy in the universe of life. Symbolized as ♂, man represents the physical world, the conscious mind, the will, and the intellect. The nature of masculine energy represented as man is to initiate thought. The masculine energy preserves and rules logical sequences through thought, desire, command, and control. It is an aggressive energy, inclined to reach beyond itself. The basic nature of men is to engage in thought and to turn that thought into action in the outer realm, the world. In this outer physical realm, the masculine nature also governs choice. The ability to choose is a function of thought. In the physical world, most choice is based on knowledge gleaned from that which can be seen, heard, touched, and perceived by the mind. Masculine nature represents the principle of God as "the Father." God as the cause, idea, order, justice, strength, and structure in the world. The purpose of masculine energy, the mind, man, is to give outwardly, to build, and to protect.

The inherent nature of the woman is to direct energy and activity inward. Symbolized as ♀, a woman represents the inner or spiritual world, the subconscious mind, and the heart. The nature of feminine energy represented as woman is to receive energy, create from the energy received, and nurture. Feminine energy is the ability to be soft and flexible in order to receive. It represents the ability to feel, which is directly linked to the subconscious mind. It is the subconscious mind that attracts, receives, and expresses or responds to external stimuli. The feminine nature is subjective, in that it creates within rather than seeking to project itself into the outer realm. Feminine energy is inclined to reach within itself and affirm itself from an inner sense of knowing and being. Feminine energy represents the heart, the ability to feel and to express that feeling by creating an environment or energy of warmth and nurturing within itself. It is the feminine nature and energy that gives rise to belief. Feminine energy is the darkness of the inner realm that cannot be seen, touched, or felt. It represents the principle of God as "the Mother." God as the medium of expression, the mystery of unseen power; the mercy, benevolence, and grace of God expressed in physical form. The purpose of feminine energy is to receive, create, express, and nurture.

When we understand the inherent differences in the natures of men and women, we can understand the differences in our behaviors and abilities to grasp certain information. Men reach outward. They think. They follow a logical sequence to a structured conclusion based on what is perceived by the physical senses. Women reach inward. They feel. They will respond to inner stimulation and may respond in ways that seem illogical. Men focus on the structure, the external representation. Women tend to focus on the process, the internal creation. The thought process of the man is an outgrowth of the intellect. The thought process of the woman is based on emotion. This is in no way a hard-and-fast rule. There are men who are extremely emotional, just as there are women who are extremely intellectual. However, both men and women carry the energy of an inherent nature, which is fostered in the way we are socialized.

My publicist recently had an experience that demonstrates inherent nature. She is a single mom. After a recent snowstorm, she and her five-year-old daughter, India, went sledding. They took a cardboard box. When they got to the top of the hill, they discovered that the slope was too steep and the box was too weak. Little boys, ranging in age from about eight to ten, were building a fortress on the hill. They informed my friend that they were building the fortress because they were going to have a snowball war. They invited my friend and her daughter to help them. They declined. It was then that my friend discovered the sled. She asked the little boys if she could borrow the sled while they were doing their construction work. They said sure.

My friend also borrowed a broom from a nearby house so that she could use it to propel the sled down the hill. After quite a few trips up and down the hill, she and India stopped for a much-needed rest. Once again, the little boys invited them to help build the fortress and join the war. My friend was out of breath and her India wasn't interested. The little boys were persistent. They explained that the other boys had more help than they did, so they really needed my friend's input. They explained how much fun they would have and how they were going to win. After a few minutes of haggling, India decided to help. She walked over to the half-built fortress and started sweeping the snow.

There were many footprints from the little boys walking back and forth. India swept them until they were level. The little boys welcomed her help because, while sweeping, India would find big balls of snow the boys could use for the fortress. When they stepped on the places India had already swept, she would fuss at them. Obediently, they would walk the other way. My friend watched in total amazement. The boys were excitedly preparing for war. India was content to sweep. They were acting out their natural instincts. India has already told us she wants to be a doctor when she grows up; we are excited about that but we hope she will also hold on to the broom. Society demands that a woman know how to do more than one thing at a time.

The inner or spiritual process of life is designed to foster the ability to strike a balance between the masculine and feminine natures that exist in everyone. You must learn to bring your head and heart into balance, your thoughts and emotions into one accord. Socialization often makes this difficult for men. Women are expected to feel and cry. Men are supposed to be strong and detached. Consequently, certain behaviors, ideas, and practices are labeled "manly" while others are considered "feminine." The spiritual transformation process is an internal process, regardless of the gender of the person involved. If you want to transform your life, you must be willing to explore the depths of your inner self. It is often easier for women to engage in spiritual practices because of their inherent ability to feel the inner stirring. This in no way implies that men do not have the ability or cannot experience the same. It is to say that men must reach, stretch, move into a realm that may be unfamiliar or uncomfortable as a result of your socialization. Change, however, is an inside job. Any lasting or meaningful change in your life must begin with your heart and mind.

On the quest of spiritual transformation, it seems that men are required to work a little harder. Your work involves a readiness and willingness to reach within, experience the depth of your emotion, respond to that emotion, and create in response to what you feel. You must be willing to seek your direction, guidance, answers, and truth from within. You must know what is going on inside you and be willing to clean it out. The bad news is, it is often dark "in there." Most of us are afraid of the dark, afraid of what we cannot see but may feel around us. The good news is, power is born in darkness. The creation of a new life is a powerful event that begins in darkness. You cannot see what is going on. At times, you will be able to feel it, but you will not always know what it is. The key to making it through the darkness is belief and trust. Believe that something good will come out of the darkness, and trust that it will.

WILLINGNESS

Prophets, leaders, teachers, and certain organizations provide us with a framework in which to work. In some instances, we get caught up in the personality of the person bringing the message to such a degree that we miss the framework of principles being offered. You can become so dependent on the messenger that the message is lost. In most cases, that is not the goal of the messenger. In high school, for example, students rarely say, "Mr. Jones is a wonderful algebra teacher. He explains those equations so divinely, let's worship him." Yet, when the matter is social, political, or spiritual, there is always the challenge of not losing sight of the teachings to enshrine the teacher. When this happens, the absence of the teacher often leads to loss of the message. No amount of information can help you until you are ready to receive it and apply it to your daily living. This readiness is sometimes called self-realization. Readiness to accept information and embrace practices leading to spiritual and personal transformation is what I will refer to as *willingness*.

When I told a friend of mine that I was writing a book to give Black men insight into the process of spiritual transformation, he said, "Good! You are preparing lunch!" I asked him what he meant. He explained that providing a process and the principles by which to employ the process is like making lunch for a man going off to work. He cautioned me, however, that unless the men are willing to go to work, there is no need to prepare the lunch. Transformation of the mind to a spiritual consciousness takes a great deal of work. It is work the individual must be willing to perform. Black men must be willing to examine themselves, tell the truth about what you see, make a conscious decision to change, and be committed to take those actions that will facilitate the change.

Some will say, "I don't know what to do." That is where the process comes in. Willingness to employ the steps of the process in every aspect of your life will result in ability. You must first recognize the need to change. This does not necessarily imply that there is anything wrong with the way you are. It means you are willing to do better and be better at whatever it is you do. With recognition comes the desire. You may know you can do better but lack the desire. Perhaps you have made yourself comfortable where you are. You may have convinced yourself that this is as good as it gets. In your case, the lack of desire will retard the transformation process. If the desire is present, you must make a decision. You must decide that no matter what anyone says or does, you are committed to undertake a course of action that will ultimately result in mental, emotional, and spiritual evolution.

You must decide that your spiritual health, emotional well-being, and physical advancement are a priority in your life. This decision requires discipline.

One of the major challenges I faced on my own spiritual journey was discipline. To do certain things, in a particular way, consistently, even when I could not see the results immediately, was a challenge. Whether it was prayer, meditation, reading, or training my mind to think a new way and my mouth to speak a new way, it was quite difficult. I was willing, but I was also undisciplined. It was so much easier to struggle along, living on the edge, putting out fires as they presented themselves, than to spend fifteen minutes a day in quiet contemplation. I bought the books. I listened to the tapes. I attended the workshops. Then I went home, got on the telephone with my girlfriends, and complained about how miserably life was treating me. It was not until the desire and decision were laced with discipline that I became consciously willing to do what was necessary. When I became willing to do it and stick to it, I reaped benefits from the daily practices. I also saw evidence of the principles manifesting as tangible conditions in my life.

The process, principles, books, and tapes are merely props. Every stage production needs props. Props help to create the set and the scenes. The props in and of themselves do not make the play. The success or failure of any production is determined by the work that goes on behind the scenes: the direction, the rehearsals, and, ultimately, the performance of the artists on stage. If the producers, director, set designers, and artists are not willing to do the arduous, time-consuming work in a disciplined manner, the best props in the world will not sustain the production. The journey toward spiritual evolution is a lifetime production. There will be many props to hold, help, and pick you up. In the end, the ability to produce in life that which you have studied and rehearsed will be a reflection of the degree of discipline you exert. You will need to be willing to practice the principles. You must believe that the principles will work for you. You must employ the principles with due diligence.

AWARENESS

Feelings lead to awareness. You are not aware that your shoes are too small until you feel the pinch on your toes. How many times have you thought to yourself that your life is not the way you want it to be? Have you ever asked yourself, What is wrong with me? What is wrong with what I do? Something in your experience brought you to the awareness, the feeling that something was not quite right. The first step of the spiritual transformation process is to become aware. You must be aware of the Spirit that lives within you. You must be aware of the truth that Spirit holds and the truth that surrounds you. You must be aware of the role that Spirit and spiritual principles play in your life.

The truth is, no degree of racism, capitalism, oppression, or disparity can alter the inherent power of godlikeness locked into your spirit. Throughout life, physical experiences and conditions can alter your state of being by affecting what you believe. The alteration affects your ability to grasp and grapple with physical experiences. The physical senses communicate experiences to your brain. If the brain utilizes only its physical capabilities, it will translate all experiences in physical terms. To utilize spiritual qualities, the brain must be spiritualized. It must be filled with information of a spiritual nature. Because men are dominated by the thought process, you tend to think in concrete terms. The spiritual impetus of physical experiences cannot be seen. The Spirit is not tangible. As a result, you can become locked into the physical perception of your experiences and remain unaware of the spiritual purpose or significance.

In order to change your mind and shift into awareness of spirit, you must be willing to know the truth and seek the truth about yourself. This will require a willingness to examine every experience from an internal frame of reference. In the midst of an experience, you must ask yourself, What am I feeling right now? In doing so, you become aware of your own internal mechanisms, what turns you on and off. The next step is to examine your feelings: When have I felt this way before? Under what circumstances? Who was involved? To your intellect, this will seem like an endless, or useless exercise of internal chatter. Once you get the hang of it through consistent, disciplined practice, it will take you only a matter of seconds to become aware of what you are feeling and experiencing. Remember, belief and trust are key in the process of becoming aware.

The truth is, nothing people say about you can hurt or harm you. People push your buttons because you are not aware of what you are feeling or remembering. Why do you respond to people, events, situations the way you do? It is because of the past. Because of things that you experienced yesterday or yesteryear. She reminds you of someone who treated you badly. He talks to you the way your so-and-so did. You know that this person has angered, insulted, hurt you in some way by what he or she did or said. Unfortunately, you are unaware of the reasons. It is not the other person. It is you responding to your old stuff of which you are completely unaware. What the other person did was touch a sore spot, open an old wound, push a button you were not aware existed.

Now comes the challenging part. Ask yourself, What did I do? How did I contribute to this situation? What was I thinking? What was I feeling when I entered this experience? We all have patterns. Patterns of thought, emotions, and behavior that are locked into our subconscious mind will attract experiences to reflect what we believe within ourselves. In the process of becoming aware, you must be willing to examine what you do and why you do it. Without guilt, shame, or blame, your goal must be to become aware so that you can make a new, better, more conscious, enlightened, and productive choice. At all times, you have the ability and the right to choose what you will think and how you will respond. Awareness enhances that ability and gives you the right.

As human beings, we adjust our beliefs and ideas to accommodate the interpretation of our physical experiences. The situations and conditions in which we live are translated by the process of logical thinking. "If I do this, then that will happen." We believe we know what will happen because we have seen it happen before or have heard of it happening in some other situation. We think in terms of the natural outcome of the physical input. We also think in terms of what will bring the least amount of discomfort or pain to the physical or mental self. These conclusions, all grounded in the physical realm, are based on physical experiences and the inherent desire to protect the physical body. Until we become spiritually inclined to trust spiritual principles, we remain unaware that every experience happens twice: first inside, within our consciousness; then outside, in our world. As long as we are thinking about, ducking around, and dodging the unpleasant physical experiences we perceive to be lurking around every corner, we are powerless. Our real power lies within the Self— the spirit of God within our being—which always has our best interests and protection in mind.

ACKNOWLEDGMENT

You can be fully aware of something and fail to acknowledge it. Alcohol and substance abusers are prime examples. They may know they cannot get through the day without a drink or a snort, hit, shot of drugs, yet they fail to acknowledge that they are addicted. Acknowledgment means being in a state of recognition of what you are thinking or feeling. It is the way in which you honor and support your right to be and feel. Acknowledgment is recognition of the truth. That truth may be painful or frightening; however, it is the path to your emotional freedom and spiritual evolution.

Men are taught it is not "manly" to be afraid, to demonstrate weakness or emotion. Yet, certain emotions will weaken your physical being. Vulnerability, fear, guilt, shame, resentment, or anger, when not acknowledged, will weaken your ability to perceive, respond, and make conscious choices. When certain emotions erupt within your being, you have been taught to deny them. You fail to acknowledge what you feel. The masculine nature is to reach or strike outwardly. Blame others for what "they made you do." Look to someone else as the cause of your response or experience. It is only when you are willing to admit that the feeling exists and that you have a right to experience it that you will be empowered to choose what to do. Emotions result from experiences. Experiences are temporary; they cannot and do not change who and what you are at the core of your being.

Acknowledging what you feel is the first step. Acknowledging what you do is the next step. It is almost impossible for any human being to always do or say the appropriate thing at the appropriate time. There are those times, regardless of how rare they may be, that you will act up or act out in the most inappropriate manner. When you do, acknowledge it. Honor yourself. It was a temporary experience. There is nothing to be ashamed of or guilty about. However, if you fail to or refuse to acknowledge inappropriate behavior or actions, they become anchors around your neck. They weigh you down and hold you back. You will be angry with other people. You will blame them for what you have done. The ego will find a way, some way, to rationalize your behavior. That is very dangerous. When you fail to acknowledge your own shortcomings, you set yourself up to be a victim. You give away your power. Once you acknowledge what you have done, how you have responded, you become aware of your behavior that may not be productive. When you acknowledge that your behavior, your approach, your way of thinking or acting out your emotional experience is not reaping the results you desire, you are once again empowered to choose. You have opened yourself to be healed.

ACCEPTANCE

At the core of every human being is an intangible and indestructible power or force that sustains life. That power is the spark of divinity called Spirit. Spirit is the universal life, sustained by breath, that remains at all times connected to the source of life: God, Jah, Allah, Amen-Ra, Olodumare. Every living creature breathes. Every breathing creature has a spirit. It is not the physical characteristics that make it godlike, but rather the nature, the potential power lodged in the spirit, which comes forth through conscious acceptance of its presence.

In every culture there are praise names for God: the Creator, Divine Mind, the One Life, the All-Knowing, the Almighty. These praise names identify and represent the hidden attributes associated with the nature and energy known as God. Acknowledgment of these attributes, combined with the practice of certain human virtues, will elevate the consciousness and ultimately enable the average person to live these attributes. All human beings are made in the image and likeness of God. This means that everyone has the same ability and opportunity to bring forth his or her spiritual nature. Peace, strength, freedom, understanding, total well-being, joy, and love are the potentials of God inherent in every human being. These attributes are our divine birthright. They cannot be infringed upon or taken away by another human being. The challenges you face are accepting that you possess these attributes, recognizing that they are always actively available to you, and incorporating into your life those activities that will activate these attributes in your spirit and mind. How do you live the benefits of these attributes as you move among other human beings? You must acknowledge that they are already present. Unfortunately, you are socially conditioned to look for and expect the benefits to come from other people and the world.

Acceptance is embracing the truth of Spirit and spiritual principles. When you embrace the truth, you are released from psychological and emotional turmoil. Whether the truth is of a personal nature or related to spiritual principles, accepting it eliminates the need to fix things to suit your needs. Acceptance also relates to a willingness to acknowledge the intangible presence of Spirit and the truth of spiritual principles. It results in an inner *knowing* that all is well, in divine order, even when there is no evidence of the same in the physical world. Acceptance is the ability to transcend judgment of right and wrong and the toxic emotions of fear, anger, shame, and guilt. When you accept the truth, you know that the truth of Spirit will prevail and reveal itself as physical circumstances for the good of all involved. Acceptance means being willing to surrender the tangible results for belief in the intangible cause, to relinquish the known facts in trust that the unknown principles of Spirit are always active.

CONFESSION

It is frightening to admit to yourself or anyone else that you have made a mistake, a poor choice, a bad decision, or that you have behaved irresponsibly. When you do, you open yourself to attack, criticism, condemnation, or abandonment. It is a humiliating experience to admit to someone that you are helpless or clueless. Yet it is only through a humble spirit that the light of Spirit can enter. Confession opens the doors of your mind to spiritual light and moral strength.

There are two very positive aspects of confession: it frees the mind of guilt, which in turn disarms defense mechanisms. When you have no guilt, your self-esteem is enhanced. When you have no need to defend yourself, you have little cause to be angry. Confession also disarms the adversary. When you point out your own weaknesses, shortcomings, and human frailties, they cannot be used against you. People cannot hit you over the head with your own bat unless you let them.

There are three distinctive levels of confession: confession to self, confession to God, and confession to others. Confession to self is recognition that you have a right to make mistakes. Whatever you do is based on who you are, where you come from, and the information you have at the time of the action. When you get more information, better information, you will make better choices and take more constructive action. In the meantime, you may step on people's toes. When you do, confess it to yourself. Give yourself the opportunity to grow up by giving up the need to be right. Once you confess to yourself, you can forgive yourself. Once you forgive yourself, you open the channels of communication and enlightenment that can bring new information that leads to spiritual growth.

Confession to God is a plea for healing. Until you admit that you can be better and want to be better, you cannot be healed. Healing is synonymous with wholeness, happiness, and a state of well-being. Confession is a sign of your willingness to be corrected. When you confess to God, it is voluntary submission. It is an admission of spiritual helplessness. It is recognition that your way is not working, is not bringing you the results you desire. When I confess to God, I usually say something like, "Help! I've messed up and I haven't got a clue about what to do next. You've got it, God. I'm getting out of your way!" At that point I stop worrying, being angry, and trying to get my way. Miraculously, I find the strength and presence of mind to do whatever comes up next. Usually, it is accepting the truth about myself and what I have been doing.

There are times when you will not be required to confess to anyone except yourself and God. This is not the case most of the time. Because we are all connected, everything we do affects everyone around us. We are like crayons in a box. If you shift one crayon, every crayon in the box is affected. The challenge of being able to confess what you have done to others arises when you begin to judge what you have done right or wrong. In spiritual principle, there is no right or wrong. People do what they do. That makes it real. People may not like what you do. You may not be proud of what you do. More often than not, you acted in fear and confusion or without enough information. You may have felt desperate or alone and you panicked. That is not wrong. That is human. When you confess what you have done and what you were experiencing at the time you acted, you are acknowledging that you are human. People can choose not to understand. They will probably be in high *pissosity*. Don't worry. They will eventually get over it. You must be willing, however, to take that risk. There is one thing you can rely on, even if your mother or wife puts you out or your best friend stops speaking to you: God knows he can't kill the kids when they mess up!

SURRENDER

The cavalry is coming over the hill. They have horses. They have guns. They have fierceness in their eyes, hate in their hearts—and they are being led by a colonel who wants to become a general. They are moving in for the kill. The natives are at the bottom of the hill. They have women and children who are running and screaming at the sight of the cavalry. They have bows and arrows and a few pots and pans. The have flammable tepees. They have some rusty hunting knives. They also have pride and a fierce tenacity.

The cavalry encroaches upon the natives' homestead, killing the elderly and some women and children. The young warriors fight back with all their might. The cavalry is relentless. The warriors eventually head for the hills. After a few days, weeks, or months of hunger and thirst, with no way around the cavalry, the natives surrender. They give up. They are alive but they are humiliated.

In a spiritual context, surrender is not synonymous with being overpowered, defeated, or humiliated. It is an act of faith. Surrender is the process of giving up your will to the will of God. It is an admission that you are willing to try a new way, do a new thing. Surrender is acknowledgment of natural law, spiritual principle, and God's way. It is a state of mind that leads to an experience of peace and well-being. When you can no longer *do* and admit it, surrender is another way of acknowledging and accepting the omnipresence of Spirit. Because you cannot do does not mean it will not be done. Surrender sets your faith into action. It shifts the focus from *doing* to *being*.

The Bible offers a wonderful parable about the act of surrender. When a wheat farmer plants his seeds in the field, he then surrenders. He relies in faith that the seeds will take root, sprout, and grow. Once the wheat grows, he must harvest the crop and separate the wheat from the chaff. When the wheat is removed, the field is left full of stubs and weeds. The farmer now has a great deal of work to do; however, he surrenders. He stays focused on the wheat. He goes home and waits for his wife to bake some wheat bread without lamenting about the condition of his field and all the hard work that lies ahead of him. In surrender, he knows that the work will get done, even when he does not know when or by whom.

Surrender happens when you can stand in the middle of all the crap in your life and be okay with it. The crap is there, smelling very bad, but you are not in fear, resentment, or humiliation. At the basic level, surrender is an admission that you haven't got a clue about what to do or what is coming. It is the prelude to confession. It means that you are willing to stop pretending that you don't know what you want. You always know what you want; however, in view of what you have been taught to believe about surrender, it is safer to pretend you do not know.

Without surrender in a relationship, for example, you are forced to play the cat-and-mouse game. You love her. She loves you. You both are afraid to admit it. That would mean surrender. Instead, you resist the attraction. You fight against what you feel and against each other in fear of looking weak or being humiliated. Surrendering to your emotions in a relationship would mean taking a risk. It would play out by you saying, "Okay, let's do this. I don't know what is going to happen, but let's go for it!" Surrender will often take you into emotionally, and sometimes physically, unfamiliar territory. That is where your faith comes in. You may not be consciously aware of what will happen, but your spirit knows. Once you surrender, you remove the resistance. Resistance causes pain. When you make the shift from pain to surrender, you come into alignment with Spirit. You provide Spirit with the energy needed to work on your behalf, teach you some valuable lessons, and support your spiritual evolution.

Because so many Black men believe they have had few personal victories in their lives, surrendering to Spirit becomes a major challenge. This, coupled with the images that surrender conjures in your mind, makes it a very unattractive option. Surrender is an act of courage and power that creates a shift in the consciousness: from being a disempowered human being struggling to make a way, to being a child of God entitled to the best. Surrender of the ego and will to the will of Spirit is an acknowledgment that you are a part of God's creation. God's will is for the good of all its creation. Surrender is acceptance that we are all connected and that if one person selfishly holds out, it will affect everyone else. When you choose a way that is not in alignment with God's will, you run the risk of pissing somebody off.

FORGIVENESS

Forgiveness is a process of giving up the old for something new. Old experiences and memories that we hold on to in anger, resentment, shame, or guilt cloud our spirit mind. They take us into judgment of right and wrong, bad and good. These thoughts take us away from the truth. Forgiveness means giving up for a change. When you give up your judgments of people and experiences, your mind is changed by the truth. The truth is, everything that has happened had to happen. It was a growth experience. There was something you needed to know or learn. If you stay angry, hurt, afraid, ashamed, or guilty, you will miss the lesson. You will be stuck in a cloud of pain.

Black men have a great deal of pain that you cannot process intellectually. It is an ancestral pain. It is alive in your DNA. It is alive in the marrow of your bones. Many of you were conceived in pain. We were all born in pain. Many of you lived through pain to grow up in pain. You can't cry about what hurts you. It is not *manly* to cry. Because your pain runs so deep, you may not know what hurts. But it is there. Your pain got you fired from that last job. Your pain encourages you to snort, sell, or shoot drugs, and to drink alcohol. Your pain makes you leave your children, beat your wife, and hate your daddy. How do you process the pain? How do you express your pain?

All emotions, even psychological and emotional pain, are the normal human reaction to experiences we cannot interpret. When the mind receives the data, the body will respond in some way. As children, many Black men were taught not to cry out in pain, not to strike out in anger, not to speak out in indignation. In effect, you were taught to suppress your emotions. It is not natural to suppress emotions. When you do, the mind takes over. The intellect will find a way to control what you feel. In order to do so, the brain waves become flat. They are suppressed. The voice becomes a monotone. You must remain tightly under control and not express your emotions. When you suppress emotions, you suppress your power. Once you start suppressing what you feel, you cannot stop. You must stay in control. You cannot run the risk of exploding, letting it all out. External and internal disempowerment is painful.

Your emotional responses to experiences are usually right on target. If someone infringes on your personal space, disempowers you, the response is probably anger. As a child, you were not encouraged or allowed to express anger, so you suppressed it. When someone slapped your face, paddled your behind, took your toys, the emotional response was pain or fear. Children are told not to cry when they are spanked. They learn to suppress pain. Unfortunately, what our parents did not understand is that there is an appropriate response to all emotions. There are times when you must act them out, should act them out, and times when you should not. Children learn to use their minds to control what they feel. They develop alternative behaviors and responses. They have to find a way to escape what they feel or it will cause them more pain and disapproval.

Another key issue many parents do not recognize is that every emotion has a complement or an opposite side. The opposite of pain is sensitivity. The opposite of anger is passion. When you suppress pain, you suppress psychological and emotional sensitivity. To be sensitive is to be kind and courteous, to have empathy. In how many instances are Black men accused of being insensitive to the needs of others? Particularly women? You are not insensitive. You are suppressing pain. When you suppress anger, you suppress passion. Passion is the ability to experience excitement, joy, intensity. Passion gives you the ability to take emotional risks without the fear of dying. Some Black men shy away from intense emotional situations. You are then accused of being irresponsible and unable to commit. You are suppressing generations of anger. I can imagine it is quite difficult to trust yourself to get excited about very much. Instead, you live in fear of exploding and experiencing shameful pain when you do.

Forgiveness is the spiritual pain reliever. Without making anyone wrong or beating up on yourself, you can forgive. Most of us believe that when we forgive others, we are excusing their behavior. In some way we think that to forgive is to admit that what has happened is all right. Quite the contrary. Forgiveness moves you out of the way and opens the way for divine justice to prevail. It takes the responsibility from your shoulders, particularly when the focus of your anger is no longer around. Spirit can find anybody, anywhere that person happens to be. When you forgive, you clear your mental and emotional airwaves so that you can get on with your life. God knows who is accountable for what, and in the end, no matter what they did to you, they will not have to answer to you for it.

Remember when you were a small child and the big kids chased you home or harassed you? Remember saying to them, "I'm going to tell my daddy or big brother on you?" You knew that your daddy could beat them when you could not. You knew they were afraid of your big brother. When you forgive, you are in effect saying, I'm going to tell my daddy on you. In this case, your daddy is God.

UNDERSTANDING

Understanding is not really an action. It is a reward. It is an emotional and spiritual awareness that creates a shift of energy in your mind, body, and spirit. Understanding is the reward for conscious acceptance of Spirit, diligent acknowledgment of Spirit, and willing surrender to Spirit. Understanding is revelation of truth. It is the ability to see beyond the physical manifestations, which are very often quite convincing, to the activity of Spirit and spiritual principles.

Another word for understanding is integration. When you can integrate the affairs of the world with the truth of spiritual principle, you will gain understanding. To the degree that you acknowledge and accept the active presence of Spirit, you will gain a deeper understanding of the experiences in your life. So often we struggle to understand, trying to make sense of events, the actions of other people, and in some cases, our own thoughts and emotions. Understanding escapes us because we use the rational mind to evaluate truth. Truth requires discernment: the ability to see beyond the thing in front of you and stand in the truth of what it is. All people, all experiences are the activity of Spirit. Spirit teaching. Spirit healing. Spirit trying to get your attention.

Spiritual understanding is not like intellectual understanding. Chemistry requires intellectual understanding. You need to know the formula and the elements of the formula. You need to know which formulas you can mix together and which you cannot. With that knowledge, you are probably pretty well equipped to make new formulas. Spiritual understanding requires courage, trust, and faith. On the spiritual path, understanding often comes after a test of faith. Your willingness, commitment, level of trust and belief in the principles of Spirit are going to be tested by your experiences in life. Once you make it through the faith test, you have a greater awareness of your connection to God. You develop a greater sense of wellness and well-being. The experiences and the tests take on meaning. It is then that you develop understanding.

The road to understanding has one major pothole: you must be willing to tell the truth to yourself about yourself. You must be able to accept what you do before you can gain an understanding of why you do it. When you are headed for understanding, the response to what you discover about yourself will be either "Oh boy!" or "Oh shit!" It is called clarity. Clarity is a telltale sign that understanding is right around the corner. Once you see the truth, accept it. Acceptance of truth is the path to healing. Understanding is the reward of your willingness to heal.

COMMITMENT

When you can focus on what you want and not be swayed by toxic emotions, negative people, or testing circumstances, you are committed. On the way to what you want, if you fall down, bump your head, and get up only to fall down again, bump your head, and burst your bottom lip and you still are not discouraged, you are committed. When you can fall down, bump your head, burst your lip, and stand up in front of a group of "negaholics" who are pointing and laughing at you because someone just stole your car with your wallet under the front seat and still not be discouraged, you are committed. When you know what you want and are willing to admit it to yourself and the world at the risk of being called a fool, you have a commitment.

RESPONSIBILITY

The word *responsibility* is synonymous with power. It is the only way to have power psychologically, emotionally, and spiritually. When you take total responsibility for everything that is going on in your life, you have the power to change those things that you do not like. When you take charge, you make your life different in response to what you decide you want. You make the conscious choice. You are no longer a victim. You now have the power to say no to conditions that do not suit you. Responsibility is the willingness to do something about what is going on or not going on in your life.

Fatherhood is the big issue encountered when the talk turns to Black men and responsibility. How can so many Black men father children and walk away? How can they relinquish responsibility for the children they cocreate? I spoke to hundreds of men about this issue. It was a frightening experience. I encountered some bewilderment, some lame excuses, and a great deal of blame and anger. "I didn't want to have a baby!" "She just had that baby to trap me!" "She told me she was on the pill!" "I can barely take care of myself. How am I going to take care of a kid?" "She had the baby. I told her to have an abortion. It's her responsibility!" My response in most cases was blunt and to the point, "Brother, it is your penis. It is your responsibility to cover it up!" At its core, responsibility is the ability to respond to the consequences of your choices and actions. You have the power to make choices. The only way to experience your power is to examine the choices and the possible consequences, and then choose those actions that will create the outcome you desire.

I had another experience when exploring this issue with my brothers. It was a sense of fear and of being overwhelmed. I am in no way making excuses for men who sire and abandon their children. I do believe, however, that the historical, psychological, and physical disempowerment of Black men has created a tremendous amount of fear. The fear of being wrong and then being criticized for it. The fear of losing and being abandoned. The fear of not doing it right and being shot down. Fear is rooted in the belief that you are powerless. In contrast, being a father, having the ability to produce life, to recreate yourself, is a powerful act. I can imagine that the biological act of fatherhood is overwhelming to a person who has been psychologically stripped of personal power. Some Black men probably believe, There is no way I can stick around to be a father. The emotional risk is too great. In response, before they can be shot down, made to feel wrong or inadequate again, they abandon a piece of their spirit.

In San Diego, there are two programs for teen parents—one for the mothers and one for the fathers. In the program for teen mothers, there are 507 participants. There are 38 teen fathers in the other program. The idea of what it means to be a man in this society has nothing to do with caregiving, nurturing, and, in many ways, responsibility for others. Men are taught to do whatever is necessary to survive. In some instances, they are taught to do what is easy. It is always easier to walk away than to change diapers, walk the floor at night, and give up your last dollar for a quart of milk. There are very few guideposts in life that teach Black men how to be men. There are even fewer that teach them how to be fathers. I believe fathering is an instinct. However, I also know that instincts must be developed with care and nurturing.

Until you believe you have the power to make choices, you cannot respond to the choices you make with conscious ability. Until you assume responsibility for your choices and actions, you will not experience a sense of personal power. As a spiritual principle, responsibility is developed through the acknowledgment and acceptance of the presence of Spirit in your life and through practices that strengthen the sense of connection to Spirit. When you are consciously aware of Spirit, you receive guidance in making choices. As your choices and the consequences of them become clear, your ability to respond is enhanced.

RIGHT ACTION

Powerful people have tremendous will. The will to do, to be, to have without the temperance of spiritual principle or purpose is a demonstration of force. In a spiritual context, the will of the human being is the directive energy behind all thought and action and is based on the qualities of the character. Willful people are controlling people. When willful people cannot control, when they cannot have their way, they become resentful and angry. When you are angry and resentful, attempting to control people and situations, you cannot take right action. Right action requires a balance of thought and emotion toward a clear intention. Intentions always equal results.

Right action is the ability to demonstrate your grasp of all other spiritual principles. To move consciously toward an honorable goal, with honorable intentions, embracing the principles of Spirit as your foundation, with willingness, and if necessary, surrendering your way to the way of divine order, is acting righteously. This does not mean that you will have all the information or resources you think you need. It means that you faithfully trust that your positive intentions will manifest positive results. Right action does not mean that you will not make mistakes, upset some people, perhaps stumble, maybe fall flat on your face along the way. It means it is not your intention to harm or to fall. Should that happen, you are willing to surrender—not stop, but seek understanding and a deeper insight. Right action does not necessarily mean that you will become rich and famous. It means that whatever happens, you will accept the experience as an impetus of growth, not an excuse to stop, blame, or beat up on yourself. If your intentions are clear and good, right action will eventually manifest the result you desire. Your level of commitment will determine the degree of your patience as it relates to right action.

John Salunek, the minister of a Unity church in Philadelphia, taught me a powerful lesson about right action. John is a devoutly spiritual white man who conducts personal-growth workshops. I took several of them because at the time I thought there was something seriously wrong with me. I was unemployed, between relationships, confused, and totally pissed off with God. Yes, that's right. We do get pissed off at God. Who else can you blame when there is no one else around? My intention in taking this workshop was to fix whatever was wrong with me. Of course, I did not say that to anyone. It was a free workshop, so I said I wanted a deeper understanding of spiritual law and principles. Actually, I wanted to figure out why I stayed broke and how I could keep a man. John was teaching prosperity principles, and there were single, eligible men in the class. Besides, you never know how your lesson is going to show up.

John saw right through me but never said a word. His intention was to provide people with the tools for healing. A person who is not telling the truth cannot be healed. I spent ten weeks in the twelve-week workshop. Two weeks before graduation, John put me out. I had missed two meetings and had been late twice. One of the boundaries of the workshop was never to let anything be more important than the work you were doing on yourself. The work you do on yourself is the work you do for God. John told me I was defying God. He told me I was wasting my talent and the blessings that God had given me by holding on to old habits and belief patterns. It was true, but I was enraged.

Right action presupposes that you will tell the truth about what you are doing and what you want. If not, your actions will not reap the benefits you desire. You cannot have a hidden agenda and take right action. When your intentions are undeclared, it is the job of the universal truth fairy to bust you. Sometimes it will happen quietly, in your own mind and heart. You will come to the realization that you are not doing the honorable thing for an honorable reason. If you act upon the revelation with confession and self-correction, you are absolved by grace. If, however, you are willful and continue to do your thing, believing you are fooling people, the spirit of life will embarrass you . . . publicly.

I got embarrassed, but in the process I learned a powerful lesson. John taught me that there are four ways of playing the game of life: playing *to win*, playing *not to win*, playing *not to lose*, and playing *to lose*. Briefly stated, when you play to lose, you find excuses for not doing what you say you want to do. This is a demonstration of simple laziness. When you play not to lose, you do just enough to say you tried and enough to let others know you are trying. However, what you do is not consistent or persistent, nor does it carry the level of commitment required to get you what you say you want. When you are trying, you are not doing. This is a demonstration of the fear of success and the fear of rejection. When you play not to win, you split your time, energy, and attention among too many things. You have difficulty completing what you start but you always take on more to do. This is called overcommitment, which results in being scattered. It is a demonstration of low self-esteem, lack of self-worth, and the belief that you do not deserve what you say you want.

When you play to win, you give 100 percent of your time, energy, attention, resources, and commitment to a goal. You have a clear, unselfish intention, and the commitment to it keeps you focused. Playing to win is right action. It is recognition of and faith in the principle that what you give will come back to you, "pressed down, shaken together, and pouring out" (Luke 6:38) ten times the amount that you gave.

STILLNESS

To see the word *stillness* slows my hand, soothes my heart, and directs my mind. Stillness is the presence of God. You can experience it about four o'clock in the morning before the day gets busy. It is a state of quietness and oneness throughout the universe and within your being. Stillness is the art of not *doing*. It is faith in action, trust abounding and belief turned into a tangible experience. It is making a decision and not judging yourself right or wrong, good or bad—because you know your Creator will love you anyway. Stillness is when you can be who you are, right where you are, and know there is a way out of no way. When you have "no where" to turn, stillness is the realization that your help is "now here."

Conscious breathing results in stillness. Meditation is the art of stilling the mind. Learning how to *be* rather than what to *do* results in stillness of the ego, which breeds fear, doubt, anger, and the need to be in control. The ability to live in the moment, casting off past regrets and fear of the future, is an experience of stillness. Sleeping is a form of stillness; however, the required level of consciousness is not present when you are asleep. Stillness is a conscious recognition of the presence and activity of God within your soul and the willingness to surrender all that you are to that presence.

DAILY MINIMUM REQUIREMENT

Learning how to walk with Spirit and walk in faith is like being a toddler learning to take those first steps. You must test your strength and build your spiritual muscles. To take a spiritual walk in faith means that there will be times when you will not act like a man. You will act like a clumsy, stumbling child of God, unable to stand on your own and figure out how your life is supposed to work. People may want to coach you or seduce you to take those first steps. They will try to make you do things you are not ready to do, not strong enough to do. In those times, you must hold on to Spirit, standing up only when you know you are ready. Then, begin by taking small, baby steps, one at a time. If you stand up or step out before you are ready, chances are you will fall and hurt yourself. A fall can make you give up. If you truly want to transform your life you must stand in faith, step out in faith, and hold on to faith. When you are ready to begin the transformation process, remember that the first step is always the hardest one to take.

Ask yourself every single day, "Am I happy with my life just as it is?" Also ask, "Am I willing to do more, be more, and feel more?" If you are willing, you may want to use the following exercise to begin your spiritual transformation.

Using the Spiritual Transformation chart, you can begin to incorporate and practice the principles listed in daily activities. Select one principle that relates to where you are and what you want to manifest in your life. Write the principle, the affirmation, and the keyword on an index card. Carry the card with you throughout the day. As you interact with others, incorporate the essential meaning of the principle into your thought process and behavior. Repeat the affirmation three to five times throughout the day. Keep the keyword in a place where you can see it to remind yourself of your daily goal. Work with the selected principle for seven consecutive days before moving on to another principle.

SPIRITUAL TRANSFORMATION PRINCIPLES

PRINCIPLE	EXPLANATION	BENEFITS	KEYWORD
WILLINGNESS	Internal process. A state of readiness. Mental openness. Seeking with an expectation of a favorable outcome. **AFFIRMATION: I am a willing spirit.**	Enhances internal drive. Awakens mental alertness. Strengthens spiritual connection with the Divine energies of life.	Readiness
AWARENESS	Internal process. Intuitive knowledge. Ability to identify and harness the spirit of truth. **AFFIRMATION: The spirit of truth is present in all people and in all circumstances.**	Fosters consciousness of spiritual activity. Opens mental and emotional faculties to the spirit of truth and spiritual principles. Strengthens the faculty of belief.	Belief
ACKNOWLEDGMENT	A physical action (such as speech). The ability to demonstrate willingness to accept truth as an active principle and awareness of truth in all circumstances. **AFFIRMATION: I acknowledge the power of Spirit in all circumstances of my life.**	Eliminates human judgment and interpretation. Introduces the divine healing energy into life events. Strengthens sense of freedom and independence.	Recognition
ACCEPTANCE	Internal process. A psychological and emotional release of beliefs and thought patterns. Recognition of the power of truth and the presence of spiritual activity. **AFFIRMATION: I surrender to the power of truth and the presence of Spirit in my life.**	Facilitates transformation. Fosters psychological and emotional stillness. Subdues the ego. Builds faith and inner strength. Creates attitude shift and shift in consciousness.	Surrender
UNDERSTANDING	Internal process. Discernment. Reaching beyond the physical manifestations to the spiritual cause. Integration and translation of the physical circumstance into spiritual principle. **AFFIRMATION: I seek clarity through understanding.**	Eliminates judgment. Subdues fear and hesitation. Fosters peace of mind. Strengthens and broadens vision.	Clarity
CONFESSION	Internal process and physical action. Purging the psychological and emotional being of fault and guilt. Acknowledging to self and/or others individual misdeeds, dishonesty, or violation of spiritual principle. **AFFIRMATION: It is safe to tell the truth about my experiences.**	Eradicates self-abuse and debasement. Eliminates blame. Restores one to sense/state of spiritual innocence. Strengthen self-image and self-worth.	Purge/ Elimination

PRINCIPLE	EXPLANATION	BENEFITS	KEYWORD
SURRENDER	Internal process producing physical action. Giving up the need to be right. Recognition of the power of spiritual activity. Obedience to spiritual principle. Demonstration of trust. **AFFIRMATION: I surrender all.**	Builds inner or spiritual strength. Conserves physical strength. Opens the way for spiritual activity. Builds character and spiritual commitment.	Strength
FORGIVENESS	Internal process and physical action. Psychological and emotional release of toxic emotions. The ability to give up perceptions and judgment of self and others. **AFFIRMATION: I forgive myself and all others totally and without condition.**	Freedom from mental and emotional bondage. Opens channels of physical and spiritual communication. Restores emotional balance. Identification of spiritual value of all experiences. Strengthens reliance on spiritual principles and the activity of spirit.	Release
COMMITMENT	Internal process. Focus. Bringing thoughts and emotions into alignment in pursuit of a goal. The result of the decision to have what you want. **AFFIRMATION: All that I give, I receive tenfold.**	Eliminates conflict and distractions. Replaces willfulness. Focuses mind on victory. Strengthens self-worth and self-esteem.	Focus
RESPONSIBILITY	Internal process resulting in physical action. Ability to make choices. Recognition of the consequences of choices and actions. Ability to accept and respond to the consequences of conscious choices. **AFFIRMATION: I am responsible for the choices I make in life. Failure to act is a choice.**	Initiates personal empowerment. Eliminates victimization. Increases self-awareness. Honors one's personal strength. Legitimizes personal authority. Strengthens self-value.	Empowerment
RIGHT ACTION	Physical action. A manner of moving or behaving. Physical demonstration of willingness, acceptance, acknowledgment, understanding, and the ability to make conscious choices. **AFFIRMATION: I live, move, and have my being in the power and presence of Spirit.**	Enhances faith and trust. Solidifies vision. Produces spiritual reliance.	Demonstration
STILLNESS	Internal process. Conscious cessation of mental and physical activity. Awareness of inner voice. Act of spiritual communication. **AFFIRMATION: My answers are revealed in the stillness of my spirit.**	Prepares the mind to receive Divine guidance. Produces calmness. Eliminates the human need to be in control. Strengthens sense of being and Oneness. Builds divinity.	Oneness

Awareness

I remember the day my godfather called to share with me a startling revelation. His voice was quiet and serene, but there was an urgency that let me know the seriousness of the situation he was about to share. He had been cleaning his temple, praying for revelations and guidance. He began his conversation by saying, "I am not a racist. In my own mind, I do not hate white people." He went on to say that he had been praying to understand why he had such an aversion to sharing information with white people and being in the company of Black men who had certain mannerisms. While cleaning his temple, he had a vision of himself four hundred years ago. It was like watching a movie. At first he thought he was dreaming; then he realized he was standing up with a broom in his hand. He said he didn't look the same, but somehow he knew he was looking at himself. He was a slave, standing at the door of a tiny cabin, watching his mother being raped. He relived the anger and fear he experienced at that moment.

In the vision he also saw his father and brother. They too entered the room in the midst of the assault and tried to help. Instinctively, they all charged the slave master, only to be stopped by the fear of striking a white man. They moved swiftly but without the required fierceness. The slave master was able to reach his weapon. The older man, his father, was shot and killed. Now rage replaced fear. In the vision, my godfather and his brother beat the slave master and then shot him with his own gun. He lay dead in the middle of the cabin. The mother suggested that they drag him into the corner, cover him up, and go about their chores until nightfall when the family could regroup. When it was sufficiently dark and still, they buried their father beneath the house and the slave master in the woods. The family and a few trusted friends huddled together to pray and vowed to protect one another.

My godfather's vision had become almost real for me too. I could see the faces and feel the tension. I imagined how the slaves' eyes would meet though their lips never parted to speak of their knowledge. I could sense the fear and energy of knowing. Bále said a number of days passed before another slave, another Black, revealed his knowledge to the master's family. Vividly my godfather relived the fury of the gang of white men who encroached upon his family's home. There was a lot of screaming and shouting. The enraged mob set the shack on fire with Bále's mother and baby sister still inside. Then they dragged Bále and his brother to a wide-open field. He remembered the anger, the fear, and the hanging. As I listened to this man whom I love and respect, the tears rolled down my face. Vividly he recalled that the last thing he remembered seeing as he hung from that tree was the face of the white man who had put the noose around his neck.

He could feel the energy of hate and betrayal moving through his body on this day in his temple. He believes that the emotional energy he lived through four hundred years ago is the impetus of his lack of trust and dislike for whites today. He also understands and accepts that there exists among Black men a lack of trust and respect that, in part, is based on the roles they have played in one another's lives at another time. This energy must be cleansed and healed. It is for this, among many other reasons, that African culture mandates ancestor worship and veneration. It is through these practices that you will heal and elevate the spirit of those whose blood still runs warm in your veins.

3

ON THE BACKS OF THOSE WHO CAME BEFORE

*Pour a libation for your father and
mother who rest
in the valley of the dead.
God will witness your action and
accept it.
Do not forget to do this, even when
you are away from home.
For as you do for your parents,
your children will do for you also.*
          *The Husia: Sacred Wisdom
                of Ancient Egypt
     Translated by Maulana Karenga*

I often tell people that we know everything we need to know in this life. We know because we are connected to the first Father and the first Mother. We know because the breath of God is our sustenance in life. We know because there is only one Mind, one Life, one Spirit. Spiritual sciences teach that there are no new spirits. We are all embodiments of the one Spirit, which has lived many times and in many places. There is no new birth. There is only continuation. Each person living today is the genetic-composite continuation of blood-linear ancestors. Those who lived before you are represented by the shape of your head and the structure of your body. You have a propensity to like and dislike certain foods, environments, and stimulations based on the intangible energies that live in your cells and tissues. You have been taught that you can inherit disease, mental and emotional limitations. You have not been taught that you also inherit memory. You have a cellular ancestral memory that lives and moves in your bloodstream, contributing to who you are, how you approach life, and ultimately how you live your life.

Many of your mental and emotional experiences are not yours alone. You are in part influenced by the experiences of your ancestors. You live with an unconscious memory of who they were and what they did. Much of the anger and animosity you experience today toward the dominant population was experienced by every ancestor in your cellular line. The fear is there. The hate is there. However, the instinctual cultural memory of greatness, wholeness, pride, and honor is also there. Those of us alive today work from a cultural foundation that was born thousands of years ago. The challenge you face today is in learning to move beyond the anger, fear, hate, and social rejection to express the inborn greatness. The memory of greatness lies dormant in your spirit, waiting to be called forward and activated. The attempt to follow the mandates of a culture foreign to your inherent nature and cellular memory can result in low self-esteem and self-sabotage. Until you are aware of those unconscious influences and how they affect you, however, you have very little power to change. Ancestor worship is one of the many practices of African culture that can assist you in bringing your spiritual energy into balance.

Your greatest grandparents, ten to fifteen generations removed, are alive today in the corpuscles of your blood and the marrow of your bones. They are the reason you are who you are. To worship your ancestors, in the language of African culture, is to honor their memory. It is a process of veneration, lifting up the energy of those who lived before you and are alive by virtue of your life. It is your duty, as a living descendant, to give praise and thanksgiving to those whose lives you continue. In order to sustain your own life, you must purify and elevate the spiritual energy within yourself. When you honor your ancestors, you are acknowledging a part of yourself with which you no longer have conscious or physical contact. It is the recognition of the intangible, spiritual force within your being that contributes to your ability to live fully. Without the energy of the ancestors, you would have no connection to the beginning, no story to tell, no heritage of which to boast. You are today the energy of who your ancestors were. They are today who you are becoming.

THE ANCESTRAL MEMORY

While it is called something very different today, every society honors its ancestors in almost every aspect of life. Societies build monuments to their ancestors. They name buildings, streets, and schools after them. Picturing deceased leaders on currency is a form of ancestor worship. The most recent president of the United States, Bill Clinton, performed a major ancestral ritual on national television before his inauguration. The majority of those who watched had absolutely no idea what he was doing. Those of us who recognize a ritual when we a see a ritual, did. President Clinton retraced the path Thomas Jefferson took from his home to the White House. Along the way, he walked across the Potomac River, the sweet water, an energy of purification. He stopped at the grave sites of several other presidents, where he lit a candle and knelt down to pray. This exercise was not solely a political or patriotic gesture. It was a spiritual ritual. He was calling on the forces of nature (fire, water, and the transmission of the spoken word) and the energy, the memory of those men who paved the way for him, his communal ancestors. When the president-elect did it, it was considered "nice," appropriately patriotic. When Black people light candles and call the names of their ancestors, it is called evil or voodoo worship. Unfortunately, many of us believe it is.

In your most ancient cellular memory is a history of African men being looked up to, bowed down to, revered, honored, and respected because they were men. They were the leaders, the decision makers. That was their role. It was not, however, without balance. The ancient African man, in return for his position in the community, honored the role of women because they provided the much needed spiritual and emotional balance. Men understood that the reverence they received was not "about" them. Men were held in high regard because of the function they served and the roles they played, which benefited the entire community. The bowing was not "to" them or "for" them as individuals, but rather to the positions they held. That memory is alive today in the spirit of Black men. There is a need and desire to once again enjoy a position of reverence and honor. Today, however, there is little understanding and balance in the pursuit of this position.

Black men have a robust assertiveness that today is often mistaken for arrogance. It plays out when you are demanding or commanding that your needs be met, your desires fulfilled. I remember how my mother challenged my father about demanding that she drop whatever she was doing and focus her attention on him. She often asked him why she should. His response, "Because I said so," prompted her response, "Well, who the hell are you?" It can be abrupt and disconcerting to deal with a Black man who does not have a philosophical or spiritual understanding of his assertive propensity. Black women, who must live with but also do not understand the role ancestral memories play in our lives, label our men arrogant, demanding, and macho. We do not remember being spoken to with disrespect. The demands of the men are no longer centered on the "we" of our common survival. More than likely, they stem from the man's fear, anger, and aggression, which he believes he has the right to impose.

The ancestral royalty who ruled a village, kingdom, or nation imparted certain "rights" to Black men. The right to be respected, to be heard, to be obeyed without question or challenge was a function of culture and communal tradition. Today, without the benefit of a supportive cultural context or the temperance gained through ritual, ceremony, and training, the ancient spiritual directives that once gave Black men the right to rule are polluted by selfish motivations to dominate and pursue individual gain. The once royal attribute of being in charge, which was tempered and spiritually grounded, comes across today as ego-centered aggression.

Forceful, powerful hunters and warriors moved strategically, using skill rather than brute force to gather food for the village and to protect tribal boundaries. The Zulu of South Africa, the Ashanti and Dogon of West Africa were warriors, trained in the arts of hunting and war. Under normal conditions, healers did not engage in war and priests did not hunt unless they had been specifically trained to perform those functions. These traditional men knew that their role was to serve and maintain traditional continuity. The Ashanti warriors, for example, never killed an animal unless the day had been divined by the priests as a good one for hunting. The animal would then be used for food and clothing. No honorable warrior ever killed another man unless it was to protect or save his family. Today, descendants of these mighty and proud men move brutally through concrete and asphalt, destroying life and limb, to claim the victory of controlling a corner or a turf, much to the dismay of those who live in the communities among them. Without proper understanding and training, ancestral energies that surge forward in the consciousness of Black men stimulate behaviors that are inappropriate and out of context for the world in which you live today.

Yoruba culture, like most traditional African cultures, provides "manhood training" in the form of rituals. Rites of passage are performed to mark significant milestones in life. At birth, the naming ceremony includes divination, so that the community can identify which ancestral energy the child embodies and what the child's role will be in life. The child is then given a name that exemplifies that energy. The Yoruba believe that the name is the nature. When you call a child's name, you are educating the child's spirit about its mission in life. When young males reach adolescence, they are taken into the woods to be circumcised and to receive mentoring from the older men about their functions as men. Young artisans, hunters, warriors, and statesmen sit with the elders to receive guidance about the mandates of cultural traditions.

Before they marry, men receive training from their fathers and elders to ensure their preparedness to take on the responsibility of a wife and family. This is a form of sex education as well as a cultural education in which the man is informed what he will be expected to honor. There is also a ceremony that signifies moving from the status of clansman to elder, a status of great respect and prominence. This is not a ceremony in which all men participate. It is an evaluation of one's life and the contributions made to the welfare of the entire community. The final rite of passage takes place at death, when priests and elders perform a ceremony to ensure a safe "passing over" from the physical to the spiritual world. The measure of the worth of the man's life is reflected in the elaboration of the ceremony and the number of people attending. If his children are present to perform the rites, contribute to his burial, and carry on his work, it is believed that the man has lived a full and meaningful life.

In African tradition, men are taught the principles of manhood according to cultural prescriptions. The goal of these rituals, ceremonies, and others rites is to inspire, uplift, and support the development of consciousness. In many ways, including divination and ceremony, young men were advised of their purpose in life, the thing they had been born to do. Young men were taught the principles of the universal and natural laws that ruled the flow of life and controlled their environment. They were taught to respect these principles and honor the laws. Armed with this information, they were provided opportunities to demonstrate their ability to survive and support, learning from the males around them. They were instructed in cultivating their God-given talents, gifts, and abilities, at a pace that matched their temperament and was conducive to their purpose. African men were instructed in the importance of both the tangible and the intangible forces with which they were expected to interact in life. Much of this manhood training as it was imbued by African culture, traditions, and ceremonies is not available to young Black males living in the Western Hemisphere today.

While the men were being trained, the women also received their life instruction through ritual and ceremony. Although the basic rites of passage were the same, the primary emphasis for young girls was on child rearing, homemaking, support of the male, and commerce. In many ancient African cultures, women, not men, ruled commerce and trading. Women ran the marketplace because they harvested the crops. Women were the foundation of the textile trade because they cured the animal skins, wove and dyed the cloth, and constructed the garments. And, believe it or not, women controlled the purse. Because women gathered the food, furnished and maintained the clothing, and provided the basic foundation for the family, many cultures deemed it appropriate for women to handle and manage the medium of trade, the money. It was the man's responsibility to do what was required to enhance the family's financial status, but the woman handled the distribution of the resources. This tradition also existed during slavery and afterward. It was not uncommon for a Black man to work all week and bring his paycheck home to his wife, who then provided for the family's needs. Today, a Black man who gives *his* money to his wife is called a fool. The treatment and status of women in the culture in which we now live gave rise to the belief that women are incapable of handling something as important as money. Your ancestors knew better.

THEY SUFFERED FROM MORE THAN SEASICKNESS

As slaves, Black men were forced to subdue their basic instincts in order to remain alive. The instinct to lead, build, rule, and protect those around them is an inherent characteristic of the male psyche. On one side of the coin, this was good. Had every descendant of a king, hunter, or warrior insisted on acting out his ancestral inclinations during slavery, mass deaths could have resulted in the extinction of Black people. On the other side, the dehumanizing, oppressive social system of slavery that forced Black men to suppress and alienate the calling of their consciousness created inner conflict. This conflict was between the fear of pain and death, which could come from the hands of the slave master, and doing what they knew and believed to be their responsibility as men. Men protect the women; men build for the community; men control their resources through cooperation with their physical environment; men initiate thought and action for the survival and evolution of the group. As slaves, Black men, fearing death, were forced to suppress this energy that lived in their being. They lost touch with their purpose. The concept of manhood that was alive as the cellular ancestral memory had to be denied. When a Black man called himself into question in the recesses of his own mind, he was deemed unworthy. He was not living up to his responsibility or purpose as a man.

It was rape and the separation of the family that devastated the psyche of the Black woman. The reality that a man could impose himself on you, without your permission, as an accepted aspect of culture, left the Black woman vulnerable and confused. Her virtue and purity no longer seemed to matter. That her father, husband, brother, could not protect her from violations of her home or body diminished the very fiber of the Black woman's existence. Although she logically knew and understood that her men could not protect her, she still wanted, needed, and expected it. A Black woman knew it was her duty, her purpose and responsibility to keep the family together. If she failed, it was a blemish against her and all the women before her. As a slave, a Black woman could keep her mouth shut, endure the crack of the whip, submit to the whims of the master, not because she wanted to or enjoyed it, but because she believed it would keep her family safe. A woman can endure and survive a rape. No man can survive being hanged.

Why does it seem that the Black woman has been able to endure, overcome, and move beyond the horrors of history while the Black man has not? The cellular, ancestral memory of service, even sub-servience, did not affect the Black woman's spirit in the same way it did the Black man's. For a woman to be subservient to a man once had a purpose and brought rewards. However, for a Black man to bow down to another man shatters the fibers of his being. For a woman to delay personal gratification for the good of the whole is not offensive to her ego. For a man to be denied the right to be who he is, do what he is capable of doing, and reap the rewards of his labors offends his very soul. The infliction of pain, the fear of death, the relegation of Black people to a position of disgrace and dishonor affected us all. Each gender has devised its own defense mechanisms and rationales to cope with the experience. Many of these mechanisms keep us emo-tionally and spiritually separated today. It is quite possible that Black women still blame Black men for not being there to protect them. Black men may still be angry at Black women for the things they en-dured at the hands of white men to ensure our mutual survival. The culture into which we were brought was in direct conflict with the an-cestral memory in our genes. The conflict in which we lived then manifests in almost everything we do today.

From slavery through Jim Crow, Black men learned to use dishon-esty as a survival tool. They could not speak the truth as they knew it. They could not demonstrate their knowledge or intelligence. They held themselves at an emotional distance from those things and peo-ple they believed would draw from them the truth of their identity, their thoughts and feelings. Lying, withholding information, and al-tering their reality to the demands of others were the ways Black men stayed off trees, off the auction block, and out of fires. For Black women, dishonesty was more of an internal process. Black women had to tell themselves that whatever was going on did not matter and that only God could help them. They too had to shut down their feelings and close their mouths, not only in the presence of the master but in the presence of their fathers, brothers, husbands, and mothers. They could not complain, could not condemn their oppressors for fear that they would be overheard or incite those closest to them to take action. Black women were not willing to sacrifice those they loved to defensive action on their own behalf. A Black man's acting to protect his family was known to be fatal. Black women lied about being in pain and being exhausted. They lied about being raped and who had done it. They lied to themselves, telling themselves that they did not matter and that they somehow *deserved* whatever they got. These memories and their effects are still alive in the cells of Black women's bodies today. They are particularly devastating when they play out in our personal relationships.

Dishonesty is the tool Black men use whenever their physical or emotional safety is at risk. Telling people what they want to hear or need to hear appears to give the Black man control over his well-being. Dishonesty as a learned behavior and ancestral memory is the way Black men today suppress their needs and fulfill the needs of others. Withholding information or altering facts to avoid confrontation is dishonesty. It is what our ancestors did to avoid being beaten, lynched, and denied the things they needed to survive. While this behavior appears to be an accepted standard among Black men today, it is not always a conscious choice. A Black man will often lie even when he does not want or need to. The ancestral memory of "truth being deadly" surges to the consciousness when you are not aware of it. When he senses danger, the warrior will hide and prepare to attack; the hunter will stalk; the king will order capture or destruction. When you cannot act on your inherent nature, the instinct is to lie in order to survive. Unfortunately, this behavior is inappropriate within the context of today's society. Dishonesty is no longer an acceptable means of emotional and physical survival.

To be emotionally vulnerable is a difficult experience for anyone. It seems particularly difficult for many Black men to feel safe enough to express their true feelings or thoughts in their interpersonal relationships. Some men believe the truth will hurt the woman and she in turn will in some way hurt him. A history of emotional pain and abuse, with Black women being used as the mechanism by which the pain was inflicted, has had a devastating impact on Black men. It is natural for a man and a woman to be attracted to each other. They are universally complementary. There is a natural emotional intensity. The attraction is often silent, intangible. Yet, when a woman evokes feelings that the man's brain cannot interpret, he becomes frightened. Once again, he is not in control. When a Black man is emotionally challenged or uncomfortable, he may resort to dishonesty to protect himself. As it operates under these conditions, dishonesty is the defense mechanism Black men have been conditioned to use to protect their sense of emotional balance and self-control.

We know when a person is being dishonest. Alarms seem to go off in the mind when something does not ring true. Black women know when their mates are being dishonest. This knowledge creates a conflict between honoring what we know and challenging the man and the "lie." Our history has taught us that if we challenge you, someone is going to be hurt or killed. In response, we dishonor ourselves by telling ourselves we believe what you are saying. Then we become angry and resentful of you. In some cases, we want to, we try to believe you. We ignore our own intuition because we, as women, can survive. The questions we ask, the actions we take based on what we feel and know, often challenge you anyway. You realize that you could be "found out." We are afraid to speak, afraid of losing you, afraid of inciting you to take action. Two frightened, dishonest people will often do and say things to reveal what they tell themselves they want to hide. They both become guarded. They both become suspicious. They are both dishonest about what is really going on. Eventually, in relationships built on this kind of fear and dishonesty, communication, trust, and respect erode. The parties become alienated.

Black men remember being used for breeding. Unconsciously, they remember not being "allowed" to choose their mates or develop emotional attachments. Today this memory seems to surface as your ability to become involved with several women without emotional commitment. It seems that some men "sleep around" because they have nothing else to do. Others do it to avoid commitment without denying themselves the benefit of companionship. Commitment to a relationship would mean an exchange of emotion and intimacy and a level of unconditional honesty that you have been conditioned to fear. Physical involvement enables you to enjoy the advantage of the relationship without the emotional risk. Physical companionship without an emotional or spiritual commitment requires only a little time and a great deal of dishonesty. You must tell yourself it is okay. I believe that you are totally unaware of the influences of your ancestral past and the manner in which it affects the choices you make about your relationships today.

Black women have an unconscious memory of being breeders and of having sex with men with whom they had no emotional commitment. From these men, they could ask or expect nothing. "Master" would take care of the children and provide for her if she was a quiet victim and a good, hard worker. The children Black women bore were a reflection of their circumstances. They had no choice but to love and care for them while they "told themselves" they cared nothing for the father. Today, even when a woman can "see" through or "feel" through the dishonest intentions of a man, she remains silent. She tells herself it does not matter or it will get better. If companionship is the goal and she is not ready to end the relationship, a Black woman will deny her feelings and accept dishonesty in order to keep the man in her life. Unfortunately, this only serves to reinforce her anger toward and lack of trust in Black men. Moreover, it further enables the man to remain emotionally dysfunctional.

My mother knew my father had another woman. When he left home Tuesday in a pink shirt and came home Friday in a blue shirt, she should have been suspicious. She says she wasn't. When he left in the morning in a jacket and came home that night in a coat, she should have asked him some very provocative questions. She didn't. The day he left home riding the bus and came home in a car registered in a woman's name, she should have packed her bags and left. Instead, she washed his laundry, cooked his dinner, slept with him, probably made love to him, and suffered thirteen years of hypertension. She had to keep the family together. To challenge him would have meant the disruption of the family. To challenge him would have made him angry. To challenge him would have forced him to take an emotional risk, which she knew would probably drive him away forever. She could not risk that. Instead, she denied herself.

Very often, slaves were afraid to reveal the true nature of their relationships for fear that they would be sold away from one another. Dishonesty and hiding were the ways they saved themselves. A wife knew her husband could be ordered at any time to "mate with" another woman. She did not like it but she had to accept it. Today, Black women often accept behavior from men that they do not want or like.

A husband knew his wife could be used for breeding or the sexual pleasure of the master. This enraged and frightened him. He could not take his anger out on the master. While he knew it served no purpose, he often expressed this rage toward and *on* his wife. Black men and women today remember, although unconsciously, being forced to suppress their feelings in relationships. When you do not openly and honestly express your feelings, you are being dishonest. When you accept less than you want or need, telling yourself that what you have is enough, you are being dishonest. These behavior patterns are alive in us today as an unconscious memory. They are wreaking havoc in our homes and communities. It is a cellular, ancestral memory that can be cleansed, healed, and altered with an understanding and practice of ancestor worship.

MEMORIES OF THE DIVIDING LINES

The memories of both ancestral greatness and imposed unworthiness are active in the ancestral bloodline of Black men today. There is the memory of royalty, freedom, cohesiveness, and duty. There is also the memory of degradation, oppression, and human control of life and limb. There is a conflict between the fear of the oppressor and the need to build, protect, and provide. Fear creates a paralysis in the mind and an inability to move forward. Today, this conflict manifests for some as the inability to hold a job or irresponsibility toward family duties. The suppression of natural warrior instincts may surface as occasional outbursts of anger and brutality in a cultural context where the role of Black men is unclear, when your innate talents and abilities are unwelcome and unwanted. Acquiescence to covert and overt oppression and feelings of "an inability to escape" may also manifest for you as alcoholism, drug addiction, or acceptance of mediocrity. The memories of the theft of the village's riches and natural resources and the violation of the women could very well be a motivating rationale for crime and pilferage in the minds of Black men today. Your behaviors and attitudes today are more than mere manifestations of a macho, ego-centered arrogance that demands respect "just because I am the man." They are, in part, the result of a spiritual pollution of the ancestral memory. This pollution has created a cellular and emotional imbalance that ancestor worship can eliminate.

I am very familiar with the Willie Lynch letter read by Minister Louis Farrakhan. When I first read it on the airwaves in Philadelphia in 1993, people accused me of making it up. In that document, Willie Lynch, a European slave owner in the Caribbean, outlined the steps necessary to ensure the mental and emotional as well as the physical enslavement of African people. In speaking to a group of North American slave owners, he instructed them to create dissension between:

1. The younger slave and the older slave.

2. The light-skinned slave and the darker-skinned slave.

3. Those who worked in the house and those who worked in the field.

4. Those who had straight hair and those who had coarse or kinky hair.

5. Those who came from the north and those who came from the south.

"Miss no manner of pointing out to them how one is better than another, one more worthy than the other." These tactics were far better than the whip, Mr. Lynch assured the slave masters, and because they were self-perpetuating, they would have lasting effects.

We all know that there were slaves who worked in the fields and others who worked in the "big house." The slaves who worked in the house lived slightly better, had access to more amenities, and were closer to the master. Their survival depended on their ability to help the master keep the field slaves in line. Many of the house slaves looked down on the field slaves for giving the master trouble, for not being appreciative of the master's tokens of generosity, and for "allowing" themselves to participate in activities that kept them in the filth and squalor of the field. I often wonder how many descendants of house slaves work for corporations, live in the suburbs, and look down on the descendants of field slaves who work at menial jobs, live in the ghetto, and challenge the corporate and governmental structures that oppress their lives.

The field slaves did not trust the house slaves then. They were well aware that anyone who could sleep in the master's house might do whatever was necessary to stay there. Some house slaves put ground glass in the master's food. Others provided valuable information to the master regarding the plans and possible uprisings among the field slaves. Today, the descendants of house slaves are called sellouts by the descendants of field slaves. Not necessarily because of their true intentions today, but because the ancestral memory still lives in the consciousness of the descendants of field slaves. The ancestral memories etched into the being of Black men today affect your relationships with one another, with Black women, and with the white population. My godfather's memory from four hundred years ago is only one example of how the influence of the ancestors can affect your life today. I am sure there are many other ways of which we are unaware.

From a man's perspective, it is quite conceivable that you would expect Black women to despise the descendants of men who committed such heinous offenses against your manhood. For us, the belief is, If we don't work, we don't eat. We have been conditioned to do whatever is necessary. Neither history nor culture, pride nor ego will fill the pots or pay the rent. We have not forgotten our history. However, we have been able to endure and move beyond it at some level within our spiritual being. We have held on to one another in faith and with hope. We have moved beyond anger through prayer and forgiveness. We have been able to internalize the concept of freedom and find ways to make the concept real in our minds. Some Black men are still waiting for an apology and an act of repentance from their captors. Many Black women realize that that may never be a reality for either of us.

ONE FOR ALL

The world today is in the midst of a spiritual revolution. All over the world, people are beginning to recognize and engage in spiritual education and purification. It seems to be accepted by and acceptable for everyone—except African Americans. When we as a community begin to embrace and practice our spiritual heritage, we are accused of being anti-Jesus or anti-God. Japanese culture mandates the placement of fruit on the ground in honor of the dead. When a Black person does this, it is called voodoo, and we are called pagans. East Indian culture mandates the practice of meditation and breathing as a means of balancing and centering oneself. When we do this, we are warned against opening ourselves to evil spirits. Christianity openly embraces the symbolic practice of "drinking the blood of Christ" and "eating the body of Christ." People line up to do it. Catholicism advocates the burning of candles and incense as a means of purifying the physical environment for spiritual communication. When Black people light candles, they run the risk of being accused of practicing witchcraft, sorcery, or black magic. In the words of El Hajj Malik Shabazz, we have been "Tricked! Had! Hoodwinked! Bamboozled!"

When you begin to engage in practices that purify your mind and strengthen your spiritual constitution, you are in effect purifying and strengthening your parents, grandparents, and all those whose blood is alive in your veins. This is what is meant by cellular memory: the energy that is alive in your cells, physically and spiritually. You cannot hope to evolve economically, politically, or socially if you do not evolve spiritually. The father who left home when you were a child, the mother who beat you or abandoned you, the grandfather who drank himself to death, the grandmother who nursed white babies at her breast are all alive in you—whether you are aware of it or not. You may be holding on to anger against them and for them, resentment or animosity toward others because of their experiences as well as your own. The energy of fear, rage, and denial that your forebears carried is alive in your cells today. When you honor and purify their energy, you give freedom to a part of your own consciousness.

I believe the behavior of Black men is often an outgrowth of their suppressed rage, the results of a process that castrated their natural instincts and now perpetuates the need to demonstrate power. I also believe that Black women's anger toward Black men is an outgrowth of the historical inability of Black men to protect and provide for us. It contributes to our willingness to overlook the contributions you have made and do make in our lives. I know, as we call forward the most ancient memory of our ancestors, we will bring clarity and peace to our minds and spirits. As we invoke spiritual understanding, the energy of our most recent ancestors will be cleansed, purified, and brought into balance. As we honor our ancestors, we will remember who we are and what our individual and collective spiritual purpose is in life. I believe the effects of ancestor worship will have long and positive effects on our lives.

HONORING THE ANCESTORS

To worship your ancestors does not mean to replace God as the object of your spiritual enlightenment. It refers to activity designed to purify and elevate the energy they represent in your being. When you honor your ancestors, you are calling forth and clearing their energy in you. In essence, you are praying for, clearing, purifying, and elevating yourself. The spirit of your ancestors was always linked to God. However, the soul, the emotional life energy, is linked to human consciousness, and it experienced fear, anger, guilt, and shame. Those memories, good and bad, afflicted or affluent, are now alive in you. These are the lessons your soul has come to life to clear, learn, unlearn, relearn, or cleanse. The Eastern traditions call it karma. Spiritual purification and elevation of the consciousness through ritual and ceremony are an intricate part of your heritage. They are means by which you can free the spirit. This is the goal of ancestor worship. Without it, memories and inclinations can, will, and do manifest covertly and overtly in your behavior.

To honor your ancestors is to honor all that you are. You are not accepting, rejecting, or condoning what they did in life; you are giving thanks that they lived. Had any of the ancestors in your life chain been other than they were, you would not be who you are. The fact that you are alive is something to be thankful for. By directing your thoughts and words, combined with the universal energies of water and fire, to the memory of the ancestors, you refresh and strengthen their energy. A spirit is strengthened when it serves another spirit. Ancestor worship also strengthens the link between the physical and the spiritual worlds, the tangible and intangible energies that affect your daily life. Most important, it provides you with the opportunity to focus on exactly who and what you are: a spiritual being having a physical experience. As you become more aware and purify the energy of your spiritual existence, you develop a deeper connection to and understanding of the spiritual influences that operate in your life.

The Yoruba term for ancestral spirits is *Egungun* (pronounced A-goon-goon). This refers specifically to family spirits. To begin a practice of conscious recognition of your ancestors, you will need to know who they were. Begin by asking living family members. Check through old family records and photo albums. Do not get discouraged if you find gaps in the chain. Gather all the names you can from both sides of the family. Make a list of these names. You can memorize the list or keep it in a place where you have easy access to it. If you choose to, you can erect an ancestral altar in your home. If it is convenient, you can erect an altar in your backyard. You may already have an ancestral altar in your home and not be aware of it. An old easy chair next to a lamp table with family pictures on it is as good an altar as any. Do not let the language frighten you. An altar is a sacred place. A ritual is a prescribed way of performing a particular act. There is nothing wrong with altars and rituals. Nor is there anything "weird" about them.

If you decide you would like to erect an altar in the home, you will need:

1. A small table covered with a white cloth.

2. Pictures, personal belongings, and the list of your ancestors' names.

3. Flowers or a basket of fruit. They are gifts from the earth.

4. A candle, preferably one that is housed in glass. The flame of the candle serves as the means of communication between the physical and spiritual worlds.

5. A large vessel of water, for purification of the energy.

Always be sure that candles are away from curtains and other inflammable materials and objects.

Outside the home, the altar becomes a shrine. Same meaning, different location. It is erected upon a straw mat on the ground with the same items. If, for whatever reason, you are not comfortable with either of these alternatives, it is perfectly acceptable simply to include calling the names of your ancestors in your prayers. You may call upon them for guidance and protection when you feel the need. You can sing for them. You may ask them questions. Always remind them to take your prayers to the feet of God. You should always give thanks to them for paving the way for you.

The prayer that follows can be used for your daily ancestral ceremony. Call out the names of your ancestors at the appropriate time during the prayer. You may want to establish a specific place and time to engage in your ancestral recognition. If you choose not to erect an altar, keep a vessel of water and a candle in the alternative location that you have selected. You are also free to read biblical scriptures or other sacred texts as part of your ritual. The most important aspect of any spiritual practice is your sincerity and your intent. After reciting the prayer or reading the text, spend a few moments in quiet contemplation of your life and those things you wish to see manifest.

It is probably worth mentioning that you can honor and praise your ancestors regardless of your religious affiliation. This practice is as much in reverence of God as any other religious rite. It is the active recognition of the one Mind, one Life, one Spirit of God that is present now and has been present in every living being. It is an outgrowth of our culture. Our ancestors taught that in honoring those who lived before us, we are constantly reminded of the many ways in which the Creator can manifest in life. We are reminded of the lessons we must learn. We are reminded of the strength and power that we embody. A frequent argument against ancestor worship is that we do not need anyone or anything to intercede with God on our behalf. This is quite true. However, every major religion teaches of a prophet or avatar who lived to bring us closer to God-consciousness. Ancestor worship serves the same purpose.

(This prayer has been adapted from a traditional Yoruba prayer and is written in keeping with the principles of affirmative prayer, praise, thanksgiving, willingness to accept Spirit in your life, and more thanksgiving.)

PRAYER FOR THE ANCESTRAL SPIRITS

Divine Father/Mother God, I praise your name and honor your presence in this time and place.

I give thanks for the air that I breathe. I give thanks for the womb in which my life was created. I give thanks for the body through which you express yourself as me.

Divine God force, I give thanks for all that I have been, all that I am becoming, all that I will be by your grace and with your guidance.

I give thanks today for all those who came before me, paving the way that the gift of life could be mine.

I give thanks to those who died in the Middle Passage. Their spirit lives today in the water that surrounds the world.

I give thanks for those who chose to live, whose names are forgotten or unknown.

I give thanks to those whose blood is alive today in my veins for their willingness to be an expression of your life.

I thank you _____. (Here you call the names of your ancestors, one at time, saying "Thank you" or "I salute you" before each name. The Yoruba word is Ache [pronounced A-shay].)

I ask you fathers, mothers, brothers, sisters, and friends to remember me in your spiritual minds.

Protect me from harm and danger. Guide me to do what is good and honorable. Assist me and all members of our family, both living and deceased.

I am in need of your assistance at all times to overcome my challenges with money, employment, and health, in my dealings with other people and my own mortal progress.

Good spirits, carry my prayers with you to the feet of the Creator that I may forever be in grace.

Guide me through my lessons, gently and lovingly, that I may be an instrument of evolution for us all.

I thank you for your guidance. I thank you for your intercession in the matter of _____.
(Here you would state a situation in which you are in need of guidance or assistance.)

Good spirits, still my heart and mind with perfect peace and understanding.

I thank you for bringing to my consciousness the perfect solution, in the perfect way, at the perfect time, for the best of all who are involved.

Amen or *And So It Is* or *Ache! Ache! Ache!*

DAILY MINIMUM REQUIREMENT

If you are comfortable setting up an ancestral altar in your home, by all means do it and practice the ceremony as outlined. If you are not comfortable with this practice, you can still recite the prayer. If you are not comfortable invoking the names of deceased family members in prayer, you can use the names of saints (Peter, Jude, Michael, etc.), archangels (Michael, Gabriel, Raphael, Uriel, etc.), or the twelve disciples (John, James, Philip, Bartholomew, Thomas, Peter, Andrew, Matthew, Simon, Thaddaeus, Matthias, James the son of Alphaeus. You must use all twelve names to establish balance). The goal is to use the power of your spoken word to invoke protecting and enlightened energy in your life and consciousness.

Acknowledgment

The story of Ogun in Yoruba culture is an excellent example of how and why differences result and people become oppressed or relegated to the status of outcasts. Ogun was an ironsmith and a warrior. His purpose in life was to protect the village from bands of roaming thieves and to use metal to create the tools needed for life and the weapons needed for war. Ogun was a very large, very black, aggressive man who did not like to wash but loved to drink palm wine. His presence was formidable. Those who did not know any better would say Ogun was a beast. Most of the villagers were afraid of him, not only because of his appearance and size, but also because he was able to kill swiftly, violently, and seemingly without remorse. Women and children ran away from him; the men approached him guardedly only when they needed his services. Ogun's presence created such a disturbance among the villagers that the elders banished him to the woods, where he lived and worked in isolation.

Ogun had no wife and no children. He would listen as the young women passed his compound, wishing one of them would come to keep company with him. He heard the children laughing and playing in the village, and wished they would come so he could teach them his craft, how to mold metal into useful implements and instruments. He heard the men talking, laughing, and drumming, knowing their hearts were filled with life and love because of the women and children. He listened and heard, knowing he could not have. He lived among the animals, working day and night to serve the others who despised him. He drank palm wine to soothe the pain of his isolation and longing.

The village people hung a bell at the entrance of the woods leading to where Ogun lived. When his services were required to create or repair an item, they would place the materials at the entrance of the woods, ring the bell, and run away. In turn, Ogun would come to the entrance, stick his hands out to retrieve the items, and "know" exactly what needed to be done. The elder women brought food to Ogun in the same manner. When there was a problem in the village, someone would ring the bell in rapid succession. This let Ogun know that he needed to be prepared to fight, to protect.

One day the village children decided to play a trick on Ogun; they would ring the bell and run away. When Ogun appeared, with his machete drawn, prepared to strike down the enemy, no one would be there. The children would hide and Ogun would have to retreat. The plan was executed to perfection. The bell was rung, and Ogun appeared at the roadside, sweating, growling, swinging his machete, prepared to strike down the source of harm. When the children who were hiding in the bushes saw the huge, black, half-naked man swinging his war weapon in the air, they could not help themselves; they howled with laughter. Ogun was growling so loud, with such intent to destroy the enemy, that at first he did not hear them. It was not until his machete chopped away the top of the bushes in which they were hiding that they scampered away.

Ogun stopped. Realizing a trick had been played on him, he retreated to his place in the woods. Hurt, confused, and embarrassed, Ogun began to drink. He had protected them, served them by furnishing everything they needed to stay alive and be protected; why would the villagers play such a foul trick on him? Although he loved them and wanted to be with them, they had made him an outcast and now they taunted him. Why? Many weeks passed. Ogun drank more than he worked. Many items had collected at the entrance to the woods; Ogun did not respond to the bell. There was speculation in the village that he had fallen ill or was dead. No one dared approach to confirm the speculations; after all, he was a beast.

The children decided they would once again draw Ogun out of the woods. They would ring the bell and not stop until he came out in response. When the first clangs sounded, Ogun was too drunk to move. He heard the bell and made every attempt to get to his feet. The bell continued to clang. Slowly, Ogun gained control of his senses and composure. Remembering what had happened the last time, he became angry. What if this was just another trick? The bell continued to ring. What if thieves were robbing the elders, killing the children, raping the women? The bell continued to ring. Ogun knew he had to make a choice: to respond or to stay in the woods. The bell continued to ring. Hurt, confused, half-blinded by the influence of palm wine, Ogun gathered himself and his war weapons and charged from the woods. The children did not hear him coming and did not move fast enough. Ogun began to howl and swing. When it was over, half of the village children lay dead, cut into pieces by Ogun's emotional isolation and drunken rage.

The village people did not understand Ogun. What we do not understand, we fear. Although Ogun was useful and served a purpose, he was different. Differences, when they are not understood, create fear. When we cannot understand our fear, we want to control. Human control generally implies physical force or psychological captivity. Because Ogun was unable to articulate his feelings and his needs, he internalized the impact of his isolation. It was his fault. He was not right. There was something wrong with him. His appearance was something he could not change. His purpose was unlike that of anyone else. His natural instincts made it difficult for him to live within the villagers' guidelines. Each of these factors contributed to the misunderstanding and fear of him. His response to the fear helped to create a cooperative oppression that kept him stuck in the isolation of the woods and ultimately contributed to the destruction of those around him.

4

THE SPIRIT OF
YOUR HEAD

*You've got to get the mind cleaned
out before you can put the truth in it.*
　　　　Minister Louis Farrakhan

Black men are different. You are different from European or Asian men. You are different from all women. This difference is not solely based on your physical attributes, and it has absolutely nothing to do with spiritual principles. To the contrary, all men, all human beings are spiritually equal. We have the same rights and abilities. We have the same connection to the divine source. Spiritually, we each have a different universal purpose. This is what we express in different gender forms. Spiritually, we all have a different mission. We come to life to learn certain lessons and accomplish specific tasks. These spiritual differences are not the ones to which I am alluding. Black men in America are different because your experiences in this life have been different.

Your grandfather's grandfather's grandfather had a very different experience from any being living on the planet at this time. Consequently, your inherent nature, combined with your genetic memory feeding into your conscious memory, creates a different experience from that of all other people. Before enslavement, the experience of Black men was unique to their culture. Following enslavement, the experience of Black men was unique to their physical attributes. Black men were not understood. Misunderstanding creates fear. In response to the fear, Black men were treated differently from Black women and white women. They were treated very differently from white men. In response to the treatment Black men received and their experience of that treatment, they learned to internalize feelings of worthlessness and self-doubt and respond to them with fear and anger. A system of degradation based on physical attributes is something to be afraid of and angry about. There is nothing *wrong* with you when you respond in this way.

When you are told you are different and are treated differently, it is essential that you find ways to honor yourself. The degree to which you learn to honor yourself will determine the degree to which you create psychological, emotional, physical, and spiritual strength in your life. If you can acknowledge that you are different and that you have had very different experiences from other people, you are honoring your uniqueness. In admitting that you are unique, you open your mind to principles and practices that will serve to honor who you are. In Yoruba culture, blessing of the head is a practice that honors and celebrates the uniqueness of your being. It is a ceremony that puts the individual in touch with the most powerful element of the self—the head, the seat of all consciousness.

WHERE THE MIND GOES, THE BEHIND FOLLOWS!

In *The Power of the Subconscious Mind*, Dr. Joseph Murphy states, "What you focus your mind on grows." Thoughts joined with emotions intensify and become a living reality in your world. Your historical experiences and socialization have conditioned you to believe that all your negative experiences in life are the result of either your human attributes, over which you have no control, or your human frailties, which are difficult to control. Reacting to your experiences, you label yourself. Those labels are usually supported by what you have heard about yourself. This is not always a conscious response. In fact, most of what you believe you can do or cannot do in life is in response to your labels being supported by evidence in the physical world.

What's wrong with me? is a common question we all ask. In response, we remember all the things we have heard from our parents, our teachers, our friends, the television and the radio. "You're lazy." "You're stupid." "You're too this or not enough that." All generate one level of experience. The perception that you are inferior, dangerous, or bad will affect another level of your psyche, depending on the degree of internal and external reinforcement received. The normal internal conflicts, coupled with the image of Black men portrayed in the world, often result in a negative self-image. When you have not been taught how to interpret correctly the inner message or decharge the negative external messages, the conflicting responses become self-affirmations that are locked in the subconscious mind. Repetition is the mother of skill. If you hear something enough, you begin to believe it, and eventually it becomes a part of your reality. Your internal mental and emotional conflict will stimulate emotional responses that will ultimately govern your behavior.

When children are born, they do not know their names. The child learns its name as a result of being called that name by others. Within the first four to six months of life, an infant learns to respond to a particular word without realizing it is a name. By the time the child is three, it knows its name, how it should sound, and that it is expected to respond when its name is called. The child has been conditioned. In the case of Black men, you are led to believe that several other inferences are associated with your name and physical identity. "It's hard being a Black man." "White folks don't respect Black men." "Ain't nobody gonna give a Black man nothing. He's got to take it for himself." "Black men are violent." "Black men are dangerous." And usually, along with these very common affirmations comes a derogatory commentary on Black women. The point being, by the time the average Black male in a major metropolitan environment reaches the age of twelve, he has been barraged by negative commentary about himself and his primary teachers—his parents.

Black men need a balancing of the negative and derogatory commentary presented by the society; they need words of praise and support from family and friends. Without this balance, you will accept as your reality what others say about you. It becomes imbedded in your subconscious mind, which means you may not be consciously aware of how it affects you. Let us take, for example, all the Black men who lived in a city where a heinous crime has been committed and attributed to a Black man. Without any fault, a group of Black men would immediately become suspect because of their innate characteristics. They become a murderer, a rapist, a thief, a suspect, even when they know they are not responsible. If there is nothing positive in the consciousness for the individual to grab on to, whether or not you are guilty is not the issue. The issue becomes, Black men are suspect. Black men are to blame. Black men are bad. The truth being revealed and everyone being appalled does not eradicate the damage. The conditioning is furthered. The conscious mind is affected.

What would happen if from birth we began calling Black male children doctor so-and-so, or attorney so-and-so? What if by the age of three that child was told what college he would attend, or what craft he would pursue? This would be supported by regular reminders. When the child was disobedient or misbehaved, rather than being spanked or punished, he could be reminded, "You are not going to get into Howard acting that way!" When he brought home good grades, he could be commended, "These grades are excellent, just what you will need to get into Fisk!" Or, ". . . to be an expert carpenter!" When the grades slipped, rather than criticizing or debasing the child for not living up to presupposed standards, why not remind him, "A 'C' is okay if that is the best you can do, but a 'C' will not get you into Morehouse"?

In the end, the child may not go to Howard, Fisk, or Morehouse, but he would be conditioned to believe he was going to some college; he would have a craft toward which he would aspire. He would know he could be a doctor—a medical doctor, a doctor of education—or have any other career he chose to follow. He would know that to be a carpenter, a plumber, a police officer is also an honorable way to live. The goal is to condition our children early in life that they are something other than what the world says they are. Implant in the subconscious mind, "You are the brightest and the best! Loving and lovable! Valuable and worthy!" This practice would give male children a frame of reference, a positive reference that they could attribute to themselves. It does not mean they would not hear negative commentary; it means there would be something to balance the effects of such commentary. Furthermore, we would prepare the child early in life to be dedicated to something, perhaps lessening the attraction of drugs, sex, and negative peer alliances, and lessening the inference of worthlessness.

To counteract the often negative portrayals of Black men in the world, your minds must be filled with supportive, self-affirming information. This is not solely an intellectual or academic process. It is a spiritual process as well. You must develop and maintain a good relationship with your own head. You must learn to trust, value, and honor yourself. You must treat yourself with affirmative support and positive affirmation. And you must believe you have the ability, right, and power to do this for yourself. Support from the family and within the home and community is also helpful. However, until you acknowledge and develop the ability to be self-supportive, you cannot alter your reality in the world. "Train up a child in the way he should go, and when he is old, he shall not depart from it" (Proverbs 22:6). In Yoruba culture, this same sentiment is expressed as "The head rules the body." What you put in the head will determine where the body will go. Randolph Wilkerson, a minister and teacher of spiritual empowerment, coined the phrase "Where the mind goes, the behind follows!"

PUTTING CLEAN WATER IN A DIRTY GLASS

Each day, hundreds of thousands of Black men awaken to the screech of the alarm clock. You get up, get dressed, and rush off to attend to tasks prescribed for you by others. Workers rush to get to work on time and finish assignments given to you by others. Those others will judge your proficiency in completing those tasks to determine whether you will be paid and how much you will be paid. Students rush off to school to study assignments for which they will be graded according to standards set by others. The standards may have nothing to do with your true ability. Rather, they reflect your ability to function within certain specified guidelines.

None of this is intrinsically bad. The effects, however, are that you live an externally stimulated lifestyle in which very little of the twenty-four-hour day is focused on the *Self*. You know what is expected of you, and you do what is expected to the best of your ability. This may or may not satisfy others. It may or may not have any relationship to your expectations or goals for yourself. As a result of socialization, most human beings are motivated by rewards, *doing* and *getting*. Few of us are motivated by Spirit. In fact, we spend a relatively small fraction of our lives in positive contact or interaction with the very source of our ability to live. Spirit, your connection to your Creator, is your ability to live.

In the workshops I give, I engage the participants in a mirror exercise. I ask them to establish eye contact with themselves in a mirror and assess what they see. Almost without fail, the majority of the participants smooth their eyebrows, fix their hair, or closely scan the face for pimples. Those who are able to establish the eye contact have one of two reactions: they will look away quickly or they will cry. We have not been taught how to take the time to look at ourselves, to be with ourselves. We are conditioned to *polish the shell*, to look good for the world. When we see, or more important, feel the energy of who and what we are, we are humbled. "The eyes are the mirror of the soul" is an ancient African adage. The eyes are also the principal connection to the mind. The first step toward your personal empowerment is the ability to connect with and see yourself. This ultimately results in acknowledgment of who you are and begins the development of the spiritual mind. Your ancestors developed many methods for honoring the head as the seat of spiritual identity and consciousness. Blessing the head is one of many methods prescribed.

THE SPIRIT OF YOUR HEAD

Spirit is the essence of life. The word *life* is an acronym for *Learning Inspired for Evolution*. The evolution of life is the process of preparation, unfoldment, refinement, and improvement for a greater, nobler purpose. The physical life is the process by which you are spiritually purified. For purification to take place, you must cleanse the negative and limiting thoughts and emotions embraced during your human experience. More important, you must be healed of your perceived separation from God. As long as you breathe, you are connected to Spirit. It is your connection to Spirit that imbues you with power. The challenges, often called problems, that you face in life teach you lessons. They are designed to bring your physical mind (consciousness) into alignment with your spiritual mind (superconsciousness). Once the alignment occurs, you develop the ability to transcend the selfish demands of ego and live according to the mandates of natural law and spiritual principle. This then results in a sense of personal empowerment and freedom that cannot be determined or deterred by other human beings.

Many religions teach about *the Spirit*. Few teach about the soul and make clear the difference. Spirit is the divine energy of God existing in everything that has life. In human beings it is called the "I Am" consciousness, which returns to a state of purity at the end of the physical life experience. What facilitates Spirit's ability to fulfill its mission in the world through human beings is the soul. Soul is born of Spirit as an individualized energy that is covered with flesh. A living soul is called a human being. When a soul drops the flesh form, what we know as dying, it returns to the body/essence of Spirit. Although Spirit and soul are often used interchangeably, there is only one Spirit. There are many souls. The soul is where the energy of Spirit fuses with the impressions of the human mind. This fusion creates what we call the personality.

In Yoruba culture, the soul is called *Ori* (pronounced Or-ree) or "the spirit of the head." It represents the unity of the spiritual and the physical being. Your *Ori* takes on the characteristics of your gender and influences your inherent nature as either male or female. Your *Ori*, or soul, is the part of you that knows your individual mission and the purpose of your life. Through your experiences in the world and your perceptions of those experiences, your *Ori* develops into consciousness. Because *Ori* is deeply influenced by the subconscious mind, the part of your nature that gives rise to emotion, it is easily blocked from the influence of Spirit.

The purpose of the physical life is to bring the soul and spirit into alignment. This is called the spiritual mission. When these two energies, the subconscious and superconscious minds, are in alignment, you are in contact with the divine Self. You recognize and are able to fulfill your life's purpose. You receive guidance and support from within rather than from the outside. You have access to divine knowledge, power, and substance. When Spirit is aligned with your soul and you are attuned to it, you are continuously provided with opportunities to learn greater lessons and realize greater spiritual fulfillment. This alignment also facilitates the development of your character, the physical attribute upon which you must rely in life.

Spiritual alignment is a great challenge for many because it requires belief in what you cannot see. In a world that dangles tangible elements of power in your face, spiritual alignment requires that you *draw your power from the invisible Source.* The woman's receptive nature makes alignment a much easier task for many of us. We can feel spirit move before we see it. For most, this is evidence enough. For men, it is a greater challenge to give up control of what can be seen. Attachment to the physical world, the struggle to be right and acknowledged for being right, is a tool of the ego. The word *ego* is an acronym for *Easing God Out.* The ego thrives on your conditioned responses to external stimuli. It points out to you what is *wrong* and what is *missing.* Ego is the means by which you are led to believe that you are separate or disconnected from God.

Ego and the human will are not in alignment with universal law. They are developed in response to experiences, judgments about your experiences, and the emotions born of your experiences. Will and ego are centered on the way things "appear" to be, which is only a portion of what they really are. The will and ego create conflict in the mind, which then feeds into the emotional being as fear, anger, hate, and greed. These emotions stimulate the need for painless physical satisfaction and/or physical control of what is perceived to cause pain. As a result of personal experiences, your personality and character can be polluted by these negative attributes. You develop what the Yoruba people call "a bad head." This is what Grandma meant when she said you were "hardheaded."

The physical body has no life of its own. It exists only as an extension of Spirit. If you are to realize the essence of your being and the meaning of your life, you must turn within. Through Spirit and spiritual understanding, you will find the guidance needed to bring the physical self into alignment with the spiritual self and the Creator's purpose for your life. It is only through the Spirit within that you will find the power you have been conditioned to seek in the physical world. Spirit is the source of all the essential elements that support the physical life. You can begin the process of alignment by acknowledging and making contact with the divine Spirit within your own head.

Africans are a ceremonial and ritualistic people. Ritual is a prescribed way of doing a particular thing in order to achieve a desired outcome. Ceremony is the manner in which the ritual is undertaken. Many of the spiritual rituals and ceremonies of African culture have been denounced by Western cultures as blasphemous. According to most African traditions, however, spirituality is not an all-or-nothing proposition. You are free to consciously choose what you will or will not do on your spiritual path to unfoldment. The ceremony presented here is available for your use if, and only if, you are comfortable with it. Performing it will not harm you. If you choose not to perform it, you will not be deterred on your path. Spirit will meet you where you are in order to provide you with what you need. The following is spiritual wisdom, based on ancestral culture, presented for your benefit. The choice of how to use the information is yours alone to make.

BLESSING YOUR HEAD

Your head is your 360-degree universe. The head rules every other part of the body and access to the physical world. In many ancient cultures, people were taught to cover their heads to protect the sacred knowledge they received. In certain cultures, it is considered disrespectful to cover your head during spiritual ceremonies. It is believed that the Spirit enters and leaves the body and makes contact with the being through the head. The head is the seat of the *crown*. If your crown is covered, it is believed that you cannot receive the energy of spirit. The *crowning* of the spirit. Caring for the head as a sacred part of the body is an aspect of ancient African cultures that has been lost by African Americans. If the head is the individual universe, close attention must be given to what goes on it, as well as into it. The head must be strengthened. It must be purified. It must be praised and blessed. *No man can receive the blessings of God without the acceptance of his own Ori.* A simple head-blessing ceremony allows you to make conscious contact with your head in order to purify and align your physical, mental, and emotional energy. The ceremony can be performed daily, weekly, or monthly. Simply put, it is a time to focus your attention on you and acknowledge the divine energy within you.

The dictionary defines *bless* as "to pronounce holy; to request divine favor for; to bestow good of any kind; to extol as holy; to declare sacred; to devote to divine purpose." You have the ability and power to bless your head. What you may not have is belief in this ability or power. As you begin to acknowledge yourself as a unique manifestation of your Creator, you deepen your belief in the inherent power with which you were born. As you shift your attention from the outer world to the inner self, you will begin to recognize how this power manifests in your life. Your head receives and transmits energy and information. Your ability to utilize the information enhances your sense of power. Your head is an instrument of knowledge. Your ability to put information to practical use empowers you to transform your reality. You are a creation of divine love and universal power. There is no one, no thing that has more influence over your head than you. If you are willing to accept your identity and acknowledge your power, you can honor yourself by blessing your head.

THE CEREMONY

As with any sacred ceremony, you should begin with prayer. Prayer focuses the mind and states your intention. Prayer also invokes divine energy through the spoken word. You are free to use any sacred text or scriptural passage you believe is fitting to prepare yourself for blessing your head. The following is the prayer I often use before blessing my head.

> Dear God,
>
> Think into my thoughts today. Speak into my words today. Work in all my deeds today. Today, let my life be a channel through which some portion of your love flows to reach the lives of all who are near me. Let my head be the vessel through which divine light and energy flow. In your name and through the power that you are, I bless the spirit of my head.

What You Will Need

You will need the following to perform the ceremony:

1. A small glass or clay vessel, with a cover, that has not been used. Between ceremonies keep the covered vessel in a place where sunlight can reach it. The sunlight will keep the water charged with positive energy.

2. A supply of spring water, which you will use to fill the vessel.

3. A quiet place where you will not be disturbed.

What to Do

1. Stand or sit so that you have easy access to your vessel of water.

2. Open the vessel and dip the index fingers of both hands into the water.

3. Place your fingers in the middle of your forehead and draw them across the top of your head, down the back of your head to the base of your neck, while affirming: "I bless the spirit of my head."

4. Dip your fingers again. Place them at the top of your head (the crown). Draw your fingers down the sides of your head to each ear while affirming: "I bless the spiritual energy of my head."

5. Once again, dip your fingers and place them in the middle of your forehead, draw them across the top of your head, down the back of your head to the base of your neck, while affirming: "I bless the masculine energy within me."

6. Repeat this step with each of the following affirmations:

   "I bless the feminine energy within me."

   "I bless the energy of the child within me."

   "I bless all the identities I have assumed since the beginning of time."

7. You will now bless each part of your head, in the following order, with the appropriate affirmation. Dip your fingers in the water before each blessing.

Forehead (Third Eye)	Draw fingers from the center of the forehead out to each side. "I bless the gift of spiritual vision. Let me see and know truth in my life."
Eyes	Strike each eye gently outward. Right hand, right eye, left hand, left eye, simultaneously. "I bless these eyes. Let me see my way in life clearly and according to God's will."
Nose	Strike each nostril from top to bottom. "I am grateful for the breath that allows my life to be sustained."

Ears	Strike each ear from front to back. "I bless my ears. Let me follow the guidance of Spirit and know truth when I hear it."
Mouth	Stroke your lips from the center outward. "I bless my mouth. Let me speak the truth of Spirit, affirm the guidance of Spirit, give praise for the blessings of Spirit."
Face	Stroke a circular outline of your face from the center of your forehead around to your chin. "I bless my unique identity. Let me be a full and blessed expression of the Creator on this earth."

Bless your head again by drawing your fingers from the center of your forehead to the back of your neck, and from the top of your head down each side while affirming: "Let there be light. Let there be light. Let there be light."

You are now ready to begin your day or week having made conscious contact with the spirit of your head. Feel free to add a sacred oil to your water: *sage* for wisdom; *frankincense* for clarity; *myrrh* for purification. If you use your water daily, you should change it every seven days. If you use your water weekly, you should change it every seven weeks. Remember that the water is a purification tool. Keep it in a place and a vessel that will not be disturbed or polluted.

DAILY MINIMUM REQUIREMENT

The prescribed head-blessing ceremony takes very little time to complete and it gives you an opportunity to program your thoughts. It is a good idea to perform the ceremony for yourself daily or no less than twice a week. As your thoughts become clearer and more focused, you can decrease the practice to weekly or monthly. Remember, what you give, you will get.

If you are not quite ready for the full ceremony, try anointing your head daily. For this ceremony you would need an essential oil such as frankincense, myrrh, rose, rosemary, or lavender. After reciting a prayer for grounding, guidance, and protection (any of the psalms or appropriate sections of the Koran will do), you can anoint your head. Pour a small amount of oil onto the index and third fingers of your right hand. Using any affirmation from the Spiritual Transformation chart (chapter 2) or one that you select, you will anoint the top of your head, the middle of your forehead, your Adam's apple, and the base of your skull. You may repeat the anointing any time you experience stress or tension throughout the day. One final word: in selecting an oil, please use a pure essential oil rather than a commercial oil. Any good health-food store in your community will probably carry essential oils.

Acceptance

When I was growing up, my grandmother frequently sent my brother and me on scavenger hunts to find missing articles. A missing glove or hat, her glasses or a shoe were generally the objects of our search. Like most children, we would conduct a cursory scan of the surface of the house, focusing on those areas that were accessible. These searches were usually fruitless. When we reported to Grandma that we did not see the object, she would direct us to "Go back and look again." The next level of the search took us around, under, and in between things. With this level of investigation, we always found what we were looking for, and more. Now we had a new sock with no match or another glove we had forgotten about. When we reported this good fortune to

Grandma, she still was not satisfied. Forcefully she would demand, "Go back and look some more!"

As we searched, we would huff and puff, murmuring to ourselves the hundreds of reasons we hated Grandma. We would wish all sorts of horrible things on her. We would get completely caught up in it—until reality hit us. If Grandma were gone, we would be alone and probably starve to death. Little did we know that our huffing was a form of deep breathing that helped us clear bad feelings and get focused on the search. Within a few minutes, we would get really clear about why we should shut our mouths. When we did, we calmed down, stopped complaining, and became totally engaged in what we were told to do.

The missing items I searched for as a child became symbolic for me as an adult. I equated the missing sock, shoe, and glove with my search for truth, peace, joy, and love. I have enjoyed some level of these experiences, but there always seemed to be a part missing. When I limited myself to the surface, the places I could easily see, I always seemed to be missing something. When I took my time, earnestly searching, moving around what came easily, exploring deeply what was offered to me, reading between the lines of what I saw and heard, the results were often more satisfying and complete. I don't know whether my grandmother had any purpose other than having us find what she needed at the time. I sincerely doubt that she was trying to teach us the benefits of deep breathing. I suspect she was trying to get us out of her way for a while. Whatever her motivations, those searches and the wisdom of her words have remained a vital part of my life. "The further you look, the more you will find." This process has led to my greatest insights in my search to discover the deeper meanings of spirituality and religion. A statement I once heard really summed it up for me, "The search for religion is for people who are afraid to go to hell. The search for spirituality is for people who have already been there." Most Black men I know have already been to some neighborhood of hell. Some of them still live there.

5

AND ONE DAY, MY
SOUL JUST OPENED UP

*No one can give you wisdom. You
must discover it for yourself on the
journey through life, which no one
can take for you.*

                          Sun Bear

Y ou are endowed with the ability
to master yourself. This ability is
a function of your connection to
your Creator. Mastery is a process of becoming consciously accountable for what you do under any given set of circumstances. Spiritual
mastery requires awareness of and adherence to spiritual principles as
the motivating factor behind all your actions. This means controlling
the responses of the human self and allowing natural law and universal
principle to stimulate your actions. Personal mastery means that you
are consciously aware of your thoughts, what you feel in your body, and
how what you are thinking and feeling prompts you to act. Spiritual
mastery requires listening to your inner self, your thoughts and feelings,
for guidance; it requires being able to recognize when Spirit, not your

ego, is motivating your actions. When you acknowledge that you are connected to the divine mind of God, you will master your ability to hear your spiritual voice. Learning how to breathe consciously is a first step toward personal and spiritual mastery.

Mastery in any area of life requires a willingness to stand by certain intangible principles. Spiritually, mastery means standing on faith, trusting in the process of divine order, knowing that in pursuit of truth, by virtue of harmlessness, all situations will evolve to produce the well-being of everyone involved. For Black men, spiritual mastery means developing the ability to see and move beyond the barriers of your own personal physical hell to the consciousness of divine mind. It means being in control of the demands of the physical self in pursuit of the development of the spiritual self. Breathing links the energy of the two "selves" and will create a balance between them. When the balance is accomplished, you have the tool to achieve a sense of freedom in life. The tool is called spiritual mastery.

My father did not scream at my mother because he wanted to hurt her or because he thought she was deaf. He screamed when he believed he was losing control of her and what she was doing. He screamed when his ego, his physical mind, was offended. *Ego* is an acronym for *Easing God Out*, when the physical rather than the spiritual mind controls the body. When the ego senses the loss of control, it will initiate a need to act within the body. Spiritual mastery requires that you recognize the internal impetus for every action you take. You must recognize and be willing to admit your motivation to yourself in order to make better choices. Conscious breathing, which infuses the body with energy, is the only way to subdue the ego and facilitate spiritual mastery over the demanding urges of the physical body.

It is human nature to respond to the demands of the physical body. For example, it is twelve o'clock and your stomach begins to rumble. You ate breakfast a few hours earlier. You ate dinner the night before. You have eaten two or three meals a day for most of your life. The moment your stomach growls, however, you are prepared to drop whatever you are doing, run off, and eat. According to modern medical reports, you have more than enough nourishment and substance in your body to carry you for at least ninety-seven days, as long as you drink water. As a human being, you will be motivated to act in response to the demands of the stomach, which has no mind of its own. Personal mastery would be knowing you are equipped to take control of the situation and subdue your conditioned response. Say to your stomach, "Hey wait! I'm in control here! You will be still and quiet! I am going to take care of you but not now!" Instead, the average person would give in to the demand.

This simple process is an example of how you are led to believe you are helpless and powerless to master internal or external forces that affect your well-being. An external stimulus elicits an even greater response. Most of us are enslaved by our physical senses, what we can see, hear, smell, and touch. Your mental, emotional, and physical well-being is constantly affected by the lure of the senses. Consider, for example, the moose, which loves the sound of music and can be lured to its death by the horn of the hunter. Or the insect that loves light. It will move to the light, where it is then killed by an annoyed human being. While most animals and insects struggle against the lure of one dominant sense, you are affected by five! The senses, combined with the demands of the ego, those of the physical body and the emotions, create conflict in the mind. But when you know how to breathe, you short-circuit these demands and conflicts. You balance the physical senses with the energy of Spirit.

SPIRITUALITY EQUALS MASTERY, RELIGION EQUALS CONFORMITY

The science of breath is a spiritual school of thought taught and practiced by yogis and other metaphysicians. The goal of scientific breathing is to empower the individual through mental stillness and mastery over physical senses and emotions. It is time for the world to break away from the conformity of organized religion and become freethinkers in search of the true meaning of spirituality. This will be impossible until you recognize the difference between religion and spirituality. Finding your own sense of spirituality does not preclude your being part of an organized religion. The choice of religion, however, will be made consciously, in search of an individual connection to the Self rather than in conformity to the way your parents and grandparents did it. Spirituality asks you to find God within and then find the religion that matches that interpretation. Spirituality demands that you seek out truth from everywhere rather than accept the dogma that has been taught to you from birth. You may still end up where you started, but at least you will know why.

Religion, in particular Christianity, has been a spiritual mainstay in the Black community. Unfortunately, many of the teachings of the Christian schools of thought have been used to miseducate and deny the inherent spiritual power of Black men. Those teachings have conditioned, trained, or programmed you to believe that the average person cannot achieve spiritual mastery unless you conform to a specific prescribed formula. Among these formulas are those teaching that human beings are naturally sinful and lost from birth. This notion, in particular, has damaged the psyche and spiritual development of Black men. It has promoted the inference of helplessness and unworthiness.

Those who follow these more dogmatic schools of thought are taught to look to and follow the example of other men, *special men*, who have been able to do things the common man cannot. Somehow, in the process, the message comes across that God has *special people*. It is understandable how the average Black man who is having a hard time paying his rent or keeping a job would believe that he is not one of God's special people. This traditional and widely accepted religious message is that you are not worthy of being one of the special people. The message does not make it clear that the secret to the prophets' success was the mastery of the mind, a focus upon and commitment to a set of principles from which you discover your purpose and mission, and sacrifice of selfish physical desires for a greater and higher cause. That cause is the will of God. The prophets were not special. They did, however, achieve a special thing. Spiritual mastery.

From a number of conversations I have had with my brothers about God, spirituality, and religion, I came away with the distinct impression that many Black men are really upset with God and the church. They are upset about their position in society as a result of *God-given* attributes. They are upset that God himself seems powerless to correct their oppressors. They are upset that the church continues to collect money in God's name but that money is not helping them. They are confused about God's seeming inability to end war, hunger, disease, and, of course, racism. Many Black men think spirituality is "a woman's thing." "How you gonna pray and have faith when some white cop is chasing you for no good reason?" "Praying don't pay the rent, and meditation has not put an end to oppression!" I tried to explain to them that God has given us all free will. As a result, people, not God, have created the atrocities with which we now live. "But

God could stop them if he wanted to, if he cared about Black men, if he *really* had the power." "How would he do that?" I asked. Silence. In a number of these conversations I reminded them, "We can stop what is going on in the world when we really believe that *we* have the power of God within us and stop waiting for it to show up via federally funded programs."

It is time to rethink the message of powerlessness and unworthiness promoted by certain religious doctrines. The Reverend Cecilia Williams Bryant calls it "bad religion and irresponsible theology," which keeps many people in a state of confusion and fear. Bad religion conditions its followers to look outside of the self for spiritual salvation. It does not, however, teach you about the *Self* within your own being. An irresponsible theology teaches that regular people can't do it, cannot find the Self on their own. This reinforces notions such as "The power of God does not live in me! I am not good enough!" and "Unless I do as I am told, I will not make it!" In essence, Black men are led to believe that they are not directly responsible for their own spiritual salvation, when, in fact, spiritual unfoldment, evolution, mastery, and salvation are born of a sincere desire within the individual. When the desire is deep enough and strong enough, you will discover the ability to see through and around all matters and issues of limitation.

MORE THAN ONE WAY TO
FIND THE SPIRIT

Max Heindel, founder of the Rosicrucian Fellowship, a spiritual school of thought, once told his followers, "To define spirituality is to define the very essence of man, yet it somehow escapes realistic description."[1] Despite the lack of definition, spirituality is believed to foster self-mastery, the ability to elevate the mind to the highest and purest form of thought to guard against being led by lower, lustful physical forces. This is accomplished by the development of an individual relationship with the Supreme or Higher Being. It is not limited to or restricted by rules, denomination, or membership. Each

---

[1] *The Power of Spirit: Rays from the Rose Cross*, September–October 1992, p. 269.

person is responsible for developing and maintaining this relationship. Spirituality subdues the human will, disciplines the physical mind, and strengthens the connection to Spirit. The path for each of us is different. Spirituality takes this into account. Individuals will need support and teachers. Your spiritual teachers are those people who come into your life to assist you in the development of whatever it is you need to master at any given time. Christ was a teacher. Buddha was a teacher. Your parents, friends, and adversaries are your teachers. And yes, your "ex" was also a teacher.

In its earliest forms, individual spiritual mastery was the goal of religion. According to the Aquarian Gospel of Jesus, the word *Christ* is derived from the Greek word *Kristos* and means "anointed."[2] The concept of this gospel is that every individual is "anointed" with breath and can achieve mastery over the lower nature of human limitation. Jesus was the name of one person who achieved this level of mastery. Christ is a state of mind represented by the ability to "overcome carnal propensities to such an extent [one] can be tempted and not yield."[3] This same concept is symbolically depicted by the Egyptian sphinx.

The sphinx is a human head attached to the body of an animal. It represents the power of thought over animal instincts. In essence, the symbolic representation is a reminder that as you strengthen your mind, your spiritual consciousness, and move beyond the perceived limitations of our human characteristics, you gain mastery. You become Christlike. Black men have not been taught to think of the sphinx as a cultural symbol representing divine or Christ consciousness. In part, this is because it is symbolically unfamiliar in the Eurocentric context. It is also a reflection of the historical fear of most things that are in any way African. An outgrowth of spiritual mastery is the ability to decode and understand symbolic representations that exist in the world.

All these issues are just as true for Black women, but women seem able to garner a greater degree of spiritual mastery through the support, encouragement, and nourishment we receive from one another. Women are verbal, more open about what we feel and think. As a re-

---

[2]*The Power of Spirit*, p. 6.
[3]*The Power of Spirit*, p. 7.

sult, we find and are open to information that nourishes our mental, emotional, and spiritual constructs. This could be explained by the scientific evidence that women are left-brained, more intuitive, less rational than men. As women's brains function, they have a greater ability to embrace intangible spiritual principles such as faith and belief, whereas men need a more concrete frame of reference. This is perfectly demonstrated by the resurrection events. When Christ appeared to his disciples after the crucifixion, some chose to continue mourning, others were afraid, and still others doubted it was him (Matthew 28:18). As he tried to convince them that he had in fact come back as promised, they wanted proof. On the other hand, when Mary saw him, he spoke to her, directed her to do something, and with no further questions, she obeyed. She demonstrated the ease with which many women are able to grasp the evidence of spiritual principle.

DON'T HANG OUT WITH PEOPLE WHO ARE WHERE YOU DON'T WANT TO BE!

When I was initiated into the priesthood (ministry) of Yoruba culture, many of my family members and friends admonished me. The general belief was that I would burn in hell for turning my back on God. I tried to explain that I had not turned my back. I was simply taking another approach. This frightened everyone, even my more liberal friends. When my grandmother asked me who would save me, who would be my salvation, I explained that I would. I would be held accountable and responsible for adherence to the laws of the universe. It would be my responsibility to incorporate divine law into my life as I worked to fulfill my spiritual purpose. It was at that point that she began to pray aloud for the salvation of my soul and the return of my sanity.

Like the majority of my friends, I was raised in the church. We were Baptists who converted to the Pentecostal faith. As a young adult, I began to explore the teachings of religious doctrines that presented a more evolved perception of human beings and were more spiritually directed. My search eventually took me into an exploration of ancient African traditions, which did not promote the concept of unworthiness and provided a broader concept of life from a spiritual perspective. According to Yoruba tradition, God is present in every living being. The presence is sustained through breath. The purpose of life is to allow the individual the opportunity to live up to the attributes and potentialities of the God presence through the development of a spiritual consciousness and nature. These ancient traditions taught also that men and women have an equal opportunity to engage in spiritual development, as they are both divine expressions of God manifesting in a unique way to fulfill a spiritual purpose. For me, this made a great deal of sense. In addition, it gave me a stronger sense of value and worth in myself as a human being and a woman. Particularly as a Black woman.

As I travel around the country, I have become aware that I am not alone in questioning the validity of religious dogma as it has been passed down to the African American community. I have heard a tremendous outcry for religious teachings that are more reflective of our history as a people, which includes honoring the role of women. This cultural awakening among Black men has raised serious questions about the validity of certain religious teachings that continue to promote dependency. In *African Religion and Philosophy,* John S. Mbiti wrote, "Religion is culture specific." The manner in which people think of and ultimately worship God will be based on the expressions of culture in which they live. Dr. Yosef Ben Jochannon, a noted African American historian, stated, "Every time I had the good fortune to research someone's religion, I found God to be in the image of the people to whom the religion belonged."

The diversity of cultural expressions throughout the world has given rise to many approaches and various interpretations of God and God's law. These approaches are culture-based, not color-based. All holy scriptures are the cultural interpretation of what is believed to be God's will for human beings living in a community with common needs and goals. Many of the religious ideological constructs passed on to African Americans as a composite part of our religious indoctrination were in direct contrast to the culture and traditions of our ancestors.

Language is also an important aspect of culture to consider as it relates to religion. The language of a people resonates throughout the mind and body. When the cellular memory of a people is not energized by the language they use, it may be difficult for them to feel the essence of that which they worship. The language of postcolonial Christian teachings does not resonate in the deepest memory of

African American people. The songs, the instruments, the verbal cadence used in some forms of religious worship do not stir the soul or jar the spiritual memory of the modern Black man. His memory is of the drum. His ear is tuned to the singsong rhythm of incantation. Like Archbishop George A. Stalling, founder of the Black Catholic movement, Black men have begun and must continue to challenge organized religion to be more responsive to your spiritual needs. Those who remain silent continue to deny a part of your spiritual self and delay your own spiritual unfoldment.

SPIRITUAL PURPOSE AND
CULTURAL IDENTITY

A friend of mine, Ralph Stevenson, shared his poignant analysis of spirituality with me. He believes that life exists in a spiritual ocean. The ocean is the oldest source of life support in the universe. Scientists have discovered that millions of years before the evolution of humankind, all life-forms existed within and were nurtured by the amnioticlike fluid of the ocean. As humankind evolved, the ocean was miniaturized into a form that still provided sustenance for all life-forms. The evolution of humankind gave rise to cultural rivers. These rivers provided men and women with the opportunity to express their abilities, talents, and habits once they emerged from the amniotic fluid of the womb. The universal flow of life is designed to ensure that each cultural river will eventually spill into the spiritual ocean, to ensure the consistent evolution of all life.

To get to the ocean, human beings must follow the river. Culture provides the philosophy, history, and traditions that contribute to the richness of the spiritual ocean. Every culture is simply a drop in the vastness of the ocean. Each cultural expression is a necessary demonstration of the diversity of Spirit. However, your cultural identity does not preclude your ability to demonstrate the true meaning of life. Rivers become stagnant when they do not flow. When culture does not evolve to meet the ever-changing demands of the flow of life, it will pollute the life force of the people. The ocean never stagnates. The tides, controlled by the moon, flow continuously to circulate and sustain life in an impersonal way. When people are stagnated by the concepts of culture, they are cut off from the life-centering force of the ocean.

"A bad religion and irresponsible theology" have not taught Black men how to tap into the spiritual ocean. Many have been stagnated by the demands of the cultural river. "Race consciousness elevates the spirit of man to a greater knowledge of self."[4] As you become conscious of the race experience, you gain a deeper understanding of your innate characteristics. Race is by no means the total expression of who and what you are. The boundless vastness of Spirit is at the core of who you are. Before you can fully express your cultural identity, however, you must tap into your spiritual identity, your purpose in the ocean. Spirit chooses a physical identity as required to teach certain lessons and to fulfill a unique mission. The choice of Spirit to be Black and male has a purpose. That purpose can only be fulfilled when the physical mind, the river, receives guidance from the spiritual mind, the ocean. When the two flow in harmony, you are guided to your purpose. This is the ultimate goal of spiritual mastery: development of the willingness to honor spiritual purpose.

Nana Ayibanwaah Bambara-Abban VII, a priest and spiritual teacher practicing in the United Kingdom and a long-distance brother of mine, puts it this way: "The genes African men have in their bodies are the houses of spirit. They contain powers which can alter their state of consciousness. The lack of understanding and improper use of these powers leads to chaotic expression and an imbalance of the Black male psyche."

Working with Black men and women throughout the world, this traditional African spiritual practitioner has come to recognize that "The majority of challenges and issues faced by Black men are the result of a lack of spiritual education and information. This is compounded by the fact that the African descendants are educated in a foreign tongue, a foreign culture, and a religious doctrine which bypasses their innate spiritual nature by teaching a theology of dependency and powerlessness."

The spiritual nature of the human being is like a rose that unfolds one petal at a time in response to the degree of care and nurturing it receives. A rose cultivated in a healthy environment, with the right climate and adequate light exposure, unfolds gracefully, fragrantly, into a

---

[4]H. R. H. Adefunmi Osegjiman I, *The Foundations of Religious Culture* (Sheldon, SC: Yoruba Village, 1989), p. 9.

thing of beauty. Roses kept in poorly lit, overheated, or overly exposed environments develop with less prominence. The appearance of the poorly nurtured rose is less appealing, and it draws little or no attention from those in search of a rose as a symbolic message. In fact, poorly cultivated roses wither and die quickly. The spiritual consciousness of the human being adheres to the same process as a rose. The better the environment in which it lives, the more nurturing it receives, the more graceful and beneficial will be the unfoldment. As with the rose, the earlier and more consistently we receive the care, the sooner the unfoldment and the longer the life. Unlike a rose, we can begin the care-and-nurturing process at any stage of our life and still reap bountiful rewards. The searches for deeper spiritual meanings in life are the methods by which we accomplish the unfoldment of our spiritual consciousness. Conscious breathing is one way in which we accelerate and support the search process.

I remember once receiving a telephone call from a man requesting spiritual guidance. He said he suffered from chronic asthma. He had worked for the federal government for twenty-three years when he began to suffer frequent, debilitating asthma attacks. He had been hospitalized several times for several weeks, which made his supervisor suspicious of the true nature of his illness. After several meetings and hearings, he was forced to take a leave from his job on workers' compensation. His income was cut by two-thirds. Eventually he lost his apartment. He was living in a furnished room, receiving food stamps, and barely surviving. He was miserable, frightened, and totally confused. He did not understand how this could happen to him. He was a born-again Christian. He did not smoke, drink, swear, or fornicate, and he followed the Ten Commandments every day. He said he knew that prayer had caused his asthma to subside, but no matter how hard he prayed, he could not get his job back, find another job, or get enough money to support himself above the poverty level.

I asked the man if he liked his government job. He said no. He had two master's degrees and his lifelong dream was to teach. He stayed on the job for security. He made a decent salary and was entitled to a very good pension. I asked him if as a Christian, was it not his duty to glorify the Christ? Christ was not miserable, unhappy, living in fear or confusion. It is one thing to know the tenets of Christ. It is another thing to be able to live them. If he wanted to be a good Christian, he should use his God-given talents and abilities to do what would make him happy and bring some good into the world. I explained that the issue for him was not asthma or workers' compensation. The issue was knowing his spiritual purpose. The issue was being connected to his spiritual Self, which would provide him with the guidance he needed. I reminded him that God is happy when we are. Therefore, we owe it to God to be happy.

If teaching would make him happy, if he had the credentials to teach, then he should teach. He said he had tried to get a teaching job in a private school but was turned down. How many times? I asked. Once. "Then you did not go to the right place." With all the schools in the country, I assured him, the right school would accept him. Immediately he went into fear about his inability to find the right school. I told him to take a few deep breaths. "I can't! I'm an asthmatic. I can't breathe like that!" The man was afraid to breathe. He was afraid that he could not get enough air and that he would die. I suggested to him that for the same reasons he was afraid to breathe, he could not find a job. He was afraid there was not enough. He believed there was a lack, or that he lacked something essential to his survival.

For several weeks this man called me every day and I guided him through deep-breathing exercises. I taught him how to use breath to calm his thoughts, to retrieve information from his memory, to relieve pain, and to control his asthma. There were times when he accused me of doing "voodoo" and playing mind-control games with him, but he kept calling. When I last heard from him, he was an assistant principal at a middle school in Philadelphia. When he learned how to breathe, he learned how to live, without fear or hesitation.

If your spiritual philosophy or religious practice is not producing what you need in life, you are not unfolding and it may be time to find another way. You can always find a reason or an excuse not to do something. Often, we use religion. We master religious rules, live according to their mandates, and wait for the results to befall us from a sacred place outside the self. This is the primary difference between the letter of religion and the principles of Spirit. "Knock and it shall be opened unto you" (Matthew 7:7). Spirituality is the knock that brings answers from within. The knowledge takes shape in your mind and form in your life according to the operation of natural law and universal order and your willingness to accept its validity. Conscious breathing supports your willingness and strengthens your ability to access information you need for your unfoldment process.

TAKING THE SPIRITUAL PATH

Religion alone will not save you. No matter how devout or knowledgeable you are, how pious you attempt to be, no religion will save you if you live in mental darkness, fear, hate, and anger. What will save you is character: the quality of intent with which you conduct your affairs in life. Character, coupled with respect for and reliance on the laws of nature and spirit to operate in your favor, will strengthen your faith in and trust in the omnipotence of God. Salvation is a holistic principle. The goal is to preserve or save the mind, body, and soul. As such, compliance with nutrition and dietary laws will strengthen and enhance the body temple as a dwelling place for the Spirit. You must determine for yourself the type of nutritional regime best suited to your needs. There are a number of wonderful books on the market that can acquaint you with basic dietary laws and practices. And finally, the sincerity of your desire to develop and maintain a personal relationship with God within yourself, without reliance on external interpretation, will result in spiritual mastery. A spiritually masterful being thinks and behaves in a spiritually powerful manner.

THE GIFT OF BREATH

Breath is the gift from the Creator that sustains life on the physical plane. As long as you are breathing, you are connected to the life and grace of God. Conscious breathing, knowing the pattern and rhythm of your breath, keeps your mind clear and your spirit strong, which ultimately results in mastery over the lower or physical nature. To become conscious of your connection to Spirit within your being and the information it may hold for you, it is necessary to (1) become conscious of your breath and (2) consciously discipline the mind to take in breath.

In his book *The Science of Breath*, Yogi Ramcharaka says, "Breath is the vital life force which connects every man to every other and all men to God." It is through breathing that you draw the life energy of God into your being. When you inhale breath and open your mouth to exhale, you make the sound of breath, Ahhhh. It is the same sound made when you speak the name of God as All-ah or Allah. The same sound of breath is present in J-ah (Jah), Jehov-ah (Jehovah), Pt-ah

(Ptah, the most ancient recorded name for the Creator), and Ori-shah (Orisha, the manifestations of God in the Yoruba tradition). We hear the presence of breath in Hal-le-lu-jah, the word used to express praise or joy in the presence of God. This is the same sound you make when you have a revelation—Ah-ha, meaning "I understand. I've got it." God is your revelation of life, present in your every breath.

SPIRIT-MIND-BREATH CONNECTION

Think back to a time when you were upset. Chances are you were breathing rapidly, trying to talk or think, unable to catch your breath. If you were ever in a situation where you were in danger, your breathing most probably became rapid and shallow. Often, you are not aware of the rhythm of your breath. Shallow breathing forces oxygen into your head. The brain is then overwhelmed from the influx of oxygen. The common expression for this is "it blew my mind." Shallow breathing also depletes the body of oxygen, so that you cannot feel what is going on in your body. When you are not in touch with your body, you do not feel grounded. In effect, the thing with which you are confronted literally "blows you away."

Conscious breathing quiets the mind, calms the emotions, and grounds the body because it fills the entire being with the energy of life, oxygen. Breathing shifts the mental focus from the external, the physical, to the internal, the spiritual, as it fills the body with the energy of spiritual elements created by God. Oxygen is the sponge of the universe. It absorbs rays from the sun, stars, moon, and all the planets. Conscious breathing enables you to circulate this universal energy into every part of your body: tissues, cells, muscles, and organs. As you circulate this energy into your physical being, the mind, body, and spirit become more attuned to the universal force of life.

The gift of breath is God's grace. As long as you are breathing, you are in the grace of the Source of life and the energy it emanates into the universe. When you stop breathing, the grace of life is over. The average adult takes very shallow breaths, circulating air only between the chest and the brain. For the masculine energy, in which thought is the dominant purpose, shallow breathing increases the attention to what is going on in the brain. There is little conscious connection to the energy flow in other parts of the body. Life is a total process. The energy stored as thoughts and emotions is constantly at work influencing behavior. Conscious breathing helps to cleanse, purify, and bring the total being into balance.

There is one major challenge to conscious breathing, however: oxygen energizes everything—the good and the bad. Some Black men have very negative memories, thoughts, ideas, and emotions stored in the crevices of the brain. Conscious breathing energizes everything, the negative as well as the positive. Unless the thoughts are spiritualized, conscious breathing can strengthen the distorted views you may have about your life.

I had a male friend once who studied martial arts. The better he became at martial arts, the more arrogant and aggressive he became in his personal relationships. His wife and I could not figure out the conflict. We knew that most martial arts are based on sound philosophy and discipline. Yet this brother became so aggressive and dominating as he progressed in his studies that his wife and children grew afraid of him. Late one night these fears were realized; this brother had an argument with his wife and beat her to within an inch of her life. When I arrived at the hospital, he was visibly shaken by what he had done. He said, "I don't know what came over me." I asked him how much of the spiritual philosophy of martial arts he had studied. He looked at me as if I were crazy. "I don't take classes to learn about God; I take classes to learn how to defend myself."

That was the core of the problem. Without the spiritual understanding of the arts, he used his skill to defend himself against any and everything, even when it was inappropriate. He did not see martial arts as a spiritual discipline. He saw it only as a physical activity. As a result, when he felt threatened by his wife, he defended himself. The breathing techniques that accompanied his studies strengthened the bad in him as well as the good. Minister Louis Farrakhan reminds us that you must clean the mind out before you can put the truth in it. This brother had not cleaned his mind out before he energized the things in it.

In learning to breathe consciously, you can become consciously aware of God's grace in your life. To do so, you must be willing to ignore the demands of the physical world and become attuned to your inner world. In that sacred space within, through the art and science of breath, you can release, cleanse, and heal the mind and emotions. It is possible through conscious breathing to subdue the ego and make conscious contact with the living spirit of the Creator within. For some, this will be a monumental challenge, since shallow breathing has kept you locked into the brain. To you I offer a passage from *A Course in Miracles*, "No learning is acquired by anyone unless he wants to learn and in some way believes he needs it." For those who are willing, ready, and eager to change, learn, and grow, I say simply, BREATHE.

BREATHING EXERCISES

You should begin your breathing exercises with a silent prayer to be held in the light and love of God. If you are unsure or uncomfortable making up your own prayer, you can recite the Lord's Prayer, the Twenty-third Psalm, a section of the Koran, or any other standard prayer you know. Once you have completed your prayer, allow your mind and body to relax before you begin your breathing exercises.

DEEP BREATHING

Deep breathing aids in the circulation of oxygen throughout the body, energizes the circulatory and nervous systems, opens the ache (power) of the spiritual crown and the third eye, and strengthens the heart. To practice it:

1. Sit or stand with your back straight.

2. Exhale through your nose to expel all air in your lungs. When you believe it is all out, exhale again with a sniff through your nose.

3. Slowly inhale through your nose while expanding your diaphragm (stomach). Do not force the expansion of the stomach; allow it to expand naturally. Try to feel your back expanding. This helps to engage the lungs in the breathing process.

4. When you have taken in as much air as possible, slowly exhale through your nose, drawing the diaphragm (stomach) in.

5. When you have exhaled normally, sniff out through your nose again.

6. Allow your body to relax for three to five seconds and then begin again.

7. Continue this exercise for at least three minutes during the first week of practice and ten minutes the second week. Increase thereafter by five minutes per week until you reach a total of twenty to thirty minutes.

At first you may notice that your heart is racing or that you can hear your heartbeat. Do not be alarmed. Your heart is breathing, probably for the first time in many years. Rest and continue. If you feel light-headed or faint, simply rest. You will also note that your body feels lighter and your mind is still. This is a good thing! The beauty of breath is that you can do it anytime, anywhere. If you feel yourself becoming unglued, nervous, or upset by what is going on around you, simply breathe. Take long, deep breaths to replenish the energy within you.

CIRCULAR BREATH

Circular breath distributes oxygen into and clears carbon monoxide out of the body, strengthens the lungs and the circulatory system, and balances energy stored throughout the body. To practice it:

1. Sit or stand with a straight back and inhale as much air as possible through your nose while extending your diaphragm (stomach).

2. Without stopping to hold the breath, exhale the air through your nose while drawing in your diaphragm.

3. Without stopping to rest, inhale again, extending your diaphragm.

4. Exhale in the same manner.

5. Repeat this breath ten times by counting the inhalations.

6. After the first ten breaths, slightly open your mouth. Inhale through your nose again.

7. Exhale through your mouth.

8. Repeat inhaling through your nose, exhaling through your mouth for ten breaths before you rest.

Three to five minutes of this exercise daily will be enough to get all your juices flowing.

BALANCING BREATH

Balancing breath cleanses the lymph nodes, balances the left and right sides of the brain, and opens the *ache* (power) of the third eye and solar plexus (center of power). To practice it:

1. Sit or stand with a straight back.

2. Cover your right nostril with the thumb of your right hand.

3. Inhale slowly through your left nostril to the count of four.

4. Using the index finger of your right hand, cover your left nostril. (Both nostrils are now closed.)

5. Hold your breath for two counts.

6. Remove your thumb from your right nostril and slowly exhale to the count of four. (Your left nostril is still covered by your forefinger.)

7. Inhale slowly through your right nostril, counting to four.

8. Using the thumb of your right hand, cover your right nostril. (Once again, both nostrils are covered.)

9. Hold your breath for two counts.

10. Remove your index finger from your left nostril and exhale slowly, counting to four.

11. Repeat this breathing sequence eight times in succession for the first week. The following week, change the count to inhale six, hold three, exhale six. Continue this pace for one week. The third week, increase the count to inhale eight, hold four, exhale eight.

12. Maintain this rhythm for at least ninety days.

PITUITARY BREATH

Pituitary breath aids in strengthening the major gland in the body. The pituitary gland controls all other glands. This breath increases circulation in the brain, improves the thyroid gland, and brings the flow of blood into the face and neck. It also strengthens and increases flexibility in the spine and stretches the vertebrae. *Do not attempt this breath exercise if you have high blood pressure or any heart ailment.* To practice it:

1. Stand with your feet about twelve inches apart. If you are more than six feet tall, use eighteen inches.

2. Close the right nostril with the forefinger of your left hand.

3. Take a deep breath through your left nostril.

4. Close your left nostril with the thumb of your left hand.

5. Slightly bend your knees.

6. Place your right hand on the top of your head.

7. Bend over by first lowering your head to your chest, then rounding your shoulders, then continuing to bend until you are loosely hanging over. Your knees remain bent.

8. Hold your breath and the position as long as you can. If you feel as though you must breathe, swallow.

9. Slowly begin coming up, unbending your spine, from your waist to your neck. Slowly roll your neck and head back to an upright position.

10. When you are straight, open one-half of your right nostril and slowly exhale.

11. Repeat this breath only twice.

This is a heavy-duty exercise to be performed no more than once a day. During your initial practice sessions, you will probably feel faint. Do not panic. Your brain just received an influx of oxygen. Your heart is probably pounding. This too is fine. If you find that you cannot bend or hold the breath, do not force yourself; let go and start again. You have nothing to prove. Take your time. Be gentle with yourself.

MEDITATIVE BREATH

Meditative breath quiets the mind while opening the *ache* (power) of the crown, third eye, and solar plexus. It pulls spiritual energy into the crown of the head. To practice it:

1. Sit with a straight back, feet flat on the floor and palms of hands on thighs facing upward.

2. Close your eyes and drop your chin to your chest. Do not force it; simply lower your head.

3. Begin inhaling and rolling your head upward to the count of seven. By seven, the head should be hanging backward.

4. Hold the breath for a count of four.

5. Slowly exhale through your nose while rolling your head back down to the count of seven. By seven, the head should be hanging to the chest again.

6. Repeat the breath and movement four times before resting.

You should now be in a meditative state. Your mind should be still and receptive, your body relaxed. The meditative breath exercise can be performed daily just about anytime or anywhere (except while driving). This is also a good time to begin infusing your consciousness with transformative ideas.

DAILY MINIMUM REQUIREMENT

The following Affirmation for Empowerment is a simple but powerful tool that you can include in your daily breathing routine. When you begin your daily breathing exercises, be sure to have a copy of the affirmation nearby. Recite it once aloud before you begin your day.

Affirmation for Empowerment

There is a universal power seeking an outlet through me.
The instrument of universal power is my mind.
Today, I believe in the power. I believe the power is right
    where I Am.
I understand this is a power for good. I realize the power
    flows through me as my divine right.
Today, I accept the presence of this power.
Today, I believe the power is operating in all of my life's
    affairs.

Today, I acknowledge that there is a divine power instructing me in all that I do.

Today, I affirm divine power as the active presence of joy and happiness in my life.

Today, I deliberately turn from everything that is confusing and denies the reality of God's power in, as, and through me.

Today, I know that every atom, every cell, every tissue, every organ in my body is brought into divine health and harmony.

Today, I know that every shadow of doubt, worry, and fear is dispelled and I Am quickened with the power of the living spirit in me.

Today, I Am graced with the presence of spirit. Today, I Am blessed with the love of spirit.

Today, I Am strong in the glory of spirit. Today, I know I Am the power and glory through which spirit is working.

Today, I affirm that the living spirit within me now breathes newness into my being.

I Am filled with good. I Am filled with light. I Am filled with faith.

I Am filled with the truth of my being, which is enduring, dynamic, and divine.

Thank You Spirit! Thank You Spirit! Thank You Spirit!

Let it be so! And So It Is!

Understanding

One beautiful summer day, I was walking with a very religious male friend of mine. I say he is religious because he virtually lives in the church and quotes scripture to solidify every point he makes. He is always talking about love, peace, and learning how to live without fear through belief in the Lord. Coming from a bookstore, we were engaged in a loving, peaceful conversation about our different and similar views on life. We passed an open, public trash can where a swarm of bees appeared to be doing the same thing my friend and I were—enjoying the beautiful day. One of the bees must have decided that we looked more appealing than a can of garbage and decided to follow us. As we continued walking, the bee buzzed around my head and darted back and forth in front of my face. I was not concerned. I think bees are really cool and I am not afraid of them. My six-foot-tall, very robust, athletic male friend had a different take on the situation.

I tried to continue the conversation but my friend began swatting at the bee. I told him not to do that, it would frighten the bee. "I don't care if the bee gets scared! Those things are poisonous!" He said he had a friend who had almost died of a bee sting. He described in detail how his friend's face blew up like a balloon, how his arms and legs became stiff as boards and eventually he couldn't breathe. The doctor said he was allergic to bees. I assured him I was not allergic to them and that I could die of far worse things than a bee sting. He looked at me as if I had lost my mind and decided we should take the bus. He, I, and the bee stopped at the next corner to wait for the bus.

Just to make conversation while we were waiting, I asked my friend why he thought God had created bees, bugs, and other creatures. I tried to explain to him that everything in the kingdom of life plays an important role in the process of life. His eyes never diverted from the bee. "Be still." I said. "If you are still, it will go away." He was now standing about two feet away from me, and his hand automatically moved to ward off an attack whenever the bee moved in his direction or my direction. I asked him if he was afraid. Emphatically he said, "No!" Again, I asked him to be still so that he would not frighten the bee. He told me I was crazy. "Bees don't get scared. They sting and they do it for no good reason." If you have ever had a run-in with a bee, you know that the more you swat the closer they come.

As nature would have it, the bee stopped to rest on top of my head. Stalking the bee, my friend approached me, his eyes fixated. "It's on your head," he whispered. Before I could say a word, he pounced. Taking his $24.99 hardcover book in both hands, he hit me on the head. I crashed to my knees on the hard cement. The little pebbles on the street were digging in my legs; my ears were ringing; I had bitten my tongue; I saw brilliant bursts of light floating around in front of me. "Shit!" he said. "It got away!" I looked at him in total amazement for at least thirty seconds before he realized what he had done. He scrambled to help me up, apologizing profusely. "I just didn't want that thing to sting you!" He didn't understand. If the bee were going to sting me, it would have stung me. I would have been hurt, but I would have survived. By hitting me in the head with a three-pound book, he could have caused me far more damage than the bee.

6

I AM

It's not the man. It's the plan!
The Honorable Harold
Washington

At all times in this life, two plans are operating. The first is the plan of the human mind, which teaches us "Every man for himself when we hit the beach." Only the strong survive, those who are strong enough to cut everyone else off at the path. Only the smart will make it, those who are smart enough to figure out the plan and a way around or through it. The human plan is that you compete for your place in life, even when you are not given all the rules for the competition. And if through your own ingenuity, you happen to figure the plan out and find your rightful place in life, you must fight to hold on to it. The human plan is that you live hard and then die with the knowledge you gained or die because of your lack of knowledge about competition, fighting, and holding on. This plan also teaches that in the midst of competing, fighting, and holding on, you must grab. That's right! Grab all you can get. If you don't grab it, someone else will get everything and leave nothing for you. If you follow this human plan, you will get very tired, very quick.

The other plan is the plan of Spirit. It is Spirit's plan that all people will have a well-ordered life and live abundantly. It is a plan designed to teach you that although lessons and tests will occur in life, there is a wellspring of knowledge within your being. The spiritual plan is for you to understand that an unlimited source of inspiration, protection, and guidance is always available to you. The spiritual life plan, which has been translated into a variety of languages and repeatedly interpreted by many human beings, says that all people are born with the right and ability to inherit God's kingdom. Your job, if you choose to accept it, is to give up the human plan. In other words, the human plan says fight to live. The spiritual plan says stop fighting in order to have life. Meditation is a part of the spiritual plan that empowers you to have an abundant life.

Because we were taught to fight, we teach our children to fight. Unfortunately, we do not always give them the proper weapons. We give them the same fears, doubts, anxieties, and beliefs that were given to us. We teach them to blame, strike back, hide, and hold on because that is what we have been taught. This is not to say that your parents, grandparents, and great-grandparents were wrong. It is to say that many of them came onto the battlefield of life improperly equipped. Through observation and conditioning, human beings believe that the only way to fight another human being is with the weapons devised by human beings. More important, those on the battlefield are taught to believe that you actually *have to* fight. It is not necessary to fight in life or for life. It is, however, necessary to give up some part of your life to the source of your life. Believe it or not, that is the spiritual plan: to learn how to live without fighting or struggling. According to the human plan, this seems virtually impossible. According to Spirit's plan, which includes the practice of meditation, it is the only way to fly!

I must admit that I was embroiled in a never-ending battle with life. Although it appeared to me and others that I was losing, I tried to teach my son how to fight. At the time, I didn't know the *other* plan. I did not have the appropriate tools or weapons. Yet I gave my son battle instructions, hoping that he would somehow make out better than I did. While I was teaching him, we fought each other. My way, his way, the way—they were all different, and I believed that no matter what his success or failure, it would always be a reflection of what I had taught him. When I realized that there were two plans, two methods for approaching life, I tried to change the syllabus. I tried to give him information about the spiritual way. It was too late. He had found a plan and had faith that it would work for him. He put his plan into action. In total horror, I watched. I beat up on myself. I almost gave up on him. Then a quiet voice in the pit of my soul said, "Be still!" When I did, things got better for me. Eventually, they got better for him.

KNOCKED DOWN, NOT OUT

My son Damon was not a good criminal. Some people are. He was not. Each time he was arrested, he would desperately plead with me to find a legal loophole that he could crawl through. He had not been read his rights. He was manhandled by the police. There were no witnesses. There was no search warrant. You see, I was not only his mother whose battle instructions had been a disaster; I was a lawyer. Damon believed it was my personal and professional duty to save him. Whenever we had the "Ma, you've got to save me" conversation, I reminded him that he had not been arrested for breaking man's law. He had broken God's law. Damon's destiny had been divined in a traditional Yoruba ceremony when he was young. He was destined to become a spiritual teacher. He was told that he should follow the traditions of his ancestors, the Yoruba tradition, and dedicate his life to spiritual pursuits. He was also told that he would eventually find his purpose and surrender to it. He was fourteen at the time and had never been arrested.

In Damon's mind, dedicating his life to God and spirituality somehow translated into not being able to have fun. He was convinced it meant he would not be able to "chase girls." Furthermore, he did not want anyone telling him what to do with his life. Not God or anyone else. He wanted to play football, make a lot of money, eventually start his own business, and live a life of luxury. He was never told he could not do the things he wanted to do. It was merely suggested that he should do them from a firm spiritual base. My son was convinced that what he wanted was not what God wanted for him. He was not able to explain it, but he "knew" if he gave in to God, he would somehow miss out on all the fun in life.

When I discovered the spiritual life plan, I told my son, "It is the Father's pleasure to give you the kingdom" (Luke 12:32). Damon, like many contemporary Black men, understood the "kingdom" to be heaven. You have to be dead to experience heaven. It made no sense to him. Either you waited until you died and got to heaven to have a good experience or you could risk dying trying to get your good on earth. Damon wanted money. That was the kingdom of good in his mind. He also understood that he would have absolutely no use for money in heaven. Instead, he wanted to prove to society that he, a Black man, could have money and do all the things money enables you to do on earth. I taught him that. I taught him that money was a valuable commodity. "With it," I said, "you can buy almost anything and almost everyone." He understood that to mean that, with money, the world would think *he* was valuable. He admitted it. Damon wanted to show off to the world. He wanted to prove his worth with wealth. He stole cars and sold drugs believing that would get him where he wanted to be quickly.

Black men rarely come into public view unless they are wealthy or in trouble. Money gets the public's attention. So does trouble. Some Black men get in trouble because they have the wrong battle plan. Others, like my son, get in trouble because they want or need money. Dr. Benjamin Mays once said, "It is not your history or your environment. It is the quality of your mind that determines the quality of your future." I understand this to mean that if you want to win the game of life, you must develop a sound mind. Very often, this means you must give up the fast-track ways of the world, take the backroads, and move slowly. I also believe it means that you must identify and heal your psychological and emotional issues related to self-value and self-worth within yourself before you can receive any recognition from the world. It sounds really good in theory—until you try to convince a twenty-four-year-old Black male who has lived just above the poverty line all his life.

Taking Dr. Mays's message one step farther, I believe it is important for Black men to have a vision, a mission, and a purpose in life. Once you understand who you are, you must also know what you want to do and why you want to do it. You cannot stand in the middle of the field waving your sword over your head just to prove you have a sword. You must be prepared to strike swiftly and precisely if you want a victory. Even though we may not use these exact words, most mothers try to teach this to their sons. Very often, the sons don't understand. When Mom fails to get the message across, a trip to prison converts many sons into fast learners.

THE BATTLE PLAN

In prison Damon had to make some difficult choices and decisions. This should have been easy because he had a lot of time to think. Money could no longer distract him. Unfortunately, his motivation in the thinking process was not emotional growth or spiritual evolution. His motivation was to figure out how not to get caught again. Damon believed that his thinking was fine. He figured out that he had been careless. Consequently, when he was released from prison, the focus of his criminal activity changed. His thinking remained the same. He was angry and resentful about his status as a Black man in society. He was frightened and confused about his responsibilities as a man. Having been raised in a dysfunctional single-parent home, he was emotionally imbalanced. Having chosen to disregard the advice of divination, he was not on purpose. He also believed that he could fool his mother and God by making commitments with his mouth that he was not obliged to keep.

In prison Damon began to understand that there were invisible forces pushing and pulling him. Some of these forces were positive. Others were not. He also understood that the strongest forces, the negative forces, were most dominant in his life and that they had nothing to do with anything I had taught him. These forces were in his own mind. When Damon first went to prison, he thought he was being punished. He had done so many *bad* things, God had to be mad at him and God was punishing him. I explained to him that God does not punish us. We punish ourselves. Guilt, shame, fear, and dishonesty about the motives of your behavior will punish you. It has absolutely nothing to do with God. Working against laws of nature such as order, harmlessness, and balance will cause you to punish yourself. It was then that I began to talk to him about meditation as a way to get still and cleanse the mind.

Your mind is the *cause* underlying every experience you have in life. What ultimately happens in your life is the *effect* of your habitual thought patterns. Damon admitted that he frequently thought that what he was doing was wrong and that he would eventually get caught. Once he understood the process of cause and effect, he was able to admit what he had done to himself. He had reaped what he had sown. He deserved to be punished. I had to take him a step farther. I explained to Damon that God always forgives you. No matter what you have done or where you have been, God will forgive you, wipe the slate clean, and provide you with the opportunity to begin again. The second time around, your failure or success depends on your understanding of what you have done and why it is not wise to repeat those things, and your willingness to submit to this Higher Authority. Unfortunately, we have so much difficulty forgiving ourselves, we do not give the divine forgiveness process an opportunity to work. Meditation also teaches you to be patient with yourself.

Damon began to meditate in prison. When he did, he was able to understand his behavior and became willing to accept responsibility for his actions without blaming anyone. It was about that same time that it seemed as if the walls of life caved in on him. His wife abandoned him. Bureaucratic delays caused him to be incarcerated longer than required for the minimum penalty. The day before he was to be released, an out-of-state warrant was produced. He was extradited to another state for a two-year-old case. Once there, he was appointed a very good lawyer, a brother, whom I spoke to on a number of occasions. Before Damon's case went to court, the brother became a judge and reassigned his caseload. Damon became fearful and impatient again. I encouraged him to continue meditating and stay calm. His main concern was getting out of jail. He was willing to try anything.

When you still your mind of human concerns, Spirit moves into the middle of your affairs. This is key when your life appears to be falling apart. Stillness is an admission that you cannot help yourself. If you could, your life would not be falling apart. Your plan would be working. Meditation brings the mind to a state of receptivity. You receive divine inspiration. For many, stillness in the midst of the storm is a challenge. Actually, it's a test. The question is, Will you once again battle with what you can see and what you know? Or will you trust that Spirit's plan is working on your behalf? It's a hard test for most people. It is an even harder test for Black men warriors, who are already battle-weary. It's also a test of willingness. Are you willing to give up the fears and desires of the flesh in order to be strengthened and enlightened by Spirit?

Damon decided to plea-bargain his case. He was offered three years. He decided to take it, which meant, with the time he had served, he would be out in two years. It sounded really good to him. It sounded like a test to me. "Ma, this case carries a penalty of five to ten years. Why shouldn't I take two years? That's a good deal!" I asked what was the point of the deal? What would be God's purpose in having him remain in jail two more years? He didn't have a clue. I reminded him of his destiny. He was to be a teacher. He could teach in jail or he could teach on the street. The point of this experience was for him to get the lesson. If he did not get the lesson, he would not make the necessary changes and he would still be in prison. The true meaning of freedom is doing what you have come to life to do, without fear or hesitation, regardless of where you are. The issue in life is not "getting a good deal." The issue is: be willing to do the work you were sent to do where it will produce the most good. When you are on purpose, no one can imprison your mind. When your mind is free, you can fulfill your mission and purpose. He told me I was crazy.

Over the next few weeks I think Damon understood most of what I was saying, but he still wanted to get out of jail. He had already been in for a year and seven months. I realized that he had actually been in prison for all of his twenty-three years of life. He was a prisoner in my home, of me—a single, hysterically frightened woman raising a male child. He was a prisoner of the society, a system that feared and misunderstood him. He was even a prisoner of his own mind because he believed what the world said about him. My heart went out to him. I prayed for him. I knew there was nothing else I could. When he got to court, the district attorney refused to offer him a plea bargain. The judge told him if he took the case to trial, the minimum sentence he would get would be ten years on one charge, five years on the other. He panicked. He prayed. He pleaded guilty. He was sentenced to seven years. He would be eligible for parole in fifteen months. When I asked him what he planned to do during that time, he said, "Be still!"

IN THE STILL OF THE NIGHT

There comes a time in your life when you simply have to be still. Being still does not mean doing nothing. It means consciously tuning in to the Self. Being still means listening within for the guidance or answers you need. My godfather always told me, "You cannot see your reflection in running water." You must take time to look at yourself, to listen to yourself, and to prepare yourself to do a new thing. The battle strategy we have been taught is that when you are confronted with a challenge, that is the time to get busy. You get busy doing the things you have been taught to believe will make the challenge go away. Most of the time you have absolutely no idea what to do or what will actually work because you don't understand why you have the problem. It simply makes you feel better to do something. What you do is get in the way. The human intellect blocks the way of Spirit. Meditation helps to still the intellect so that divine or spiritual understanding can take place.

It is a given that Black men in this country have been misinformed about your true identity and miseducated about life. We know that now. You now realize how being miseducated has affected every aspect of your life. When you have the wrong information in your head, your thinking becomes disorganized. This disorganization eventually invades every aspect of your being. What you may not know is that it is not only political, social, economic, or political oppression that perpetuates the continuous destruction of Black men. It is also disorganized thinking. It is ignorance of your spiritual nature. It is the belief that you are disconnected from God. All these elements contribute to your inability to live from the inside out.

Authentic power is an inward experience. When you do not draw your power from an inner source within your own being, your power is not real in the universal scheme of things. Why do so many Black men feel powerless in the world? It is in response to reliance on external forces and the belief that they can give you something you do not have. It is the result of the failure to relentlessly challenge the overt and covert messages in the world that say if you are Black, you lack certain qualities essential to your survival. It is the outgrowth of the failure to integrate the laws of nature into your life philosophy. Most important, it is the result of the failure to understand and acknowledge the power of the Spirit within your Self that continues to make you feel incomplete and inadequate. Meditation is a process of tuning into Spirit in order to gain a spiritual understanding of your experiences.

I can imagine that being a Black man in a hostile society is most analogous to hanging over the edge of a cliff. You are trying to figure out whether to hang on or to let go. It is difficult to hang on. You will eventually get tired and fall. While you are hanging there, your mind is racing. You are trying to find a way off the edge. You would rather jump to safety; that way you are in control. If you hang there until you fall, you have no idea what may happen to you. If you let go, it is a sure thing that you are going to hit the bottom. Where is the bottom? You cannot see down that far. You have no idea what is waiting for you down there. If you fall, you will probably die, but you can't hang on forever and you are afraid to let go. What do you do? Take a deep breath. Inhale slowly. Exhale slowly. Now, *be still!*

MEDITATION

Meditation is the art of being still. It is said that prayer is when you talk to God and meditation is when you listen to God. It is a process in which you can release everything that is going on in your mind in order to hear what is going on in your soul. Meditation is a time when you consciously fall off the cliff of life. It is an opportunity to fall to the bottom of your soul, the dwelling place of Spirit. We should all take time each day to let go of fear, anger, responsibility, and ego in order to allow Spirit to show us the way off the cliff. For a Black man who may feel you have spent your entire life hanging off one cliff or another, meditation is your safety net.

So many men believe they do not have the time to get still. They are too busy. In effect you are saying, There is no way off the cliff. When you are in trouble or darkness, meditation is an opportunity to retreat to the darkness of your own being. In darkness, something new is born. Spirit will bring the light of guidance, direction, and inspiration when your mind is still and receptive. The longer you persist in the battle, trying to figure out what to do and how to do it, the more exhausted you will become and the greater the chance that you will fall.

Every great spiritual leader, regardless of religious affiliation, culture, or ancestry, knew the power in mastering the art of meditation. Buddha, Gandhi, Dr. Martin Luther King, Jr., El Hajj Malik Shabazz (Malcolm X) all practiced some form of meditation. It is the only way you can move the little self out of the way so that Spirit can enter your mind. Meditation is an act of self-healing. The root *medi* means "to heal"; it is the same root we find in *medicine.* The center, *ta,* means "to take or have." The suffix, *-ation,* means "action or result." Meditation means "to take a healing action" or "to have a healing result." Meditation heals the mind by giving it time-out from physical stimuli. It focuses the attention inward, through breath. Breath is the energy of God that will fill your mind with truth. Knowing truth leads to spiritual understanding.

Within your body is a masculine energy and a feminine energy. The masculine nature is to think. The feminine nature is to feel. Thought directs action. Feeling creates the frame of reference from which you act. When the head and the heart—thought and feeling—are not balanced, there is inner conflict. When there is no balance, the experience is one of being forced to say yes when you want to say no. Or of making a decision and then second-guessing and doubting yourself. To develop self-trust and confidence you must balance your internal nature, the masculine and feminine energies. This balancing process also requires the integration of both aspects of the brain. The right or masculine nature, which is linear and produces logical and sequential conclusions, must be infused with the left or feminine nature, which is intuitive, creative, and receptive. The union of these two energies results in balanced and illumined thought.

Meditation leads to spiritual balance and illuminated consciousness. Illumination is light, in which there is the ability to see. Illumination is a concept that describes spiritual understanding. In ancient Kimetian (Egyptian) culture, light was analogous to "the Father." It was believed that the spiritual quest for illumination would lead you to the Father God. In order to get to the light, you would be required to move through the darkness. The darkness of your soul. The darkness of your mind. The darkness of your little self. To get to the tomb of any king you had to pass through the darkness of the tunnel. The tunnel was like a womb. Darkness represents the feminine principle of "the Mother." In this sense, darkness meant mysterious. Like the activity of the womb, that which is hidden from the eyes of man.

No one can come into the light without going through the darkness. You will not experience the illumination of Spirit without experiencing the mysteries of Spirit. You cannot get *to the Father* without coming *through the Mother*. Most ancient cultures understood the concept that God is both masculine and feminine energy. Modern religious theologies refer to God as "he," demonstrating the human attachment to *doing* as the fullest expression of life. In the quest to conquer and control through religious doctrine, theorists ignored the Mother. She could not be seen. She could not be controlled. In repressing the concept of feminine energy and its contribution to wholeness and balance, man repressed the feminine energy, the mystery of Spirit within himself. He began to *do* and forgot how to *be*.

Most people think that to meditate means *to do* something. Dr. Deepak Chopra, an internationally recognized teacher of spiritual and metaphysical principle, has written, "To meditate means to do nothing. It is the inactivity that heals. It is a time of rest. Rest always rejuvenates." In your attempts to meditate, do nothing. Do not think, do not try to stop thinking. If thoughts come into your mind, leave them alone. They will eventually go away. When you are ready to meditate, simply get still. Focus on your breath and let go of the need to do. This is a time to bring your physical and spiritual being into alignment. These two powerful aspects of you already know what to do. Your only job in the practice of meditation is to get still.

Meditation should not, and definitely cannot, be forced. It must be a relaxed, conscious, disciplined activity to focus inward. Breath will take you within. There are no set rules or procedures to follow; however, your practice must be consistent and purposeful. You can declare to yourself that you want to meditate and state what your goal is, what you want to experience. Try the goals of peace, relaxation, enlightenment. Choose a location in which you feel comfortable and safe and a time when you will not be disturbed. The key to learning how to meditate successfully is practice. If you declare your intent consistently, every day, at the same time, in the same place, you will soon discover how easy it is to get still and go within. As you develop the ability to let go of your thoughts and the world around you, Spirit will come through. It will guide you as to what you must do next. Eventually, you will be able to meditate anywhere, at any time you feel the need to be quiet.

Those who experience difficulty in getting the mind quiet may want to try the following exercise.

1. Sit quietly and relaxed, with your back straight and your feet flat on the floor.

2. Take three or four deep breaths, inhaling and exhaling through the nose.

3. Begin to monitor your breath, noticing the rhythm as you inhale and exhale. You can count mentally to establish the rhythm.

4. Once you have established a breathing pattern, turn your eyes down to stare at the tip of your nose. Continue the breathing pattern.

5. Continue staring at your nose for two to three minutes, after which you can close your eyes.

At first, you may experience a strain in your eyes from holding them downward. This is fine. You are also working your eye muscles. Focusing on the tip of the nose locks the brain down and lessens your ability to be distracted. Since the purpose of meditation is to quiet the mind, this will let your brain know it is time to *cool out*.

Another wonderful meditation practice is to activate the "I Am" or Christ consciousness. The following exercise is designed to accomplish this.

1. Sit in a relaxed posture, with your back straight and your feet flat on the floor.

2. Take seven to ten deep breaths, inhaling and exhaling through the nose.

3. Once your breathing pattern has returned to normal, gently roll your eyes upward as if you were trying to see your eyebrows. Hold them in that position as you repeat the deep-breathing pattern for eight repetitions.

4. Allow your eyes to close; however, keep them focused on the center of your forehead as you affirm mentally, "I Am."

5. Continue repeating the affirmation for two to three minutes. If your eyes feel strained, allow them to relax as you continue the affirmation.

6. Once you have completed the "I Am" affirmation, roll the eyes upward again and mentally affirm yourself, beginning each statement with "I Am." "I Am loved, loving, and lovable . . . I Am peaceful and peace-filled . . . I Am a beacon of light and a vessel of knowledge . . . I Am one with the Father." These are examples of self-affirming decrees using the Christ-consciousness power of "I Am."

USING BREATH AND MEDITATION

People often say they will "meditate on a problem." This is not a very wise thing to do. The mind is an extremely powerful instrument. Remember, where the mind goes, the behind follows. It is more appropriate to meditate on *the solution* to a problem, since that is where you want to end up. If there is a challenging or difficult situation you wish to work through in meditation, follow this process:

1. Sitting in a comfortable, relaxed position, take two or three deep breaths.

2. Focus on the tip of your nose and establish a breathing pattern. Continue focusing and breathing for at least three minutes.

3. Close your eyes and bring to mind the situation that confronts you. Identify and imagine the people involved, if there are any. In a very simple (ten- to fifteen-word) statement, identify the exact nature of the situation.

For example, "I am sixty dollars away from paying my car note, which is due tomorrow." Not "I lent my brother sixty dollars. He promised to give it back but didn't, so now I can't pay my car note." The difference in the two statements is this: the first simply states the situation; the second statement places blame and responsibility beyond your Self. The word *can't* indicates you have made a decision that it *will not* get done.

Once you have defined the situation, see, feel, or imagine the words you used floating out the top of your head. *See* means if you were looking at you, you would see these words come out of your head and float away. *Feel* means you are able to take the energy of the situation and push it out of your head. *Imagine* means simply to think about the words leaving you through the top of your head. Once you have done this, take several deep breaths and relax again. Sit quietly for as long as you choose. If you do not get an idea of how to deal with the situation right away, do not be alarmed. Do not allow yourself to entertain the problem. Do not speak about the situation. Wait and listen. An answer must come when you need it, for that is the law!

Enough cannot be said about the benefits of quieting the mind. You can meditate when you first get up or before you go to bed. You can meditate on your lunch hour or while riding the bus. It is advisable to start off with small intervals of five to seven minutes at a time. Work your way up gradually to thirty, forty-five, even sixty minutes. It is a practice that puts you in touch with you. It is designed to align the physical and spiritual minds. As my father once told me, "The best way to figure out what you should be doing is to sit down, shut up, and listen!"

THE UPPER ROOM

When I was a little girl, my grandmother sang a song entitled "In the Upper Room with Jesus." As I child, I actually thought this was a place you had to go and be. As a young adult, my political orientation turned me off to Jesus. The Upper Room was not a place I desired to be. I was well into my adult life and spiritual journey when I came across the teachings of Charles Filmore, author of *The Science of Mind* and founder of Religious Science. In studying Filmore's work it became clear to me that the Upper Room is a synonym for the deepest part of your being, your soul. The Upper Room is the highest, most enlightened aspect of human consciousness.

The Upper Room is your Christ consciousness. It is the part of you that recognizes and accepts that you are always connected to God. The Upper Room is a place of retreat from the pressures of the world. Conscious breath and meditation are the keys to the Upper Room. Once you are there, the world has no effect. There is no racism, oppression, fear, or anger in this place of being. There is only peace and unconditional love. All that you look for in the world, you will find in this place. All that you want to be, you become. It is for this reason that conscious breathing and meditation must become an integral part of your life. It is the way you will transform your thoughts. When you change your thinking, you will have the power to change your life. When you spend time in the Upper Room, the highest element of our being, you will find your way off the edge of the cliff. It is in this place, the Upper Room, that you can be inspired, enlightened, and guided about what you must do in the world. In the Upper Room, you must surrender the world in order to make it through the world. Breath is the ultimate battle plan. Meditation empowers you and assures you of victory.

DAILY MINIMUM REQUIREMENT

Meditation is the ultimate tool of mental, emotional, and spiritual transformation. Use any of the practices listed or devise one of your own, and make a commitment to spend no less than five minutes every morning and evening in the contemplative silence called meditation. Add breathing exercises or music to suit your needs and temperament.

Confession

We needed a retreat. We had been working very hard, without a break, for eighteen solid months. We had been *doing* a lot. Answering telephones. Answering mail. Filling orders. Traveling across the country for lectures, book signings, workshops. I was exhausted. My team of fourteen women was senseless. We needed time to think, time to plan, time to rest and regroup. A retreat was exactly what we needed. We went to Virginia Beach, to a beautiful conference center. We wanted to rest, be at peace, to have the time and space we needed to plan what we would *do* next.

I saw the tent first. It was a huge white thing that reminded me of the revival meetings I attended with Grandma when I was a little girl. A revival in the middle of a retreat was exactly what I needed. I asked people on the grounds of the conference center what was going on in the tent. Most of them were guests like me and had no idea. When I saw some men huddled together right next to the tent, I assumed they were workers. I ran over to ask them what was going to happen in the tent. They didn't work for the conference center and they did not know. I was obsessed with this tent.

Later in the day, the conference manager introduced himself to me and several members of my team. After answering the obligatory how-are-you-enjoying-yourself questions, I asked him about the tent. I knew he would know. He explained that every year the center served as host for a revival meeting called Seven Days of Blaze. The event draws about two thousand people from across the country. My heart was pounding. Then he told me that it had just ended and they were waiting for the rental company to come and take the tent down. My heart sank. I never realized I was so into revivals. Especially not now. I was a Yoruba priestess. A metaphysician. Why was I so obsessed about a Christian revival meeting?

After a wonderful dinner where we all ate everything we had no business eating, we postponed all meetings until the next day. We needed to rest or walk off the enormous amount of food we had just consumed. Meetings would begin at 8:00 a.m. The night was free. It had rained all day. The two hundred or so acres of land on which the conference center sat was pure mud. I went for a walk anyway. The moon was full and I love to walk at night under the moon. I heard the singing as soon as I walked out of doors. It was off in the distance. I thought it was piped elevator mood music coming from inside the main hall. With no particular destination in mind, I walked toward the tent. The singing seemed to get louder. As I rounded the corner of the main building, I could see there was light in the tent. As I got closer, I could see there were people in the tent. The tent was full of people singing. My heart was racing again.

I entered from the back. There were about two hundred people. I found an empty seat against the back wall of the tent and sat down. I began to listen to the songs. They were singing spiritual songs. Not the foot-thumping gospel I knew from revival tents but slow, melodic, New Age songs. They were singing about love, peace, and the goodness of God. The words to the songs were being displayed by an overhead projector. As the singing continued, people were standing up and praising. They were clapping their hands and shouting. There was a very peaceful presence in the tent. I was sitting in total amazement. I could actually see the presence of Spirit. It looked like a haze descending from the top of the tent. It dangled around the heads of some people, the feet of others. At first I thought it was fog, but when the big, hot, salty tears began to roll down my face, I knew exactly what it was. What was so amazing about the situation was, I was the only person of color I could see in the tent.

I wanted to leave, but my behind seemed to be glued to the chair. I figured the moon had something to do with it, so I sat there. Three or four songs later, I was wiping my nose on my sleeve when the presiding minister stood at the podium. He talked about the glory of God. The goodness and grace of God's love, and how tonight was a special night. He asked all the ministers in the audience to come to the stage. Twelve men walked up to sit in the empty seats behind the podium. Eleven of them were white. One was Black. The minister then talked about the power of confession. He said that this would be a night of confession. A night to heal the body of God, the church. He introduced each minister by giving the name of his church and the denomination he represented. He then asked them to come forward to confess.

One by one the ministers took the microphone and began to confess how their denomination had taught them to despise and distrust all other denominations. My mouth dropped open. It was amazing enough to see Lutheran, Presbyterian, and Pentecostal ministers on the same platform. Add to that a Baptist, an Episcopalian, and a charismatic Presbyterian. I had never heard of a charismatic Presbyterian! They exist and they were present. Each of the ministers told his story. They told how the church had taught them to turn against their brothers and sisters because of a difference of opinion in how to approach God. Not only did they tell their story, some of them cried. If you want to create a stir in a revival tent, give a crying minister the microphone. The place was in an uproar.

The haze was still visible when they finished. The presiding minister was back. He too had a story. He was the charismatic one. He shouted and spoke in tongues. His church told him he was a demon and removed him from the pulpit. He organized his own church and still criticized other faiths. As he talked, he invited people from the audience to come forward and confess. I distinctly remember his words, "Let the Spirit move you to cleanse your heart tonight." He was still speaking when the first man approached him. The man revealed his pain about being raised Catholic and converting to the Baptist faith. He talked about being excommunicated and the fear and pain it had caused him. Another man talked about being a homosexual and hiding out in a marriage. These were all grown men crying out in pain. The next man came up to pray. He prayed for forgiveness. He had been spreading hate through the church by criticizing other faiths.

The voice was so loud, I turned around because I thought it came from behind me. I never imagined that this loud, booming voice was in my own head. "Go up there and confess that you hate white people!" I didn't move. I was dumbfounded. People were still walking up to the stage, but I was no longer listening. I was having my own personal minicrisis. I was hearing voices. "Go up there and confess from your soul that you hate white people!" Even for me, a professed spiritually enlightened being, this was deep. *But I don't hate white . . .* The thought trailed off as my ears started ringing. Now I was scared. Let me listen! Just let me listen to the people talking.

There was a Black woman standing on the stage. I don't know where she came from, but she was confessing. She talked about her anger with the church for its denigration of women. She talked about how she had been treated and how she had seen other women being treated. My body was standing up. She reminded everyone that it was a woman who carried and gave birth to the *Word* of God. My body was walking to the nearest aisle. The name of that Word was Jesus. She also reminded them that before Jesus there was Abraham, who had no church or temple but had a mother. My body was halfway up the aisle. She reminded them that Moses had a mother who was barely mentioned in the Bible. All the women in the tent were standing up. They were crying and screaming and clapping. I was trying to figure out where my body was going. Now the woman on the stage was informing the audience that before Moses there was Isis, and she gave birth to Horus without the benefit of the company of a man. The women were absolutely beside themselves. I'm not even sure they knew what she had said, but they agreed with her. I was now at the foot of the steps leading to the stage.

The presiding minister was at the woman's side, thanking her. He admitted that sexism is a problem in the church. Then he admitted that an even bigger problem is racism. He stated that right there in Tidewater, two blocks from where we stood, was a church that did not allow Blacks, Latinos, Asians, or Native Americans to become members. He asked the audience to pray for that church and all other churches like it. I was now standing next to him. He looked me dead in the eye and asked, "My sister, is that your prayer?" I nodded that it was. He handed me the microphone.

My grandmother taught me that when you don't know what to do, you better know how to pray. When I looked out at the audience of two hundred white people staring at me, I closed my eyes and started praying. I know I asked for forgiveness for being disobedient. I told them I had been ordered to the stage but had refused to come. I know I said I had no intention of coming up to the stage to confess anything, but God obviously had another plan. I know I asked to be healed. I asked to be healed of hate. Then I actually opened my mouth and asked God to forgive me for hating white people. I don't remember much of what I said after that. I think I told them why I hated them. I think I told them about what had happened to my father. I think I told them about being a little girl in Brooklyn and about the white butcher who gave my family meat on credit only when I allowed him to touch my budding breasts. I couldn't hear what I was saying because the people in the audience were wailing; they were screaming out loud. I vaguely remember asking God to forgive me for hating white people and to forgive white people for the atrocities they have committed against Black people. When my brain finally caught up with my mouth and my body, there was a very tall man standing next to me. He was one of the ministers on the stage. I think he was thanking me. He asked me to stand there with him. I had no choice. I think I was paralyzed.

Before I could recover from the shock, trauma, hysteria of that experience, I was bombarded with another one. The minister who had just been standing next to me was now on his knees in front of me. He was on his knees begging God to forgive him, his father, and all his grandfathers for the crimes they have committed against Black people. My bladder was getting weak. I heard this man say, "Forgive white men for selling their Black brothers into slavery. Forgive us for raping little Black girls. Forgive us for believing we are superior to our Black brothers and sisters." I stared at him in total disbelief. From the corner of my eye I could see that all the ministers on the stage were on their knees. Some of them had their hands raised over their heads. Others held their faces in their hands. They were crying out and begging for forgiveness. The audience was in much worse shape.

People were on their knees on the damp ground. Some were standing up but I could barely see them. The haze was very thick. I stood there crying and shaking my head. The minister in front of me was semiconvulsive. He had his hand stretched out to me. I was trying to hear what he was saying. Then I heard it. "Lord, if you forgive us, let my sister take my hand. Lord, I repent and I repent for every white man I know." My brain was back in my body. This was a decision I would have to make on my own. Maybe this was a dream. Maybe I was losing my mind. Maybe this was a test. I heard my own words play back in my mind, "God, please heal me of my hatred of white people." I took his hand in both of my hands and placed it on my heart.

There was never anyone else in the tent during the entire weekend. I kept checking. When I told my team what had happened, they cried. We all cried. I had just about convinced myself that the entire thing was a dream when another guest at the center walked up to me, took my hand, and thanked me. Every time I peered outside at the tent, it would happen again. One man asked me if he could hug me. When he did, he whispered, "Thank you for helping me heal myself." The rest of the retreat was wonderful. I arrived home feeling rested and renewed, focused and ready to be my best. The neighborhood in which I live is multicultural. However, it is not unusual to be in the bank or the store and realize you are the only person of color present. I was in a very crowded deli the first time I noticed it after the retreat. I also noticed that for the first time I had no anxiety or stress about it.

7

TRYING TO GET
TO GOD

*If I have to die for something, let it
be for the truth.*
        Medgar Wiley Evers

At one time in my life, I was a
Black woman. Now, I am a
child of the Most High. Do
not misunderstand the point I am making. I know with every fiber of
my being that I am a descendant of Africans. I am proud of my heritage. I know my culture and I embrace it wholeheartedly. I also know
the truth about who my people are and I love them. I am well aware of
the issues and challenges you must face when you are the descendant
of Africans living in America. I am psychologically, emotionally, and
spiritually committed to contributing every resource I possess to alle-
viate the effects of the social and political disempowerment of Black
people. I must confess, however, that I have experienced a shift in my
consciousness. I can no longer accept being just a Black woman. The
pain is too great.

I remember being just a Black woman. I also remember my anger toward Black men. I was angry about all the things you did not do and could not seem to do. I was angry at my father for being emotionally absent. I was angry with him for being angry when he was present. I was angry with my brother for being angry at my father. I was angry with my husband for being just like my father. Not only was I angry *at* Black men, I was angry *with* Black men. I was angry at the same people you are angry at, for the same reasons and for different reasons.

I was angry at white men for the manner in which they systematically debase and deny you. I was angry at white women for stealing you away. I was angry at those Black men who do things that make other Black men look bad. I was angry at Black women, my sisters, who were also angry at you, for talking about you. I was angry at the people who get jobs before you do. I was angry at the people who create negative images of you. Even when I am angry with you, I don't want anyone else talking about you. In the midst of my anger I was looking for a husband and trying to raise a son. It was a painful experience.

I believed that my life was going down the tubes because I was a Black woman. I was poor because I was Black. I lived in one of the roughest neighborhoods in New York because I was Black. My relationships kept falling apart because it's hard for two Black people to make it in the world. I understood that people are accountable and responsible for what they do, but it just seemed harder for Black people to get anything done because they are Black. Each day I did the best I could to raise my children, keep a roof over our heads, and make it through the world. Still, it seemed like I was getting nowhere because I was Black. The supermarket was always crowded in my neighborhood and never had what I needed. Of course, I attributed this to the fact that the supermarket was in a predominantly Black neighborhood. The tellers at the bank moved slower in a Black neighborhood. The garbage collectors came less frequently, and the mail carrier came very late in a Black neighborhood. When I looked around my immediate world, I concluded that everything that was not working in my life had something to do with being Black. That made me angry.

Angry people always believe they have a good reason for being angry. In most cases, they do. The key is to get angry, express the anger, and move on. When you do not know how to express what you feel, it stays locked up in your mind. Even when you are not aware of it, that hidden, unexpressed emotion will cloud your thinking and color your actions. What it also does is attract people and situations into your life that reflect back to you what you are thinking and feeling. I attracted angry people. My husband was angry. Many of my friends were angry. There was usually something going on in my life that I could be angry about or someone to be angry with. When you are as angry as I was, for as long as I was, you eventually become afraid. I was afraid of what I might do to myself or someone else. I was afraid of what the angry people in my life might do to me, if they got angry enough. I was afraid of what the angry world might do to my children because they were Black and poor and living in a neighborhood full of poor, Black, angry people.

Fear and anger make you weak. They make you tired. I was a young woman but I was always tired. Even when I was having fun, I was tired. Raising three children alone meant that I had a lot to do, but I was usually too tired to do it. I would have blamed my husband for leaving me with the children but that would have made me angry. I was too tired to get angry. I wanted the children to be quiet so I could rest. When they were not, I got angry at them. I wanted them to keep the house clean. When they did not, I got even angrier at them. I knew I was angry about being left to raise three children alone. But I also really thought I was angry with the children just because they were noisy and would not keep the house clean, which made me tired. Most of the women I knew were tired and angry. We would sit around and talk about the things and people that made us angry, which usually made us all feel worse. There were times when we would make jokes about it and compare notes. But under the jovial, sisterly exterior was a seething rage grounded in our disappointment with Black men and sometimes directed at our children.

SPEAK YOUR TRUTH AND SPEAK IT QUICK!

Confession is a requirement of spiritual transformation. Confession clears the mind and soul of toxic emotions. Confession is an act of telling your truth exactly as you see it and feel it. It has absolutely nothing to do with anyone else. It is not blaming or excusing. It is an act of self-redemption and healing. Confession is like brain surgery in that it releases the pressure from the brain. It is also a powerful form of therapy. When you confess, you validate your experiences. You validate what you feel about what you have experienced. Confession is not about being right. It is about expression, validation, and release. Until you confess, you are weighed down by your experiences and your perceptions of those experiences. You judge yourself and others in response to the weight you feel. The heavier the weight, the greater the judgment. The greater the judgment, the more intense the anger. We have already established that anger makes you tired. When you are tired, it is difficult to move forward. You are stuck, which makes you even more angry. I could go on, but I think you get the point. Until you confess at least to yourself what you are feeling, you remain stuck and weighed down by the failure to validate your own experiences.

I had no idea how angry I was until the day I stabbed my husband. I wish I could say he had it coming, but I can't. There is nothing in the world he could have done that would have given me the right to take his life. I didn't kill him, but I was angry enough to do so. Had I not been so tired, I probably would have. I must confess. I stayed in an abusive marriage for nine years because I was afraid. I was afraid no other man would want me because I had three children. I was afraid of being alone. I was afraid people would talk about me. Men can walk around alone in the world and people think very little of it. When a woman is alone with her children, there is a covert inference that something must be *wrong with her*. Even if it is understood that there was something wrong with the man, she gets blamed for picking him. I must confess. I picked the wrong man because there was something wrong with me. I was angry.

My husband was so angry he would beat me. I think he was angry at his father for dying. I know he was angry at his mother; I just don't know why. I believe he was angry at the world for the same reasons many Black men are angry at the world. I finally recognized he was angry at himself for the things he had done and not done. For the life of me, I can't tell you why he was angry at me. I think our unexpressed anger attracted us to each other so we could see how angry we were. Was he a good man? Yes. He was a wonderful man. Under his anger, he was supportive, generous, and gentle. He was also very frightened. He was frightened that the world would find out that there was *something wrong* with him and use that to validate its harsh treatment of him. What was wrong with him? He was a Black man. He was a former substance abuser. He had a criminal record. He read on a sixth-grade level. He was raised by a single Black woman, and he was angry and afraid.

My husband never mentioned any of this to me. During the course of our marriage, it came out in a variety of ways. What I have learned is that the very thing you do not want someone to know, you ultimately show her in the way you behave. My husband did all the things a man was expected to do. He did them well. He did them with great flash and flare. If, however, he ever made a mistake or forgot to do something, he blamed it on someone else. Usually me. I made him forget. I made him mess up. I didn't do what he told me to do and now people were going to blame him. This made him angry. This usually led to our fights. My husband did not take criticism well. Even when it was constructive, criticism sent him into a rage. I now know that he felt so *wrong*, anything coming at him that pointed out his wrongness was overwhelming. Unfortunately, I did not know this at the time we were married.

My husband had frequent asthma attacks when he could not breathe. He could not get enough air. In our marriage, he could not get enough life. We never had enough money. He could never do enough work. We never had enough of the things he felt would make him a better man. This made him angry. I must confess. As I watched him, I could see he was doing it all wrong. He was pushing, forcing, fighting too hard. He did not like to talk. Had he talked to me, I could have told him what to do. On those occasions when I tried to talk to him, I usually started out by saying, "You're doing it all wrong. What you need to do is . . ." This made him angry. He would cut me off. That would make me angry and I would challenge him. The results were a disaster.

A FLAWED DIAMOND STILL HAS VALUE

After my husband and I separated, my anger got the best of me. It showed up in everything I did. It showed up in my relationships, my work, my friendships, and ultimately in my children. They started fighting with one other. Not your normal sibling arguing, but physical fights. Now they were angry too. One day I heard my younger daughter talking to her doll. She sounded so harsh, but as I listened closer, she was saying the very words I would say to her. It stopped me dead in my tracks. I knew I needed help. I began talking to people about what I was feeling. My mother and friends were my usual sounding boards. I began talking to people about what I had experienced. One day, in the midst of a conversation with my mother, every ounce of anger in my body came to the surface. It felt like I was having a heart attack. It felt like my brain was about to explode. I was very frightened. Very quietly my mother said, "The only way you are going to get through it is to go through it. Just feel it. Then, it will go away." I did, and it did.

I talked to my mother about my father. I asked her all the questions I had had all my life about him. I talked to her about her, what she did and did not do in relation to my father, my brother, and me. I told her what it looked like to me. I told her how I felt about it. Since we were talking, I told her about many of the things I had done in life that she knew nothing about. Most of all, I told her how I felt about myself and about her. Then I told her how I felt about my father, my brother, my husband, and about being a Black woman. I confessed from the deepest part of my soul. I was shocked to hear some of the things I was saying. It poured out of my mouth and would not stop until I was empty. Then I looked at my mother, who had not said a word for at least thirty minutes. She was totally still and staring at me. The silence was deafening. She broke it with a huge sigh. She took off her eyeglasses and placed them on the table. She wiped her eyes, held her face in her hands for a few moments, and then looked up at me. What came out of her mouth changed my life forever. "Now that you have told God what's wrong, I am sure he will do something about it."

GOD ALREADY KNOWS

You will never realize your true spiritual potential if your mind is clogged with negative emotions and painful memories. Most of what goes on in your life is not intrinsically bad. However, the meaning and judgment you attach to your experiences make most situations seem insurmountable. Add to this the influences of the world that make you feel wrong, that point out what you are not doing and cannot do, and the results create inner conflict. Conflict makes you beat up on yourself. Conflict in your mind and heart attracts conflict from the world. The normal human response to conflict is blame, and once you start blaming, you are going to find yourself embroiled in anger, fear, and more conflict. In order to tap into the essence of your spiritual self, the essence within your being, you must evolve beyond blame.

Confession is one way to end the vicious cycle of anger, blame, and conflict. Once you say what you feel, you release the negative energy of the emotion so that the positive energy can emerge. Once you admit what you have done, no one can use these things to badger you. Once you admit that you are frightened, helpless, confused, exhausted, or angry, you are acknowledging your human vulnerability and asking for help. When you ask for help, Spirit can respond. Until you acknowledge what you need, you cannot ask for it. If you do not ask for what you need, the need continues to grow until it overwhelms you. Confession is the way to eliminate being overwhelmed. It is an empowering act of humility. To admit that you are vulnerable or that you have made a mistake humbles the soul. When a soul is humble, it is teachable; it is open to new information. Until you confess, your soul remains closed to the light and knowledge of Spirit.

It is not necessary to have *done* anything bad before you confess. Have you thought harshly of someone? Have you spoken harshly to someone? Thoughts and words are as powerful as actions when they are laced with negative emotional energy. In addition, what you think and say is a very good indication of what you feel. What does it feel like to be a Black man? What does it feel like to be denied? Oppressed? Judged unfit by the world? Confession not only clears what you are feeling today; it clears what you were feeling last week, last month, or last year. It helps you to clear self-doubt, self-criticism, and self-denial. Confession releases energy. What negative energy are you carrying in your mind? What have you done in your life that you are not proud of? Ashamed of? What experiences have you had that you do not understand? Or are angry about? Each of these questions is a topic for confession. When you confess what you are thinking, you are, in effect, calling upon the wisdom of Spirit to shed light on you.

PRAYER CHANGES PEOPLE

Confession opens the soul. When the soul is open, the light, love, and peace of Spirit can enter. Confession is a form of prayer. It is the most empowering prayer I know of, because it is a form of surrender. You are giving up something. And whatever you give up to Spirit will be re-placed by something better. Confession as prayer is the way to fine-tune the spirit. The demands of the world fall away when you tune into Spirit. Prayer is the way to tune into Spirit. For those who have turned away from church or are in spiritual limbo, you may think you do not know how to pray. If you do not consider yourself religious, you may think you cannot or should not pray. Prayer is an internal experience. It is communication between you and the spirit of the Creator within you. The issue is not whether you know how to pray. The issue is whether you acknowledge that there is something/someone to hear and respond to your prayers. If you accept that the life force of the Creator is at the core of your being, you realize that when you pray you are praying to yourself. The divine self. For this reason, prayer need not be set or fixed in any particular way. The words you choose can be your own words or those you have been taught. Prayer is communion. You can express your thoughts and feelings in any way that is comfort-able for you.

You do not have to beg or make deals when you pray. What you get in answer to your prayer is a direct reflection of what you expect to re-ceive, not necessarily what you pray for. You can pray endlessly and never see the manifestation you want. If you pray in doubt that what you want is possible, your fear and doubt cancel the prayer request. The key to prayer is to pray with faith, knowing and believing that whatever you ask for, you already have. Prayer is the request to bring your desire into manifestation. Prayer must always end by giving praise and thanksgiving that your desire is fulfilled.

When confessing in prayer, do not blame yourself. State as suc-cinctly as possible what you have done or what you are thinking. Once this is done, ask for what you need. That could be forgiveness, clarity, strength, or wisdom. You can also write your prayer of confession. This means you would write down everything you want to confess. You can go as far back as you like when writing your confession. Also in-clude what you were feeling or thinking at the time. If you were afraid, ashamed, given the wrong information, or if you acted in anger, be sure to include those experiences in your writing. Do not spend too much energy writing about other people or what you know and feel about their part of the experience. If your confession in-cluded your actions toward others, simply ask for forgiveness and do not forget to forgive yourself. Write until your mind is clear and nothing else comes up in thought. When you have finished writing, you may tear the pages up and flush them in the toilet or burn them. This facilitates an additional release of energy.

Affirmative prayer is a traditional African concept that has been recognized by the New Age movement. Affirmative prayer begins by addressing the Creator with praise names, giving thanks for all that you have. Praise is a statement of gratitude; it communicates that you are ready and willing to receive more. After offering praise and thanksgiving, state your request or dilemma. Speak about it as clearly and precisely as possible, and state your cause in positive terms. (For example: "I know there is a divine solution to this situation. Thank you for revealing the truth of this challenge I am facing.") When you pray, do not lay blame, draw conclusions, or make demands. Prayer means you are open to divine results and revelations. Remember, you cannot see with the bare eyes all elements of what you live.

In prayer, it is counterproductive to pray for harm to come to someone else. You should gently express your thoughts and feelings and ask for guidance and clarity. You must ask for the best outcome and claim it by giving praise and thanksgiving. Once you have issued a prayer, do not negate the effects with negative thoughts and words about what you have requested. Prayer is like planting a seed. Negative thoughts dig up the seeds. Pray for what you want. Release it by giving thanks. Begin acting as if you already have what you asked for in prayer.

Every thought you think, every word you speak is a form of prayer. Thoughts and words are an expression of your life force. When this force is released into the universe, your environment, it takes shape and form. *O'fose* (pronounced Ah-fo-shay) is the ability to create through utterances. In the Bible it is stated, "Whosoever thou shall decree [speak] shall be established unto you." When you utter negative affirmations such as "I don't know," "I'm confused," and "You make me sick," you are in effect creating conditions. Those conditions are created by the power of your decree. Thoughts or words of fear, anger, hate, greed, and jealousy are also prayers. Experiences that arise in response to what you say are the answers to a prayer, that which you have thought and spoken. Remember, you are divine energy. The energy of the divine is represented by "I Am." Whatever you think or speak in connection to "I Am" must be created. Be mindful not to give power to things you do not want to experience in your life.

WHEN PRAYER CHANGES PEOPLE,
PEOPLE CHANGE THINGS

Prayer, confession, confessions in prayer are powerful tools. They are the tools I found most useful in my life for releasing anger and fear. They are also the tools that supported me in finding, defining, and refining myself. Once I discovered that I could confess to God the worst things I thought about myself and not turn into a puff of smoke, it was easy to confess what I thought and felt to other people. What can people do to you that you have not already done to yourself? More important, what can people do to you that is more substantial than what God can do to you or for you? Once you confess to God what you are thinking and feeling and ask for clarity, insight, or release, healing can take place.

Always remember that your life is a temporary, human experience. As such, you will make mistakes, poor choices, and bad decisions. This is how you will learn what to do and what not to do. When you make a mistake or when someone points out one of your human frailties, do not get angry. Confess. If you have nothing to confess, you have nothing to be angry about. When people criticize you, don't get mad at them—they are human too. Confess what is on your mind; explain to them how you feel. In this way you will avoid the backup of toxic emotions you later take out on your dog, wife, or children. Through confession, I learned how limited I was as *just* a Black woman. I found out I was bound to the same errors and weaknesses because my Blackness, my womanness, and my social and political status carried intrinsic limitations in the world. Once I was able to expand my consciousness beyond the expression of my physical self, I found that life was far more flexible and I was much more open.

As a child of God, I see all Black men as my brothers. You may get angry with your brother, but it only lasts a minute. Then you pray for yourself. You pray for the strength to accept people just as they are and the strength to overcome the need to be angry. As a child of God, I realize that I am connected to my brothers. I now know I cannot be angry with you without being angry with myself. As a child of God, I see the good in you no matter what you do or how I feel about it. I know you are powerful. I know that your experiences in this life are lessons. As you learn your lessons, you will do better.

As a child of God, I realize it is not my job to judge or criticize my brothers. In confession I discovered that the only things my brothers do to me are the things I do to myself. I have learned to love, support, and nurture myself, and I know it is my purpose in this life to nurture, support, and love you. I have learned the power of forgiveness. I believe that God has forgiven me for all the things I did when I was angry and afraid. In return, I have forgiven my father, my husband, and my first boyfriend from the first grade. I have even forgiven myself for the things I have done to you and said about you when I was angry. I have forgiven myself for being disappointed in you and for disappointing you. All of this I was not able to do as a Black woman. I was too hurt and too angry. As a child of God, I realize it is my responsibility to the universe to maintain my own spiritual and emotional health. It is also the key to my own healing. As one child of God heals, all the children of God are healed.

DAILY MINIMUM REQUIREMENT

Each day for the next seven days, be very conscious of what you are doing and feeling. If you verbally lash out at people or find yourself having negative or unkind thoughts about other people, stop immediately and pray. If you find that you have made a mistake, forgotten to do something, or failed to honor your word, admit it. First to yourself and then to the other people involved. When people speak to you or approach you in a manner that makes you uncomfortable or upset, let them know your feelings without accusing them. Use statements such as "When you do that or say that, it makes me feel _____" or "It makes me feel _____ when you speak to me that way." If for some reason you cannot say these things, write them down. Write what you feel when you are feeling it.

Surrender

"Ma. I've got a problem."

"What's the problem, Damon?"

"Remember I told you about the guard in here who keeps harassing me?"

"Yeah."

"Well, we had a shakedown the other day and they found five packs of Black & Milds and . . . "

"What's a Black & Mild?"

"You know, those little cigars."

"Okay."

"Well, this is a nonsmoking dorm and they found these cigar things in the shakedown. So this guard, the only brother in here, said I came to him and told him they were mine."

"What?! Has anyone ever seen you smoke? Damon, they know you don't smoke!"

"That doesn't matter, Ma. Me and this guy have been having problems for a while now. He is really out to bust my chops."

"He can't do that, Damon."

"Ma, listen, okay. A few weeks ago we had another shakedown. They went through all the lockers and took everything out, looking for contraband. I had a book in my locker that I had borrowed from this other brother. I mean I am responsible for this guy's book, right."

"Were you supposed to have the book or is it contraband?"

"I can have the book. It's a paperback book. I just borrowed it, but in the shakedown this same guard ripped the cover off the book and ransacked my locker."

"How do you know he did it?"

"Ma, I know he did it, okay. He didn't deny doing it either. He ripped the cover off the book and threw my stuff all over the place. I asked him why he did it. Then I asked him to clean it up. He said he wasn't cleaning up shit, so I went to the captain, his supervisor. The supervisor asked me why he should clean up my stuff, and I said because it is the right thing to do."

"Did he clean it up?"

"No. So I put in a grievance against him. When he responded to the grievance, he wrote that I called him an Uncle Tom nigger who was fronting for the white man."

"Damon! Did you say that?"

"No, Ma, please! I'm telling you, this guy hates me, but he is always talking to me. He's always asking me if I think he is fair. If I think he is a decent guard. I told him I thought he was selling his soul and his brothers for a paycheck by doing the white man's dirty work."

"Damon, did you call that man an Uncle Tom?"

"No, Ma. I told him he was a soft ass trying to be liked by the wrong people for the wrong reasons. I guess he didn't like that, so now he's out to get me. Now he's lying on me!"

"Damon, people can say whatever they want to say. If you know the truth, stand by it."

"Ma, if these charges stick against me . . . "

"What charges?!"

"He's bringing me up on charges. He said I used vulgar and profane language in the presence of an officer, and he's saying I had contraband, the Black & Milds. If these charges stick, they could give me two more years."

"That's not going to happen, Damon."

"I know, because I went to the chief. I told him I want to bring the guard up on charges. I told him the guy is lying. I asked him why would I tell this guy I was holding contraband if I had a grievance in against him. If the cigars were mine, why would I admit my guilt to him? The chief had to agree with me that it didn't make sense, so he asked me what I wanted."

"Well, what do you want? Do you think this guy is going to admit that he lied?"

"He kinda did. When the chief spoke to him, he said that he got it from a reliable source that I said the cigars were mine. When he wrote the charges up, he said I told him. Now they want to give me a written reprimand."

"What's that?"

"It's when they write you a warning. I told them if it was an admission of guilt, I don't want it. I told him I would go on a hunger strike until the hearing because I want my name cleared!"

"Is it really an admission of guilt?"

"They can write it either way. They can write it as a warning or as charges for which they waive the hearing. The chief told me I was being too severe, threatening not to eat. That's not severe! This is my life! I am willing to die for the truth!"

"Damon, don't be so dramatic! You do not have to die for anything they can do to you in prison. Besides that, God is the only one who can take your life."

"This place isn't like that, Ma. These people don't care nothing about God. They will destroy you any way they can. The chief asked me why I was so upset. Why do I care what people say about me? I told him I stand for the truth and that I want the truth to be told about me. If the truth destroys him and sets me free, so be it!"

"It sound like you're standing on facts, not truth."

"What? What facts? The facts are the truth."

"No, they are not. Facts are subject to change. The truth is consistent."

"The truth is, this guy is lying and that's a fact. The truth is, he is out to get me because he doesn't like me. I think he's afraid of me and the things I say. All those things are facts, Ma. That's the truth, isn't it?"

"The truth is, he is a child of God. He may not know it but he is. The truth is that the only power he has is the power that God gives him, no matter what he believes. The truth is, he can't hurt you unless you let him. The truth is that you believe he can hurt you."

"Ma, that stuff don't work in here!"

"God works everywhere, Damon."

"If the guard lies and his supervisor knows he's lying but can't, won't, doesn't tell the truth, what is God going to do?"

"What are you reading?"

"What?"

"What have you read today?"

"The paper. Acts of Faith. I read my Acts of Faith every day."

"Did you read Psalm 37?"

"No."

"Psalm 37 says, 'Fret not thyself because of evildoers. Neither be afraid of the workers of evil.'"

"Yeah, I know that, Ma, but . . . "

"Did you read Psalm 109? Psalm 109 says, 'Hold not thy peace oh Lord of my praise for the mouths of the wicked and the mouths of the deceitful are opened against me.' Do you know what that means, Damon?"

"I think it means that God will take care of my enemies."

"Yes, it does, but it also means that the guard is your brother and that he can't hurt you."

"Ma, that guy doesn't know he's my brother. He's a corrections guard working for the white man and I am a Black prisoner. That guy knows he has the power to tell me when to eat, how to walk, and what I can and cannot say. If he was my brother, he wouldn't lie on me and he would treat me with respect."

"What about Joseph? Joseph in the Bible? What happened to him?"

"His brothers threw him in the well and let him be sold into slavery. Then they lied and told their father that he was dead."

"And what happened?"

"He was a slave."

"And . . . "

"He became prominent in the king's court, and eventually he saw his father again."

"And what did Joseph say when he saw his brothers?"

"He told them that they did it for evil reasons, but God meant it for his own good. That is what you must always remember, Damon. You must know the truth and invoke it when your head is in the lion's mouth. When you know the truth, the lion becomes interesting company, not a threat to your life.

"Damon, you have no idea what that guy lives with at home. You don't know if his wife hits him in the head with pots or if he lives in a basement or a trailer park. You don't know if his mother or father is dying from a terminal illness or if his only child is mentally retarded. This job may be all he can do right now. It may be all he believes he can do right now. How he does his job is not your business. It is a symptom, a symbol of who he is. And you know what, Damon, his psychosocial history doesn't matter either. Your psychosocial history doesn't matter. Right now, those are all facts that are subject to change. In a minute those things will be history, but the truth is consistent, immutable, and unchangeable. The truth is, when people act out, when they lie, when they strike out against other people, they are asking to be healed.

"You cannot heal him, but you can invoke the Spirit of healing. You can stand in truth for him and know the truth about him. The truth is, he is your brother and he cannot hurt you without hurting himself. When he strikes out against you, Damon, know that God is your defense and your defender. Surrender your ego and the need to be right. Surrender your anger at yourself for being in prison. Remember 2 Timothy chapter 1, verse 7: God has not given you a spirit of fear, but of power and of love and of a sound mind."

"Ma, I know these things, but it's so hard. It's so hard in here."

"Damon, keep God constantly in your awareness. Be aware of the presence of God no matter what is going on; be aware of God in your midst and invoke that presence in your consciousness. When it gets hard and you can't do it, surrender it to God."

"Ma, please pray for my strength. I really want to be stronger, Ma, 'cause I don't want to give in to this garbage. I know I can make it through this if I am strong in my faith."

"Are you willing to be strong, Damon?"

"Yes, Ma, I really am."

"And so it is!"

8

HE IS WHO HE
SAYS HE IS

*America's greatest crime against the
Black man was not slavery or the
lynching, but that he was taught to
wear a mask of self-hate and self-
doubt.*

　　　　　El Hajj Malik Shabazz
　　　　　　　　(Malcolm X)

In his book *Living the Infinite Way*,
Joel Goldsmith wrote, "We must
learn not to try to bring God
down to us, to mold God to our will, but rather we must seek to understand God's will and bring ourselves into harmony with it." Surrender is the way that we bring ourselves into harmony with God's will. I
think this is also what is meant in the passage of the Koran that says,
"Knowledge must reach for ignorance because ignorance will never
reach to knowledge." God knows that you have so much invested in
your thoughts and feelings and the trappings of the world that you
often forget who he is. God is the source and the substance of life,

but when you get too busy or too wealthy or too angry, you are prone to forget who God is. Knowing the frailties of his human children, God has provided you with a way to get to him, no matter where you are, what you think, or what is going on. The way is called surrender.

In their book *Your Needs Met*, Jack and Cornelia Addington offer more than one hundred formulas for getting out of the way and allowing the Holy Spirit to bless you. Surrender is the principle underlying the ability to "get out of the way." Surrender can be one of the more difficult concepts to grasp, and even more difficult to practice. The foundation of the law of surrender mandates that you *let go*. You must stop helping people and trying to fix or change circumstances in order to allow Spirit to enter and create divine order. Unfortunately, when you have been programmed to believe or conditioned to think that holding on is the way to demonstrate power, surrender is interpreted as an act of weakness and failure.

Surrender in a spiritual context is the ultimate act of faith. It is a demonstration of your willingness to trust the process of life and an expectation of a divine resolution. This does not mean you must give up, sit back, and do nothing. Giving up, as it relates to surrender, is mental and emotional stillness. It is acknowledgment of a power greater than the physical self. Surrender is the way you demonstrate your awareness of and faith in divine order. Order will be the best possible outcome for everyone involved in the situation, even when it is not what we "think" it should be. This is, in effect, the challenge of surrender: giving up what we "think" about things or people.

When you look at a tree, you see a source of wood, perhaps shelter. You see a thing of strength and beauty. If you open your mind, you may see a chair, a table, even the frame of a sofa. Your physical senses coupled with imagination give you the ability to see what a thing can become. Yet there is so much you cannot see. You cannot see the age of the tree, how deep its roots grow, the number of people who have sat at the foot of the tree to picnic or cry. You do not know how many animals, insects, or people have eaten from the fruit of the tree, or have survived a storm because of the position of the tree. The tree may have medicinal or sentimental value you cannot see. Rest assured, the tree has a value, purpose, and meaning beyond all that you can see or imagine.

When faced with a difficult situation, a challenge in life, you do not always see the intangible value and worth of the experience. Unlike when you look at a tree, when your life, loved ones, or physical well-being is involved, emotions cloud your vision. Your imagination runs wild, not always in the most positive vein. When you are threatened, angry, or frightened, it is your nature as a human being to defend yourself. You may strike out in an effort to overtake the difficulty and gain control of the people and situation. It is this response that inhibits your ability to master the art of surrender.

How many fathers have tried to *make* their sons do a particular thing in a particular way because of what they *know* about the situation? How many mothers have warned their sons against behaving in a certain way because Mother can always *see* what is bound to happen? How many times have you acted or failed to act because you *knew* what could happen or might happen? How many times have you given advice, attempted to stop or help someone because of what you feared would happen if the person continued in his or her path? You respond to what you see and know based on your perceptions and experiences. Under emotional stress, you forget that there is much more that you cannot see. You forget that no matter where you are and what you are facing, Spirit has the power to bring peace, harmony, and balance into the situation. You forget that no matter how hard you try, you are not in control. Natural law will prevail. When you have done all you can do, you must surrender. Surrender in faith, with prayer, calling upon the power and the presence of Spirit in your own being to bring you peace and establish divine order. To surrender, you must give up what you think might happen. You must give up the need to be right. Surrender means to accept, without doubt, that there is a purpose and value beyond what you know and see that will benefit your growth, understanding, and evolution. To surrender is to rely on and trust in the presence, power, and goodness of Spirit working through immutable principles to protect and propel you forward. If you believe only in what you see and what you know, you will undoubtedly be forced, pushed, beaten by the events in your life until you learn to surrender. If you resist, you will strike out physically or emotionally against what you believe is not right, unfair, or out of your control. In the end, you may find yourself physically diseased, emotionally distraught, spiritually unfulfilled, and doubtful. You will be forced to admit that you do not know what to do or that there is nothing else you can do. In the end, you will surrender. The choice of whether to do so willingly or *willfully* is yours.

I was raised on a television diet of Westerns and combat movies. From that I came to the understanding that the goal of war was to overpower the enemy with such force that they would either surrender or be killed. Those who surrendered did so in disgrace, with lowered heads. Others fought to the death. I watched Native Americans surrender, weary from battle, to reservations and other indignities. I watched the Germans surrender in the face of bigger, better guns and better strategy. From this I learned that the weak, powerless, and inferior surrender to the strong and powerful or they die. Who wants to die? More important, who wants to live in powerlessness and disgrace? It is quite a dilemma, which makes surrender to an intangible power all the more difficult to understand. In the accepted practices of society, which are tied to human power and control, surrender is not an honorable position. It is more like an admission of weakness and submission to a stronger force. In society, that force is the physical man. Spiritually, surrender is the only position of power. When you surrender, you are allowing the power of God and the laws of the universe to be in control.

Men must learn that it is all right to give up. It is all right not to know what to do. It is really quite fine to admit to a weakness, to being confused, or simply to having reached the end of your knowledge or ability. From a spiritual perspective, to give up really means to *give over*. It is not a reflection of your manhood, character, or vitality. It is a willingness to give up what troubles, frightens, confuses, or limits you. To give up is to give yourself over to being shown a new way, to gaining a better understanding, to strengthening your character with faith and patience. To give up in surrender does not mean you cannot have control. It means you acknowledge who is really in control. Control is not pushing, shoving, forcing your will. Control is knowing "Thy will be done." When you know that the will of your Creator is for your good, it is easy to face any situation and "Let not thy heart be troubled" (John 14:1).

My grandmother would always say, "It's in God's hands now." She made herself content with this knowing and was willing to accept the outcome as *God's will*. This woman was no pushover, either. She once beat a guy to the ground for attempting to snatch her purse and tearing her *good* stockings in the process. This grandmother was five-feet-ten-inches tall and wore a size ten shoe. She was not a wimp or a sissy.

She simply understood how to get out of the way and let Spirit work. My father, on the other hand, would say, "This is not God's business. This is my business. If I don't take care of it, it won't be taken care of!" He, by the way, was the reason I watched those Westerns and combat movies.

My father believed he had to demonstrate control by having things go the way he thought they should, said they would. My grandmother would simply shake her head in dismay. "Why?" she would ask him. "Don't you believe that the One who created you also knows what you need?" This infuriated my father. Faith and peace and trust were nice, but they would not save a Black man in America. If a Black man was too quiet, too nice, people would step all over him, disrespect him, and eventually do away with him. My father would tell her that was the reason women were treated so badly in the world. They were too nice. Two days after my father's funeral, his mother, my grandmother, said, "Well, I guess he has finally learned how to surrender. I hope he knows now, it has nothing to do with being nice."

DAILY MINIMUM REQUIREMENT

A *God Jar* is an excellent way to master the skill of surrender. You will need an empty jar and several small sheets of paper. Keep some of the papers with you during your day to identify persistent or recurring issues. Formulate the situations into clear and concise statements, and write each statement on a separate sheet of paper. Fold each paper by holding it away from you, folding out rather than toward you. When you have folded the paper three times, place it in the God Jar. The issue is no longer yours; it belongs to God. When thoughts about the situation pop into your mind, remind yourself, "God is handling that. I surrender."

You can also use the jar to write down situations you would like to create in your life. Follow the same procedure as above, except this time you will fold the paper toward you rather than away from you. Should you become anxious or experience any stress or tension regarding this situation, affirm to yourself, "I surrender to God."

With regard to those situations you want to experience, be on the lookout for clues and opportunities. This is how you will demonstrate that you *expect* God to respond.

Commitment

Sitting at the feet of the master, the student asked for enlightenment. When the master asked him to explain what he meant, the student said that he wanted to do all the things that would transform his life to the vision of goodness of which the master spoke. The master asked the student what he was willing to do to attain the enlightenment he desired. The student said anything and everything. The master smiled and asked the student if he was sure. The student said that he was willing to give his life, if necessary, to attain enlightenment. The master assured him that he had no idea of the power in the words he had just spoken.

The master gave the student a schedule of activities to follow, which he assured him would lead him to the path of enlightenment. The schedule made no sense to the student, but he agreed to follow it. The schedule required that he awaken at four in the morning, walk to the nearest tree, and stand in front of the tree on one foot until 7:30 A.M., at which time he was to change feet and stand until 9:30 A.M. Following the tree-standing exercise, the student was to sleep until noon and then return to the tree and repeat his morning exercise for another four hours. After that, he was to retire for the day. The student followed the schedule for three days before he went to complain to the master.

"How," the student demanded to know, "is standing on one foot going to lead me to enlightenment?" The master smiled as he asked, "Have you been following the instructions exactly as they were given?" Self-doubt immediately crept in as the student thought, I must have missed something—that's why he's asking me this. Tentatively, the student responded, "I think so." Firmly, the master ordered him to follow the instructions specifically as given until he knew whether or not he was following them. Obediently, the student did as ordered. He read and reread the instructions. He had not missed a single thing. He got up on time, stood for the prescribed time, and went to bed on time. He continued the routine for another three days before he went back to the master.

This time he was adamant. This was an exercise in futility. The only thing he was gaining was stronger legs, not enlightenment. "Go back to your schedule!" the master demanded with as much outrage as the student had displayed. "If you are going to be enlightened, you will carry a heavy load. You will need strong legs!" Feeling somewhat sheepish, the student resumed his schedule, but with much less enthusiasm than before. In fact, on the very next day when he went to the tree, he took a book to read. Several days later, he took several books and lunch. Over the course of three months, the student read hundreds of books and gained several pounds. When summoned by the master, the student stood in guilt and defiance. "Have you learned anything from your exercise?" the master asked. "Oh yes!" he responded quite honestly. The master peered at him, which made the student nervous, but then he smiled and said, "Good! You are ready for the next step." The student was noticeably relieved when the master ordered him to get the boat. They were going for a ride.

It was a beautiful day. The student prepared the boat, and once the master was aboard, they pushed back from the dock. The student did all the rowing. He anticipated having an in-depth and intense conversation with the master about the path to enlightenment. For three hours the master sat in total silence while the student rowed with no destination. He was just about to complain when the master ordered him to stop the boat. The student obeyed, believing that the conversation would take place in the peaceful silence of the middle of the lake. To the student's disgust and dismay, the master sat in stark silence for another two hours before he spoke. "Put your face in the water."

This is it! thought the student; he wants to teach me something about enlightenment. He was so lost in his thoughts he forgot to do as the master instructed. "Put your face in the water!" Excited and confused, the student did as instructed, lowering his face into the cool, clear water of the lake. The student didn't want to miss anything so he tried to keep his eyes open. After what seemed like an hour, but was in reality a few moments, his eyes closed involuntarily. It was exhausting and confusing to try to find the path to enlightenment in the water and hold his breath at the same time. The student held his face in the water until he felt that he was going to burst. In fact, he was sweating and his legs were trembling. Now he felt really bad about not following the master's tree instructions. He had missed an important step on the path, but he couldn't take it any longer.

Just as the student was about to free himself from the prison of water around his head, he felt a powerful hand on the back of his neck pushing his head deeper into the water. He couldn't believe it! The master was trying to kill him! At first, the shock rendered him motionless, but then he tried to wiggle and squirm his way out of the powerful grip. The hand pushed him farther down into the water. He was submerged to his waistline. As he struggled, he held his breath. His hands had a death grip on the side of the boat. It was the only thing that kept him from falling out of the boat and into the water. Now he was struggling for his life. He couldn't breathe and he couldn't let go, and he couldn't wiggle hard enough to get away from the grip of the master. He was just about to lose consciousness when the master loosened his grip and yanked the student out of the water.

Coughing and choking, gasping for air, the student fell to his knees in the center of the boat. He did not know whether to be frightened or angry. He decided to be angry. Wiping his face, coughing, and trying to back away from the master all at the same time, he tried to speak, "What the . . ." The master was smiling. Looking directly into the student's eyes, the master said gently, "When you want enlightenment as badly as you want air, you will find it."

9

THE POINT OF
NO RETURN

*The most painful thing to me in the
1990s is when I am walking down
the street and I hear footsteps behind
me. If I turn around and see a white
man, I am relieved.*
                    Reverend Jesse Jackson

Long before slavery, oppression, and racism, African people forgot their legacy. As Dennis Kimbro says, we forgot our "designer genes." In our DNA are the genes of those who designed the universe. We became preoccupied with being human, with the human desires of power, and with pleasure as an escape from perceived human pain. We forgot the proverb of our ancestors which cautioned us to "Honor God in all thy ways and your path will be directed." We forgot that the purpose of coming to life was to make manifest on earth the nature of God: peace, harmony, balance, and unconditional love. The will to conquer and control became more important than God's will that we support, serve, and love

175

one another. We forgot about our inalienable powers, akin to the nature of God. Instead, we embraced the notion of conquest, the demonstration of physical power. The more we sought personal or individual power as human beings, the farther we grew away from the power of God.

Today, despite your lineage as a descendant of the first Father and Mother, you believe that it is by your *will* alone that you live, die, succeed, or fail. Yet you embrace habits that defeat the attainment of the very things you want: freedom and power. In this day and time, you do not suffer only because of the color of your skin or your gender. You do not suffer solely because of the supremacist notions of white men. In the universal scheme of things, there are no victims. There are those who *know* and those who *do not know.* You suffer because you do not remember who you are. You suffer because you do not believe you have been given, by virtue of your breath, everything you need to master the circumstances of your life. You suffer because you dishonor your Selfhood with thought patterns grounded in distorted perceptions that are supported in their existence by bad habits.

WHAT ISN'T WORKING FOR YOU WORKS AGAINST YOU

Habits are a series of actions that are executed so regularly they become automatic. Habits are like chains whose power you do not notice until you try to break them. Patterns of thought are habits that silently determine the degree of happiness and success you can attain in your life. When your thought patterns become filled with distorted images void of worthiness and value for the Self, you develop habits that are self-defeating and self-destructive. Richard Wright addresses the issue of developing destructive thought patterns in response to distorted images in his acclaimed novel *Native Son.*

> You are trying to believe in yourself. And every time you find a way to live, your own mind stands in the way. You know why that is? It's because others have said you were bad and made you live in bad conditions. When a man hears over and over and looks about him and sees that life is bad, he begins to doubt his own mind. His feelings drag him forward, and his mind, full of what others say about him, tells him to

go back. The job in getting people to fight and have faith is in . . . making them feel that their feelings are as good as those of others.

I have witnessed how the scenario plays out by watching the men in my life. My husband would wake up in the morning feeling good. We would make plans for the evening or the weekend. He would go to work, where he would be verbally assaulted by a hostile supervisor and served up for the verbal abuse by nonsupportive co-workers. By the time he arrived home, he was hungry, angry, and what I can best describe as temporarily insane. On the days when he was particularly insane, he became violent. When it was all over, he was remorseful. I can recall the number of times he would say to me, "They are right, you know. I'm just no good!"

My husband was not a bad person but he had very bad habits, the most damaging of which were negative self-talk, expecting the worst, people-pleasing or seeking validation from an external source, and blaming others for what he believed he could not do in life. He learned these habits from an environment in which there was a political motivation underlying society's decision not to teach him his true identity. He learned the habits in a home where his mother intimidated him into submission in fear that unless he was submissive, he would fail in life. He learned them in an educational system that was grounded in historical distortions and blatant dishonesty. The motivation of each of these environments was control. I believe the world is designed to control the minds of people and the inherent nature of Black men. In the midst of the internal and external conflict, my husband, like so many Black men, tried to acquire the sense of power society told him he must have as a man. Unfortunately, that same society forgot to tell him that his *real power* lay dormant in his soul.

My brother had a bad habit of feeling sorry for himself and blaming others for his position in life. My brother is a powerful Black man. His radiant dark skin, profoundly keen features, and lean, angular body are a credit to his maternal Dahoman lineage. His mind is sharp. He is extremely resourceful and skillful. He loves children and is great to have around the house. My brother, however, is stuck in the pain and trauma of his childhood, which fosters his bad habits. Our mother died when he was three. Our father abandoned us long before that. We have a younger brother who was raised as our cousin by our mother's best friend. My brother lived in a series of relatives' homes, waiting for Daddy to come and make it all better. Daddy rarely showed up, and in those homes my brother never felt wanted or loved.

After many years of watching my brother suffer, I came to the understanding that he is angry at my mother for dying. He is angry at my father for not being there in the way he needed. He is angry at me because I am not angry at the people who raised us. He is angry at the world because he never seemed to receive the appropriate compensation for losing his mother or for being the son of an emotionally unavailable father. Anger distorted my brother's perceptions and beliefs, rendering him a powerless victim of his circumstances. He had no sense of Self. As a result, he embraced habits that made him *feel* better about himself.

When he is centered, my brother is a hardworking, loving, and supportive Black man. When the pain of the past and the anger take hold of him, he drinks. When he is not drinking, he engages in other mind-altering habits. When he was under the influence of these stimulants, he was as obnoxious as he was pitiful. It was a pattern of behavior that I watched unfold, helpless to do anything about it. Every Christmas, New Year's Day, his birthday, or my birthday, my brother would alter his mind and call me. On those occasions, I was always his "little sister." He wanted me to know he loved me. He would ask for an update on my children; then, the drama would unfold. He would recall how terrible it was when we were children. He would remember what an awful person our father was. Did I remember when so-and-so did such-and-such? Didn't they know how we felt? Nobody cared about us. We were never loved. Everybody treated us so bad.

When I attempted to give him my perspective of the situation, he would get annoyed, "I know that, Ronnie, but . . . ." By this time he was screaming, swearing, and using totally unrelated events to prove his point. "You're confused!" I said. That would really set him off. "No! You're confused, little sister!" Holding the telephone at arm's length, I would listen to him blame and agonize until he wore himself out. As gently as I could, I would remind my brother that there was a part of him that nothing could touch. It did not matter how awful he had been treated or by whom. His *real* Father and Mother loved him and would never leave him. Once I made that astute observation, our conversation always ended the same way. He would tell me, "You know, you are the smartest one in the family but you are so dumb!" We would make promises to get together and hang up. I would not hear from him until the next significant holiday, when he would replay the old tapes.

If there is a drama going on in your life that you do not want, you must pull the stage out from under it. After several years of playing a role in my brother's drama, I pulled the curtain down.

He called on a New Year's Eve.

The minute he started, I told him, "No! You are not going to make me go through this drama again. I do not feel the same way about Daddy that you do."

That shocked him.

"I have forgiven him and released him."

Before he could get a word out of his mouth, I said, "I am not angry with the aunts, uncles, cousins, or anybody else."

"What about what they did? What they said?"

"It's over. It is time to move on."

"What the hell are you talking about?"

"I am talking about being tired of you dragging me with you through the muck and mire of the past. I am tired of watching you destroy yourself over something you cannot do anything about now. Let it go. And if by the next major holiday you have not let go of this pain, please do not call me."

I hung up and did not speak to my brother for almost two years.

BEYOND THE POINT OF NO RETURN

Life is a series of lessons, the purpose of which is to strengthen and purify the soul so it may regain the memory of its godlike nature. Each soul knows what it must learn from the physical experiences we call life. When the soul is granted permission by its Creator to inhabit a physical body, it must have the exact conditions and circumstances needed to facilitate the learning process. The soul will choose the time, locations, and conditions of physical life in order to purify and strengthen itself. Your soul chooses your parents and the conditions into which you will be born, along with the major players and events of your life. This is the precise reason your African ancestors performed divination rights when a child was born. They wanted to identify the soul. In this way, your soul is assured it will have the perfect environment to produce lessons it must master on the way to fulfilling its purpose for coming into the physical world. When you are born, you lose the conscious memory of your spiritual purpose and lessons. The experiences the soul has chosen are designed to teach the physical mind the truth and facilitate the unfolding of your spiritual memory. The goal of this process is to actualize and empower the Self in response to the physical experience.

What are the godlike qualities the soul must learn in order for you to be your true Self? Truth, harmony, order, balance, mercy, justice, and unconditional love. In every situation you face in life, you are spiritually accountable to exercise one or more of these qualities. To do so, you must learn to practice trust, faith, compassion, patience, cooperation, discipline, and forgiveness. Through the conscious practice of these spiritual attributes, you will experience freedom, joy, abundance, peace, and total well-being. Your physical mind will become *at one* with the energy of the divine Mind. In this state of being, you are powerful. You have an inner knowing, a silent, peaceful assurance, because you are in direct alignment with your life source. I suspect this is what is meant by the Ashanti proverb "You must act as if it is impossible for you to fail." When you live in conscious contact with your spirit, doing all the things you have come to life to do, learning your lessons and accepting them gracefully, you cannot fail in God's mind. You learn your lessons, evolve in consciousness, live in balance, and hold the Self in high esteem.

You cannot accomplish the unfoldment of the soul as long as you embrace limiting human habits. We as human beings hold on to those things that limit us primarily because we do not know our spiritual rights. In the world of physical man, the rights of Black men have been violated, changed, and ignored so often, you may believe that the benefits of these rights are no longer attainable. It appears as if your rights are determined and controlled by other human beings. Physical rights can be controlled by man. Spiritual rights are given and controlled by Spirit. They are immutable and unchangeable. The key is to know your spiritual rights, to embrace them as principles, and to act upon the principle of those rights in the physical world. Remember that everything is born of Spirit. What Spirit creates and controls cannot be destroyed and must, as a principle of creation, manifest in the physical world.

When you know what your rights are, you are able to protect and defend them. When you know what your rights are, you know what to expect from the environment in which you live. This is key to the concept of spiritual mastery, because what you expect must be in harmony with what you accept. You can have expectations while the events and people in your life do not live up to those expectations. In learning to master yourself, it is critical not to accept less than you expect. For a number of reasons, Black men have developed the habit of accepting less than you expect and less than you deserve. This is the outgrowth of an habitual thought pattern that convinces you that you cannot have what you want or deserve. It is also an outgrowth of the belief that other people stand between you and it. When your expectations are dependent upon the actions of others, you cannot attain Self-realization. More important, you cannot have an experience until you agree to participate in it. Your participation hinges on the belief that you deserve it. The belief that you deserve it is an outgrowth of knowing your rights and the entitlements thereof.

THE RIGHTS OF SELFHOOD

By virtue of your ability to breathe, you have certain inalienable spiritual rights. They are the right to have, to feel, to act, to love and be loved, to speak and create, to see, and to know. You have the inherent right to have anything that ensures your basic survival in the face of nature's elements. There is no guarantee of the quantity or quality of these elements you will receive; you must determine that for yourself by conscious choice. The right of Black men *to have* has been hindered by society's use of currency that is distributed by inequitable means. Society has taught you to equate your *self-worth* with your *net worth*. Consequently, the more you have of money and the "stuff" money can buy, the better you feel about yourself. When your ability to accumulate "stuff" is limited, your self-perception becomes distorted.

You have the right to feel safe in your environment, and to participate in the experience of whatever you feel. No one can validate your feelings, and no one can dismiss them as wrong or incorrect. The socialization and education process to which you have been exposed is designed to control the appropriate expression of those feelings to meet the needs of the society. Your feelings are yours, although they may not match the models established by society. You have the right to feel and express them. Most Black men have not been allowed to freely express what you feel and still be safe. You cannot feel safe in a society that demonstrates contemptuous disrespect for you and people who look like you. You cannot feel safe in a home where you are constantly reminded of how much you are *not* doing and how much *trouble* you are and cause. You cannot feel safe in intimate relationships when you have not been taught how to express your feelings, or when you do express them, you have not been taught how to handle the vulnerability of your experience.

You have the right to act on your thoughts, feelings, and ideas without hindrances from others. Acting is a reflection of who you are and what you believe to be true about yourself. All basic instincts are good. When you act on your basic instincts, you are acting on the belief in your own goodness. It is only by acting on the deepest desires of your soul that you develop a sense of inner worth to yourself and others around you. Black men have been taught to believe that you are not free to act in this society. Your parents were afraid you would not survive if you acted out who you were. They were also afraid that you would repeat their mistakes. They designed parameters and boundaries within which you could act. The educational system that indoctrinates you starts from the premise that you do not know anything, or that what you know is not worthy because you have not been sanctioned by the system. Social constructs such as educational degrees, labor unions, accumulated work experience, and corporate ceilings create boundaries that covertly and overtly serve as subtle reminders that "you are not good enough." This then prohibits you from acting on the urges of your soul. Each of these constructs, along with your own self-imposed restrictions, inhibits your right to act.

You have the right to love anyone and everyone and to be loved by everyone simply because you are alive. There is nothing you need to do to make yourself more lovable or to prove your love. As Hugh Masakela says, "There is nothing more to be added. The only thing left to do is, to do." Your color should not be a barrier to loving or being loved. Your income should not be a barrier to loving and being loved. The attainment of credentials, the neighborhood in which you were raised, the type of work your father does, and your net biweekly salary do not determine your right to express the bonding of souls or meeting of minds called love. You were stripped of the ability to love when you were made into a stud. It is a legacy of the African's history in America. You have been taught that in order to get love or be loved, you must give something. And when you give love, you must get something in return. Many Black men have also been taught to believe that love is not enough. You have been taught that you must do things to get love and have something to give in return for being loved. You have not been taught that because God is love, love is what you already are.

You have the right to speak your truth and create your world as a reflection of the truth as you know it. Truth is not demoralizing. Truth is not oppressive. Truth is not devoid of mercy, justice, or love. The so-called truth that Black men in America have been taught has stripped you of the right to create a reality reflective of your soul's purpose. This truth, which has demoralized and oppressed you in the name of justice, is a lie! This truth comes from the religious and political motivations to control. It is a truth designed to convince you that you were born wretched and powerless. This truth comes from an irresponsible theology declaring that your salvation is in the hands of other men. This truth, born of greed and fear, has taught you that you cannot speak or create your truth unless it is authorized by another human being. You have the right to deny this truth. And it is only as you begin to speak out against the lie that you will be able to create a new reality.

What you see, you will become. You have the right to see images that reinforce the meaning of yourself and the life you would choose for yourself. Is it by design or neglect that Black men do not control the images you see or the images that portray you? You have a right to see beyond the moment. Your ancestors could see. They practiced meditation. Meditation helped them to see, know, and understand how things happen. "Meditation grounded them in the infinite."[1] When you understand that the eyes reveal only a portion of the truth, you can be empowered and train yourself to see and know the truth.

You have the right to know who you are, to know why you are here on the planet at this time. You have a right to know that you have a meaningful purpose in life and that by living that purpose you will make life better for yourself and others. You have the right to know your mission in life and to know that what you have to contribute is valuable and worthy. The social constructs of the society have a responsibility to help you know yourself and fulfill your mission. All institutions created for the benefit of the society must be designed to

---

[1]John Heider, *The Tao of Power* (Atlanta: Humanics New Age, 1985), p. 27.

help you know. When they are not created in that manner and you do not know, then it is they, not you, that have failed. Once you know that the society is not fulfilling its responsibility, however, it is up to you to seek, determine, and decide how to accomplish what you know you must do. To accomplish this, you must develop a plan of action and a manner of behavior that will support you in fulfilling your responsibility to yourself. The manner and mode of your behavior is called habit.

DO IT IN A WAY THAT WORKS

Every moment in time is an opportunity to begin again. There are some things that you can never undo. Some things have lasting, long-range effects. Every minute you are alive, however, you can seek freedom in your spirit. Before you can be free, you must know that your freedom does not depend on what anyone else thinks or says about you. Freedom is a function of your consciousness. When you live who you are from the inside out, you do not need to seek approval or authorization from another living being. We are all human. We are all striving for perfection. Why would you ask another imperfect being to approve your imperfections? The ego's function is to show you how much better you are than everyone else. In the same manner you want to prove that you are better, everyone else has the same goal. Your freedom is an outgrowth of your habitual thought patterns, which grow into energy we call complexes. You may never notice your complexes because your thinking is often an involuntary reflex. Until you can master the habit of conscious thought, you remain as much a slave to your own thought patterns as you do to the world of living beings who are trying to prove they are better than you.

There are ten good habits you must develop in order to master your mind and evolve at the soul level. You must develop the habit of *having faith*. Faith is the energy that brings the invisible to the visible level of reality. You must develop the habit of *having a purpose* for everything you do. *Having a positive mental attitude* about yourself and life is a habit that is developed when you *have a positive image of yourself*. "You cannot have self-esteem until you have a self." When I heard J. California Cooper utter those words, my soul opened up. Because I believe one of the major issues facing Black men today is that you do not have a sense of Self. You do not recognize or understand who the Self is. The Self is not what you bathe and dress every day. The Self is the core, the essence, the lineage that you represent. The Self is the mission, the purpose, the lessons and challenges covered by a physical frame. The Self is not your psychosocial history or your economic status. The Self is the part of God that you are. The Self is the "I" that you are when you say "I Am." With those words, you are invoking the divinity and immutable rights that are your true Self.

When you know your true Self, you develop the habits of *sincerity* and *commitment to growth*. You realize your connection to everyone and everything. You assume your share of responsibility for the evolution of the whole by undertaking every action with a sincere intention that you and all connected to you will experience some level of growth. Sincerity and commitment to growth support the two habits of *seeking and applying information*. In your process of spiritual evolution, you cannot just *know*. You must be willing to apply what you know to yourself and everyone else. Knowing that life is a series of hard or long experiences will not lead to mastery or the development of good habits. You must go through life's experiences applying what you know to every situation as a demonstration of your faith in the process.

You must also *develop the habit of being enthusiastic*. In all things, expect the best. Your expectations, not your actions, will determine the results. Enthusiasm is one of the powerful emotions that stimulate activity in the nerve centers and cells. All habits generate a wave of energy in one cell that travels through the entire nervous system to create thought, feeling, and ultimately action. Enthusiasm is a positive emotion that quickly stimulates the entire nervous system. While toxic emotions and hardened feelings give rise to most bad habits, enthusiasm is like a quarterback. When enthusiasm is present, it throws the entire system into gear. You don't have the time or inclination to be angry or frightened. Your focus shifts to the protection of the quarterback. The habit of being enthusiastic is a reflection of your desire to have a victory. *Planning* is another good habit you must develop. Planning is related to the habit of *economic restraint of your time, energy, and resources*. When you know what you have, you can plan how to maximize its availability. Planning and the development of good habits lead to systematic activity that transforms potential into reality.

TOWARD SELF-EMPOWERMENT

It is an awesome responsibility to know who you are. When you know, you can no longer be a victim. You can no longer hold on to philosophies that limit and confine you. You can no longer play games, make excuses, or pretend that you do not know what you want. When you know who you are, you are willing to move beyond the demands of the ego and its attachment to the physical world. This scares the hell out of men who want to be in control and in charge. These men are convinced that this spiritual stuff is weird and unreal. I believe that somewhere deep inside they know that if they surrender their lives to spirit, they will have to do all the things they say they want to do. They might even have to like some people they swore they would never like. When you know who you are, your primary focus and purpose in life is to work continuously with yourself and live up to your greatest potential. When you think about who you are, the ego reminds you that your identity can be dangerous to your health, so you conveniently forget your nature. When you really know who you are, you know that there is nothing stronger than a commitment to the Self.

My godfather once told me, "You may not know how to raise your self-esteem, but you definitely know how to stop lowering it." Self-esteem is a sense of value and worth that comes from a positive self-image. It begins with you and extends to all you do in every aspect of your life. Self-esteem begins with the belief that you have a responsibility to always do your best, that your best is always good enough, and that no one other than you can destroy your self-esteem. You destroy your sense of Self and the esteem you have for that Self when you live without commitment. Commitment is the sense of purpose and vision that fuels the mission of the soul. When you are committed, you have self-imposed standards of effectiveness that do not rely on external factors. As a result, your empowerment grows from the inner self as an affirmation of inner worth. Just as self-defeat grows from bad habits that confirm inner doubt, self-empowerment grows from good habits grounded in a sense of value and worthiness.

There is always a reason for not doing something. Bad habits that confirm self-doubt are some of the reasons. Commitment provides you with a reason to do a specific thing in a specific way. It is the outgrowth of your decision *to be* and *to have*, whereas bad habits and self-doubt are outgrowths of what promises to be. Commitment is a decision demonstrating your willingness to do what comes next and to do it in a way that works. Without this decision, you can always find excuses for not doing what is necessary to make the potential a reality. With commitment as the fueling force, your desire and willingness to transform your reality become stronger than the grip of bad habits. Understanding who you are and the rights imposed upon you by your identity is a major step toward the development of commitment.

You must know why you want to change before you can commit yourself to the necessary steps. Your desire for change, which will ultimately determine your commitment to change, requires that you eliminate all self-defeating assumptions from your consciousness. It is self-defeating to believe that you can be denied because of your race or gender. It is self-defeating to assume that because certain people think they are better than you, they are better than you. It is even self-defeating to engage in arguments with other people about who they are and what they believe. Commitment alters the reality in which you operate. It becomes your reality, determined by your systematic application of good habits that are in alignment with universal principles. Commitment transforms anger at others into courage to create your own reality. It transforms fear of what someone can do into a passion for what you are doing. Commitment is your willingness to be dependable and accountable to yourself to such a degree that you are unable to compromise yourself. You will not accept into the realm of your reality less than you expect to have for yourself.

Your ability to make a commitment hinges on your willingness and ability to forgive. You cannot get to point B if you are stuck at point A. Moving the mouth or the body does not translate to moving the soul. The soul responds to the impulses of the nervous system that are fueled by your emotional being. If your emotional self is attached to self-defeating beliefs created in the midst of disempowering events in your past, you will have extreme difficulty making a commitment to your future. Until you forgive, you will remain stuck in the cement of negative experiences and emotions. You will stand firmly in that place of disempowerment because you believe, consciously or unconsciously, that those experiences keep you from moving forward. The only thing that inhibits the development of your soul and mastery of your Self is the inability to let go of the past. When you forgive yourself for past mistakes and others for their role in the imposed or chosen drama of your life, you set the stage for a new beginning that is determined by your commitment to evolution.

THE ONLY WAY OUT

The Black man's search for Self and identity in this day and time reminds me that "Inside the tiny acorn sleeps the mighty oak." You cannot see it. You cannot logically imagine how an oak tree can fit into a tiny acorn. Yet it is scientifically proved— and confirmed by nature— that oak trees grow from acorns. Imagine that you live on a side of the earth where there is only darkness. Occasionally, you get to see the moon and the stars, but you have never seen the sun. If some strangers came along and attempted to tell you what the sun looked like, you would have no concept of what they were describing. If they told of the sun's powers to heal and to cause growth of green objects, of its ability to fade away and return, you might be frightened. You might think they had lost their minds. Or something inside you might stir up inspiration. It is much the same way with revealing to Black men the ancient mysteries, secrets, and power of spirituality and spiritual consciousness; some will remain clueless, while others will be stirred.

One of the reasons human beings in general continue to struggle for their place in the physical world is that we fear giving up all that we have created. We must believe in what we create. To give up the belief would mean admitting that we were *wrong*. I know in my heart that Black men do not want to be wrong . . . again. In your mind, to give up the political struggle would mean to admit you were wrong about its value to you. To give up the fight for historical accuracy feels wrong because you have decided that would mean ignoring your history. For Black men to give up the battle for justice, equality, acceptance, and reparations has been translated to mean that they would no longer have anything to live for.

In my spiritual journey I have learned a great deal about living and dying. There are some things you must *die to* in order to *live for* something better. In the case of Black men, to surrender the things that you fight for would actually mean you no longer had anything to *die* for. It would demonstrate your commitment to live in peace and freedom as a divine right. It would mean not having to prove who you are, because you would already know. Once you know, you cannot be denied. The larger issue with which Black men must somehow come to grips is, If there is a Creator, a God force, and you are not in balance or alignment with that force when you die, how will you explain having spent your life fighting for something you were never able to achieve? If you believe that the injustices you have suffered in this life are the cause of your wounds, does not fighting them infect the wound? More important than that, I would like to know how you expect to win a war with so many wounded soldiers.

"Man is God's representative. God is realized through His qualities as they emerge from the realized human being."[2] The realized human being is the Self. It is only when you ignore the Self by diverting your attention to the demands of the physical realm that you lose all esteem for Self. You cannot live beyond the level of your self-esteem. The things to which you have been exposed and programmed, as well as the emotions charged by your experiences, all contribute to the image of the Self. If that image can be limited by mere words, physical attributes, and selfish desires, you cannot feel good about it. When you do not feel good about yourself, you cannot, do not, *will not*, take care of your Self. As a matter of fact, you become self-destructive. We see evidence of this every day as young Black men use drugs and guns to do away with themselves. These young men have embraced very bad habits. These young men have no commitment to life. These young men have lost their Self. If the wisdom of African culture is correct, it will take a legion of committed elders who teach by example to demonstrate to these young men who the real Self is. How committed are you to the wisdom of the ancestors?

DAILY MINIMUM REQUIREMENT

Make a list of all your activities for three or four days. Reduce each of these activities to its simplest form. Notice those things you have done consistently. Separate those things you would consider good from those that are not. Ask yourself, Which of these things is good for me? Which of these things is a bad habit? Make a list of those

---

[2]Mitchell Gilbert, *An Owner's Manual for Being Human* (New York: Samuel Weiser, 1980), p. 33.

things you consider bad habits. Next, make a list of the things you can do to replace these habits. How can you cut these things down in your life, or cut them out of your life? The next step is commitment. Why do you want to change these behaviors? What do you expect to accomplish by eliminating them? Make a list of your expectations. Create a plan of action. Throughout the day, remain conscious of your thoughts and behaviors that reinforce bad habits. Make a conscious decision to do a new thing.

Forgiveness

The wounded buck lay quietly, away from the herd, unfamiliar with his surroundings; the animal was frightened and desperate. Once keen senses were
now weak as his strength drained slowly from his body. With his naturally instinctual mind hazy from pain, the buck wavered between confusion and
helplessness in the darkness of the woods. The doe stood very still; sensing a
kinsman in danger, she relied on an intuitive bond and connection to help her
locate the wounded buck. That bond led the doe over the horizon, through
vastly unfamiliar territory, to within ten feet of the wounded buck. Again, she
stood silent and still.

The buck sensed something in his midst. At first there was relief. Then fear.
The buck became very cautious. The doe approached slowly, sending out

signals and sounds of support. The doe now stood in full view of the buck, conveying—as those who are connected do, in silence—the desire to assist. The wounded buck, struggling to remain alive, grappled with the overwhelming fear of death. The approaching doe looked familiar, smelled familiar, and vibrated a familiar radiance. Fear, however, turned caution into suspicion. The doe approached slowly. Not knowing how or where the kinsman had been injured, the doe reached out and unwittingly touched the exact place of the wound.

The buck is confused. This familiar-looking one has approached and created more pain. This familiar-looking one has touched the wound. Fear, pain, and suspicion translate as the need to defend. The buck strikes out, injuring the doe. The doe, now stunned, intuitively knows that the buck is off-balance and does not understand. Again the doe approaches, slowly, more cautiously. The wounded buck, knowing he is weak, feeling vulnerable and unprotected, must find the strength to defend himself. As the doe approaches, the buck strikes again with more force and vengeance. The doe now becomes defensive. What she knows intuitively is not working; the doe is unable to put knowledge into action or language. The doe has been wounded and must now struggle to survive or escape. She strikes back at the buck to forestall an additional attack. The buck retreats, confused, frightened, and angry. The doe retreats, wounded and betrayed. The two animals—one wounded, wanting support, suspicious of how it will come; the other, wanting to help, knowing what to do but not how to do it—turn away from each other. Whatever one does, the other holds suspect. Both are in a weakened state. Both are defensive. One having wounded the other, they distance themselves until they both die, alone, from their wounds. What a pity that animals do not know the power of forgiveness.

10

GIVING UP FOR
A CHANGE

*God already knows what we have
done. He is just waiting for us to
admit it to ourselves.*

Iyanla Vanzant

There are those situation in
which you want to help people
but you do not know how. The
same is true of people who want to help you. They are at a loss as to
exactly what you need and how to give it to you. Arriving on the same
boat, having lain in each other's body excretions, Black men and
women drew strength and the courage to survive from each other. We
were separated from the same familiar land, family, language, culture,
and traditions. We both suffered equal damages. Yet today it seems as
if we are two wounded beings who do not know each other. Suspicious of each other, having forgotten who we are, we attack. Sometimes in defense of ourselves, often because we are suspicious. Individually and collectively, we have forgotten the bond, the connection
that kept us both alive. We want to assist each other, but instead we

inflict pain. Eventually we retreat. In our separate places and ways, we both die of the same wounds: anger and fear.

The relationship between man and woman is interdependent. Black men and women must relearn the purpose for which we have come to life. We have not come to suffer together or because of one another, we have come to help one another heal spiritual and emotional imperfections. Only two whole people come together to support each other, serve each other, and grow together. We have not come to prove superiority one over the other, to compete with or to rule one over the other; we have come to fulfill a mission. When we find that mission and support each other in fulfilling it, both of us will find the way back to a state of grace and spiritual perfection called God. As long as we see ourselves as *opposites* rather than *complements,* we will not remember the purpose of our union. If we continue to *take from* rather than *share with* each other, we cannot serve or support each other. If we continue to hurt, we will not heal. As long as we stay on opposite ends of the wilderness, allowing fear, anger, and suspicion to direct our actions, we will not find our way home.

Black men and women each have individual healing work to do. Men must heal their minds and find their way back to their hearts. Your hearts have been closed by the pain of our history. Your hearts have been closed by fear and ego. As long as your hearts remained closed, you will not remember who we are or who you are. Women must heal their hearts and bring them into balance with their heads. We have been told so many lies. We have been given such incorrect information. We have become so addicted to our physical senses that even when our hearts speak the truth to us, our minds tell us not to trust it.

In the healing process, we must each begin where we are, with what we have, if we are ever to remember the truth of who we are. We cannot fix or change the past, but we can heal who we are right now. To begin the healing process, we must be willing to admit that we have turned our backs on divine law. In part, because of ignorance resulting from miseducation. Most recently, because of our choices that make us disobedient to the law. We must become conscious of our behaviors that are unloving and unsupportive, even when we are acting out in fear. Most important of all, we must be willing to forgive ourselves individually for the poor choices and bad decisions we have made, and we must be willing to forgive our complementary kinsmen for the same.

YOU FIND YOUR SELF BY FORGIVING YOURSELF

In his book *Working with the Law*, Raymond Holliwell writes, "A man who is great enough to forgive is always greater than the forgiven." Forgiveness means that you are willing to let go and move beyond the mistakes you and others have made. When you forgive, you make room for change, because whatever you give up will be replaced by something better. Like surrender, forgiveness may be difficult for you; you may believe you are doing something for the other person, usually a person who has hurt or harmed you in some way. You judge and determine the rightness or wrongness of what has occurred based on your perceptions and degree of intellectual understanding. Usually, that understanding does not take into account the lessons you must learn or the challenges you must master. As a result, you believe you can withhold forgiveness as a way of punishing others for their mistakes. I must confess, this is exactly the way I felt until I began to study *A Course in Miracles*. It teaches, "What you see in others, you strengthen in yourself. What you hold against others, you hold against yourself."

Forgiveness is not what you do for someone else. It is what you must do to free yourself from distorted perceptions and judgments that create fear, anger, and hatred. It is what you must do to eliminate internal confusion and conflict. I know how hard it is to be angry at a parent. I know the pain and confusion it causes in your life when you carry a broken heart and wounded ego into relationships, into a career, and into the role of being a parent. These toxic emotions create patterns of behavior and cycles of fear that are handed down generation to generation until somebody finds the strength and the courage to say, "Enough! No more! The pain stops here!" Forgiveness stops the pain, breaks the pattern, and ends the cycle of psychological and emotional dysfunction. Forgiveness, like surrender, calls upon the divine wisdom of Spirit. The difference between the two is that surrender is an internal state of stillness that creates an external manifestation, while forgiveness is an external course of action that creates an internal state of stillness.

In the spiritual support I have given people, I have received letters from hundreds of men and women who say they want peace, prosperity, and love in their lives. I always write them back saying, "Forgive somebody." People are rarely willing to accept that such a simple act can bring them the very thing they claim they want. When women write me about problems in their relationships, I tell them to forgive their father. When men write me about the same concerns, I tell them to forgive their mother. In more than half of the situations, these people will write back and say they do not understand the connection. I explain that we pattern our relationships after what we saw at home or what we missed at home. Even when we are unaware of it, our perceptions and judgments of our parents and their relationship become the model we create in our lives. I once heard that all men marry some version of their mother and all women marry some version of their father. Unfortunately, we don't marry what we see; we marry what we think about what we have seen.

Our parents do the best they can to help us. Sometimes they don't know what to do, so they do who they are. If they are wounded, afraid, angry, guilty, or just clueless about their own identity, they pass their patterns on to us. As children, most of us get angry at our parents for something. We create images about them. We convince ourselves that we are right and they are wrong. These thoughts and emotions become locked into our subconscious mind, influencing our perceptions throughout our lives until we become willing to forgive. I had a friend who had a wonderful, loving, and supportive father. I never heard this woman say one bad thing about her dad. Unfortunately, long after he had died, she kept looking for him to show up and marry her. No man was good enough, right enough, and loving enough. She kept looking for Daddy's approval and presence in her relationships.

Once she became aware of this, she took a few of her father's pictures and belongings out to the backyard and buried them. She conducted a private funeral ceremony for her father and forgave him for refusing to let her go. She forgave him for keeping her a little girl for so long. Then she forgave herself for holding on to him, looking for him, and dismissing so many men in her life because they were not her father. The relationship she was in quickly fell apart; however, she was real clear that she was not going to find Daddy, so she stopped looking for him.

Forgiveness opens your brain waves so that you can receive new impulses and ideas from the universe. As long as you hold on to old ideas and concepts, you cannot move beyond those images, ideas, and beliefs. Forgiveness breaks through to new ground, new levels in your consciousness, because it relieves the tension and stress caused by the initial impact of your experiences. Forgiveness is also an evolutionary process that opens the heart. When you forgive, hate evolves to understanding, anger evolves to compassion, shame evolves to self-value, and guilt evolves to courage. When toxic emotions evolve to universal principles, you feel better. Feeling is an activity of the heart. The heart is the home of love. Love is the presence of God. Forgiveness opens the heart so that you can experience the love of God.

LOVE MAKES THE JOURNEY
WORTHWHILE

Black men must forgive Black women for the things we have done for the survival of our people. Black women did not want to sleep with the slave master. We did not want to nurse the white babies at our breasts. We did not want to work in the big houses. We did it because we believed that, by our submission, fewer of our men and children would die. It may appear that we have abandoned you, that we have been taken away from you, that we are insensitive to you. But the eyes only tell a portion of the truth. It is the nature of woman to support. If that support involved working in the big houses of the world, learning to read and going to work, leaving you in order to save the children, we did these things because we believed they were necessary for our collective salvation at the time.

Etched into the consciousness of the Black man is an ancestral memory of anger, resentment, guilt, shame, and fear created by the rape of Black women. Today, you direct these old feelings toward your grandmothers, mothers, sisters, wives, and girlfriends. These dark emotions emerge, even when you are not aware of them, as anger, contempt, and disrespect for the women in your life today. You must forgive. You must forgive yourselves for not being able to build for us, protect us from the harm of our mutual oppressor. How can you feel good about your lovers and wives with such painful memories entrenched in your being? You must forgive. You must forgive Black women for the things we have said about you, the things we have done to you, the things we have not said or done when we had the opportunity. You cannot love a woman totally, openly, and unconditionally as long as you are nursing a wounded ego. You must forgive. To forgive means *to give up for change.* If you want to have a good relationship with your Self, your brothers and sons, and the women in your life, you must forgive. If you want to remember who you are, who Black women are, and what we must do together, you must forgive. You must do it not for our sake but to heal your own souls.

The hearts of Black women today ache with the pains of our great-grandmothers and mothers. Although we have continued to bring forth sons, we have borne the burdens of the mothers whose sons were hanged or beaten to death. We bear the guilt for the nights we were visited by the masters. We bear the shame for the daughters that we could not save from the same pain our grandmothers experienced. In the midst of our pain, we point our fingers at our fathers, husbands, brothers, and sons who could not protect us, did not save us, still have difficulty providing for us. We want to hold, embrace, love our men without conditions or demands. Yet, we are still so damn mad and disappointed, we forget that they did the best they could do under the circumstances of the time.

Black women must forgive themselves. We must forgive ourselves for giving in, for fighting, for running, and for not running. We must forgive ourselves for being afraid, being ashamed, and feeling guilty. We must forgive ourselves for not knowing what to say to our daughters. We must forgive ourselves so that we will have the strength to forgive our men. Not until we forgive can we remember the ships, the chains, and the whips that separated us from our divine mates. When we remember that, we must forgive our father's father for not protecting our grandmother. We must forgive our husband's father for not knowing what to do or say to save his son. We must forgive the men who have left us, hurt us, forgotten us. We must forgive what they have said and done. We must forgive ourselves and them in order to heal the holes in our hearts through which pain continues to seep. Once we begin the forgiveness process, we will also remember, "What you give, you receive tenfold."

DAILY MINIMUM REQUIREMENT

Pay particular attention to your interactions with people throughout the day. When you notice that you are angry or upset with a person, take a deep breath and mentally utter words of forgiveness. Once you have forgiven that person, forgive yourself for being angry. Remember, we are all here to learn lessons. While we are learning, we will make mistakes. If someone says or does something that upsets you, consider it that person's mistake. Do not judge it. Do not attach any meaning to it. Simply forgive.

Responsibility

The Jones family had lived on the Porter land for 103 years or four generations. The first Joneses were slaves, bought by old man Porter when the Joneses moved north. When slavery ended, the Joneses had no place to go, so they stayed to work the land for room and board. Actually, it was for a shack and some crumbs, but the Joneses were grateful. When old man Porter finally died, his son, a college-educated man, offered the Joneses a small payment for their upkeep of the land and harvest of the crops. That is the way the Jones family took care of itself for more than 50 years, one Porter after another paying it a little something to work the land.

Jake Jones was born on Porter land, worked Porter land all his life, brought his wife to live on Porter land, and fathered three healthy children in the same bed under the same roof where he and his father were born. He had added the extra rooms onto the shack that now made it an official house. Jake had also tilled the barren land of the Porter property so that he and his family could plant more and make a little more. Jake was headed up north. He wanted his only son to go to a northern school and get a northern job. To make that happen, Jake was willing to work long, hard hours for as many days as it took. He was not willing, however, to have another Jones body buried on Porter property.

Jake insisted that his son, John, start his education right there in the deep south. Every day, Jake's wife would make John a bag lunch, give him a nickel, and send him off at 5:00 A.M. to walk three miles to school. Since John was the oldest, he went alone. His sisters would probably be just about school age when they got to the north. John loved and respected his daddy and trusted him enough to take that long walk every day to the one-room schoolhouse. It wasn't a bad walk. On a good day John actually enjoyed singing with the birds, playing with the bugs, and outrunning any number of critters who showed up to escort him. The only part of the trip John hated was the ten or fifteen minutes he spent every day running away from the dog.

The Porter family lived on the outskirts of the property the Joneses worked. They lived in a big, beautiful house that had been in the family for as long as the slaves had. A lovely garden and a huge orchard of fruit trees surrounded the house. And then, there was the dog. He was an ugly little thing with a pushed-in face who slept in his own house right next to the Porter house. Although the house sat about a half-mile off the main road, every morning like clockwork, as John passed by, that ugly little dog would come tearing out of the yard and chase John for at least half a mile. John wasn't really afraid of the dog, although he imagined that his tiny teeth were probably very sharp. His biggest concern was that he did not want that dog to tear a hole in his good school pants. Mama would be mad. Daddy would be mad. And the kids at school would laugh at him. So that is what he told himself: he had to protect his pants.

One day, the dog surprised John. Before he even got to the gate of the Porter property, the dog was going at him, yelping and barking. It seemed to John that he was running extra fast. John knew if he ran back, he would have that much farther to go to get to school. He knew he couldn't run past the dog without being bitten. John did the next best thing. He ran across the road, heading right for the bushes. John made it across. The dog did not. There was a car coming and it was able to swerve around John, but it hit the dog and kept right on moving. John heard the dog's loud yelp and heard the dog's body hit the dirt road. When he walked back to the middle of the road, he saw the blood trickling down the side of that ugly face and the little legs twitching. All of a sudden, the dog's body started to convulse and then it got still. That's when John knew. He knew the dog was dead and that it was his fault. It was then that John panicked.

The first vision that crossed John's mind was that of his father hanging from a tree. White folks still hanged Black men in the south when they were mad at them. The Porters would surely be mad about Jake's son killing their dog. Then an even more frightening thought crept in. John was now eight. He could be hanged all by himself! "Jesus Lord! What am I gonna do?" God always answers prayers, you know. No sooner had John uttered those words than the thought popped right into his brain. Bury the dog in the bushes! Without a second thought, he scooped up the lifeless dog and headed back across the road into the three-foot-high bushes. On his hands and knees, using sticks and whatever else he could find, John dug a shallow grave, gently placed the lifeless ugly little dog in it, and then covered it up. He found some brush and leaves and used them to cover the grave. When he was sure no one would see the grave under the leaves behind the three-foot-high bushes, he dusted himself off and ran to school.

You cannot think when you panic. When you cannot think, you don't remember your times table. If you don't remember your times table, you get cracked on the knuckles with a ruler. When you get cracked, you try not to cry, but when you are riddled with guilt, cracked knuckles hurt, so you cry. Then the other children laugh at you and tease you. When you put a cold chicken sandwich on top of this kind of drama, you get diarrhea. John was a murderer with the runs who ran all the way home. By the time he got there, he was an ashen gray. Mama took one look at him and knew something was wrong. When she inquired, John began to cry. He couldn't take the guilt or the cramps in his belly. Now Mama was in a panic. She sent the oldest daughter out into the field to fetch Jake.

John was in the outhouse when Jake arrived, sweating and panting like a dog. They met on the front porch. John figured God would forgive him for killing the ugly dog, but there was no sin greater than lying to your daddy. John told him exactly what had happened, exactly the way it had happened. Mama gasped in horror. She knew about the hangings too. Jake wiped his face on his sleeve, took a long, deep breath, and murmured aloud, "It was an accident, that's all. Just an accident." The cramps in John's stomach vanished instantly. But when Jake opened his mouth again, they came back. "Where'd you bury the dog?" John told him. "Let's go git it." John headed right out the door to the outhouse.

John and his daddy walked in silence to the burial ground. Jake dug the dog up all by himself. He took the lifeless body out of the grave and carried it all the way back to the Porter house. Jake knocked on the door, and when the Porter matriarch, old man Porter's granddaughter, opened the door, she screamed and clutched her bosom. Porters came from everywhere. Jake stood tall and proud. John stood somewhere between his legs with half of his head under Jake's shirt. Jake explained what had happened and offered his humble apology. At various intervals in the story, the matriarch would scream or cry and stroke the dead dog she was now clutching to her breast. When Jake concluded the story and the apology, he half-turned, half-backed away from the door. The matriarch screamed at him to freeze. Jake obeyed and John almost fell over his feet.

The matriarch was livid. After calling Jake and John a few choice names, she demanded the ultimate. She ordered Jake to take off his belt and "whip the tar" out of John. Time stood still and so did everyone present. John figured it was better than a hanging, even though it was a bit severe. The matriarch repeated the order, but this time she demanded that Jake draw blood. Without saying another word, Jake unbuckled his belt. John stood stock-still. The matriarch whimpered. The Porter clan glared. When the belt was completely undone, Jake ordered John to lower his pants and bend over. This was his daddy talking and Daddy knows best. John did exactly as he was told.

Time was still again. The next wave of activity began when the matriarch screamed, "Go ahead! Do it! And don't stop until I see blood!" Jake didn't move. The belt was doubled up in his hand, ready to go. John was doubled over waiting, but Jake didn't move. He whispered to John to stand up. Then he turned to the matriarch and whispered ever so softly, "It was an accident. He didn't mean it, and I'm not going to beat my son because of an accident." Jake grabbed John's hand and together they walked off the Porter property. Several months later, the Jones family moved to Chicago.

11

THE LEFT HANDS
KNOWS

*The key to success is to keep growing
in all areas of life—mental, emotional, spiritual as well as physical.*
                    Julius "Dr. J" Irving

I made a list of all the things I was
responsible for and had been responsible for the better part of my
adult life. I paid the rent and all the utility bills. I made sure the children ate something three times a day, every day. I bought the children's
clothes, washed and ironed those clothes, and made sure the children
wore matching clothes until they were too short or too ragged to be
worn. I made sure the children got to school. I spoke to the teachers; I
went to the plays, recitals, football games; and when the children misbehaved in school, I picked them up from detention. I took the children to the clinic and the emergency room. I spanked them when they
misbehaved and rewarded them when they deserved it.

I plunged the toilet. I cleaned out the refrigerator. I made the beds,
all the beds, and swept or mopped the floors when they needed it. I

vacuumed the welcome mat at the front door. I scooped water whenever something was stopped up. I took out the trash. I shoveled the
snow. I hung the pictures on the wall. I tried to balance the check-
book but I usually bounced checks. I bought the Christmas tree,
dragged it home, put it up, bought and wrapped anything that went
under it, took it down, and dragged it back out to the street. I bought
the cars, paid the notes, and changed the tires if they were flat. I went
to the political rallies and community board meetings. Even when I
had a man in my life, I did most of the things that needed to be done
in the relationship and for the relationship.

After I had made the list and examined it, I asked myself, Where
would a man fit in my life if one were to show up? More important,
what would he do? I get very territorial about the things I do, the
things that I consider my *stuff*. I have had difficulty sharing my responsibilities, and when I put something in a particular place, I want
it to stay there until I move it. I have created a system in my life and I
am devoted to it. When you are in a relationship, you must be willing
to change or at least open your personal system to change. You must
be willing to share responsibility. There are times when I am not sure
I am open or willing to change. I want to, but I have been doing things
my way for so long, I am not sure I can. The way this plays out in my
life is that when I am in a relationship, the man tends to get in my
way. When he isn't in my way, he never seems to do things the way I
want them done. I know this has nothing to with the man, his ability,
or his willingness to do what needs to be done. It's about history.

Black men are being called upon to show up in the Black community. They are being called upon to show up in political and community affairs. They are being called upon to show up with economic
resources. They are being called upon to show up for the women and
children. Black men are being asked to be present. They need to be
present in the home, the school, the church, the PTA meetings, and
the supermarket. Being present does not mean that your body is
there. It means that men will be present to do their part for the collective evolution of whatever arena they show up in. There is a desperate void in the Black community that only the mind, body, and
spirit of Black men can fill. The challenge is for the women to allow
the men to show up and share the responsibility for what needs to be
done. The men are being challenged to accept and assume responsibility for their part of what needs to be done.

Things are changing so dramatically in the world. I think most men and women are confused about who is responsible for doing what. As I see it, the men must show up and remain psychologically, emotionally, and spiritually present to build the fortress. The women must show up and be willing to sweep. When the men need help with the fortress, women must do what we can to help. That does not mean we push the men out of the way and move all the bricks the way we think they should be moved. It means that we communicate with each other, reach an understanding about what we are doing and how we can get it done, with each of us doing an equal portion of the work. If it is sweeping that needs to be done, women must sweep willingly and joyfully, realizing that sweeping is just as important to the goal as moving the bricks. Let us be clear, this also means that there may be times when the men sweep while the women are making, searching for, or dusting off the bricks. The bottom line is that each of us must do whatever is necessary to build.

Women have been doing so much for so long, we must learn to be willing to share responsibility. When a man shows up and is fully present, we must be willing to share all of our life with him. We must recognize that he may not do it the way we would do it. He may not do it as fast as we think it should be done. A man is not going to decorate the interior of the fortress the way a woman would decorate it. This does not make him any less a man, nor does it make him stupid, weak, or any less willing. What women must realize is that if a man shows up in the room and meets another man, there is no space for him to assume his share of the responsibilities.

I guess the big question is, Are Black men willing to show up? If you are, do you know what your responsibilities are? If you do, are you willing to be present and accept your share of responsibility for the collective good of our community and the world? You cannot show up angry. If you do, you will get in the way; the women will get pissed off and force you out again. You cannot show up confused. We have more than enough confusion to last until the end of this millennium. You will need to get clear, and communicate what you are clear about, so that the channels of communication can once again be opened between Black men and women. You cannot show up and take over, push the women aside, flex your muscles, and expect us to quietly sweep. We have been sweeping and building for far too long. When you show up, you must be willing to talk. Talk about where you have been. Talk about what you feel. Talk about your vision, mission, and purpose for yourself and for us. Women not only want to know that you are ready to assume responsibility, we need to know you can handle the responsibility. We need to know what you are bringing to the table.

I don't think most women care what kind of work you do or what model car you drive. We do, however, need to know that you are doing something you like and are good at, that you can get to work on time and pay your car note on time, without drama or depriving us of what we need from you. If for some reason you cannot do these things, be responsible: admit it. Don't lie to us about who you are and what you are capable of doing. We are willing to support and assist you as much as possible, but we need to know the truth. If you lie to us and we find out, you're in big trouble! We will take over again. This time we will do it with the vengeance of anger, fear, and frustration. And we will force you out . . . again.

Are Black men ready to show up, be present, and be responsible? I hope that is what the Day of Atonement was about—your willingness to assume your share of the responsibility. Your willingness to atone, forgive, and redeem yourselves by opening yourselves up to a new way. I believe this new way includes incorporating very clear spiritual principles into your modus operandi. These principles include telling the truth, learning to be humble, learning to serve, give, share, and receive. I believe this means you must be willing to, as Gladys Knight says, "take God out of the closet and put him squarely in the middle of your life." I do not feel we will be able to heal ourselves by any other means. Too much time has passed. Too many wounds have festered for too long.

My intention in writing this book was not to put Black men down or criticize you for what you have not been or have not done. This book has been about the exploration of the power of Spirit. I believe with every fiber of my being that it is only through the power of Spirit that we can wipe the slate clean and pick up where we left off. And remember, we stopped before the ships arrived. I don't believe that we can *fix* what has gone wrong between us. I believe that we must now shift our gears from fixing to *healing* and to the pursuit of God-given rights as opposed to human-controlled privileges. We may never get the forty acres and a mule, but we can live together in peace, joy, and balance, even in the projects. The projects that we keep clean, together. We can get our children off the streets and into schools that will teach them the truth about who they are. And if the schools will not do it, we can do it at home, together, sharing the responsibility. We can do anything we set our minds to do when our minds are aligned with the mind of God.

I once heard Dr. Wade Nobles, a noted Black psychologist, refer to Black men as "warrior-healers." I do not recall the content of his entire speech, but one thing he said has remained in my consciousness: "An eagle must know it is an eagle before it can do those things an eagle is expected to do. An eagle must know the appropriate eagle behavior." The concepts of warrior and healer are not often used in relation to Black men. You are often called fighters. You are often referred to as sick. *Warrior* has a completely different connotation from *fighter*, and healers are almost always associated with Spirit. In the spiritual context, a warrior is one who walks in balance and harmony with his environment and wages war to protect nature. Spiritual warriors fight. They fight to preserve nature and the sanctity of Spirit. A healer is one who is trained in the art of restoring balance or endowed with the ability to do so. Healing is about balance. As I see it, Black men as warrior-healers must assume the responsibility for the preservation of nature and Spirit in order to restore balance in the Black community. To do this, you must live and work in harmony with natural laws and universal principles.

THE LETTER OF THE LAW

Many of us were raised on a steady diet of the elders' affirmations: "What goes around comes around!" and "Be careful of what you ask for because you just might get it!" These elders rarely took the time to explain exactly what they meant, and I'm not sure Grandma or old Aunt Lizzie actually knew that these were restatements of universal principles. What they did know from practice and observation was that there is a rhythm and order in life. They also knew that these things operate in life to create real circumstances and conditions. As a child, and even as a young adult, I thought I could outsmart these principles, avoid my comeuppance, and reap only the good of what I had sown. I was wrong, and life proved it to me time and time again. After many trials and errors, usually when I was flat on my face, I began to understand that the principles and laws of life and nature obeyed you to the exact degree that you obeyed them.

According to *The Metaphysical Bible Dictionary*, law is "the orderly working out of principles." Natural law or universal laws are principles that govern the state of being—how you live and the quality of your life. Used here as a spiritual concept, the term *principle* refers to "a source or cause from which a thing results." Consciousness is the source or cause that determines our mental, emotional, and physical state of being. Consciousness is the manner in which we use the mind, our ability to think and discern the validity of information. Universal law responds to the energy of our consciousness by creating circumstances and situations that mirror the mental and emotional energy we send forth.

There is an order to everything in life. The sperm unites with the egg. Over time, this union results in the creation and evolution of life. The order and the process that create life are the result of universal principle and natural law operating. They are a reflection of the interdependence of the tangible and intangible forces, the physical and metaphysical energy. Natural law is also the orderly flow of patterns, symbols, and events that affect all aspects of life, even when much of the interactive process cannot be seen with the naked eye. Sound creates vibration. Vibration creates energy. Energy creates life. At the foundation of all life are principles and laws that do not change. These principles are indestructible. They are the foundation of universal life as you know it.

Everyone in the universe of life is held accountable to natural law. These laws are impersonal and immutable. Whether we are ignorant of their existence or willfully attempt to break, alter, and subvert them, the consequences are the same. When you do not honor natural law and principle, you fall out of balance with nature and lose the supportive grace of Spirit. The most common way to break natural law is to blindly follow the demands of ego. This is when you attempt to force life's events to conform to the personal will without consideration of nature's will. The weather as a function of natural law is the most common example.

Heavy rainfall, snowstorms, tornadoes, hurricanes, earthquakes, and all other forms of weather or natural disasters are nature's attempts to cleanse and heal the environment. They are also clues from the universe that it is time to slow down, go within, and be still. I watched as people made very earnest attempts to get to work in the middle of an earthquake. In the midst of snowstorms and hurricanes, people continue with their schedules as if nothing is going on. Human beings have become so arrogantly consumed with our physical lives and so out of touch with nature, we will find a way to do our thing in the midst of nature doing its thing, which is usually for our own good. When you conduct your life without regard for your environment and the messages it gives you, you are operating outside the boundaries of natural law.

In the Western world, there are seven root notes on the musical scale. All musical compositions originate from combinations of seven principal chords. There are seven colors of the rainbow. All colors have their origin in one or more of the seven primary hues. There are seven points of power in the body and seven main organ systems sustaining it. If any one of the power points or organ systems is defective, the quality of life within the organism is affected. Seven is the number of Spirit. It represents interdependence, balance, and harmony. To live in balance and harmony with one another, we must honor our interdependence with one another and with the tangible and intangible forces that sustain life. Universal laws, as they operate, are the mechanisms designed to keep us in harmony and balance with one another and with all other living forces.

THE LAW OF MIND

There is only one Mind. It is the supreme controller of the universe, the principle of life, the creative force of all things, often called divine mind or God. The energy radiated by this creative force affects every human being. The effect is called an *idea*. Ideas give rise to your patterns of thought in response to your objective and subjective awareness. Objective thought is the ability to think, decide, and discriminate based on stimulation received from the outer or physical world. Subjective thought is the creative impulse within the being that responds to the patterns of objective thought. The *mind*, as it relates to an individual, is actually the brain. The brain receives and creates in response to the patterns of objective thought and the subjective impulses, ultimately causing the individual to respond or react.

The brain with which you are endowed is a vehicle that gives form and structure to the creative energy and impulses of the divine mind. Think back to a time when you had an idea, thought, or great inspiration. You may never have revealed that idea or inspiration to anyone.

Yet somehow, within a matter of moments, days, or months, someone else will give voice to your idea. Someone else had the very same thought! This is an example of how the one Mind affects all minds. The idea is radiated throughout the universe of life and everyone receives the impulse. Some of us pick up on it. Other do not. Just as divine mind radiates ideas that affect the body of all living things, the individual mind radiates ideas that affect the individual being. Everything begins in the mind. The body does not function, the organism does not move unless a split-second command is given by the physical mind. When the mind is operating in alignment with universal principles, nature will instantly create based on your pattern of thought.

The superconscious component of the individual mind is the spiritual energy. It is at this level of consciousness that you receive direct impulses from the one Mind. It is also here that information is stored about your spiritual mission, your life purpose, and the lessons you master in life. The superconscious mind provides your link to the attributes and qualities attributed to God. This component of the mind works best when the conscious (objective) and the subconscious (subjective) consciousness are in a state of stillness. That is the goal of meditation. The most important thing to remember about the superconscious mind is that this is your *higher mind* or *higher consciousness*. It is the *Christ* in you. The *I Am* energy of your being.

THE LAW OF CAUSE AND EFFECT

The merging or coming together of thought and feeling is the ultimate act of creation. Your thoughts and emotions will cause the creation of conditions. The conditions are the effects created in the physical world in response to your dominant thought pattern and the intensity of your emotions. Thoughts and feelings create and direct words and actions. Remember, the subjective mind, the internal feeling nature, is the mold that receives the impulses of the objective mind. The universe then responds to that energy by creating a mirror image of the mold in the physical world. This is the law of cause and effect in operation. The thought patterns and emotional convictions you have today reflect everything you have heard, seen, and thought during your entire life. When you work from a foundation of distorted images and beliefs or toxic emotions, you carry that energy into everything you do in life. Nature then creates in response to your mental and emotional energy. In other words, your thoughts and feelings are the underlying cause of every experience you have in your life.

The nature of divine mind is such that it will not argue with what you believe. Divine mind is the element of truth always present in the universe. The universe does not seek to determine the validity or truth of your thoughts or feelings. You must know the truth and infuse it into your thoughts. As a function of cause and effect, your objective mind unites with your subjective mind to absorb thoughts and create from the energy of those thoughts. What you feed your mind will create a mold from which real conditions and experiences will manifest. When you understand and apply the principle of cause and effect to your belief systems and thought patterns, it is possible for you to transcend the limitations of the physical world. As you surrender reliance on the physical world and tap into your superconscious mind, you become aligned with the creative energy of divine mind. It is the law of cause and effect that gives you the power to create the circumstances of your life.

THE LAW OF CORRESPONDENCE

Everything draws to itself things of a like nature and kind. Colors, sounds, organisms blend to create more of their kind. There is nothing in and of itself that will not draw to itself exactly what it is. According to the natural law of correspondence, what you draw to you is what you are. The people, conditions, and situations in your life are a mirror reflection of what you believe. They represent your most dominant thought pattern and the essence of your emotional being. The law of correspondence does not dismiss the validity of your experiences, which serve to justify your particular belief system, nor does it justify your beliefs. The law, in operation, brings into your world the corresponding reflection of what you believe about yourself, the world, and others in the world.

Even when you are not aware of it, you are a powerful and creative force in the universe. The presence of Spirit in your being makes you powerful. Life is a spiritual environment operating on spiritual principles. In life, nature serves the will of Spirit. It responds to the purpose of Spirit. The one common spiritual purpose of all life-forms is to create and evolve. Thought is the medium of creation. Evolution is an outgrowth of creation. Your spiritual purpose in life is to create those things and forms that will support the evolution of the species and the world. Nature is not concerned with your failure to adhere to its laws. The laws do not change because you are unaware of them. You are here as a creative expression whose duty it is to create more of what you are. If you think hate, you will create and experience hate. If you think angry thoughts or hold limited ideas, you will create and have experiences that evoke anger and keep you limited to the realm of what you believe. That is how the law operates.

THE LAW OF SUPPLY

Divine mind is the substance of the universe, the force behind all things. Divine mind lacks nothing. The secret of unlimited supply is belief that divine mind, not people, is the source of your good in life. There is nothing you can desire that does not already exist. It exists in divine mind, which is how you got the idea in the first place. What you have been taught is that people can supply or deny your needs. The truth is that people are merely the vehicles used by divine mind to produce the supply. If you do not know the truth, you hold people responsible. Remember, these are the same people who want to prove they are better than you. If you believe they are better or more powerful than you, you in effect give them power over your supply.

Anything you desire must be supported by an expectation. You must expect to have your desire fulfilled. In this way, you will attract the corresponding result. Desire, belief, and expectation will produce themselves in form through the operation of the law of supply. For this to happen, you must understand that it is divine *mind*, acting in concert with the operation of natural law and your application of it, that will supply your desires in life. People cannot withhold divine supply. If you are psychologically, emotionally, and spiritually receptive, the thing that you desire and expect to receive must manifest in the physical world. If a particular person is unwilling to bring forth that which you have created and expect, divine mind will simply find some other channel. When you believe that there is only one way, one channel through which you can receive, you violate the law of supply. As it operates, you will be supplied as you believe and as you demand. It is the job of divine mind, working in concert with the universe, to determine the channel for the supply to come forth. It is not your job.

THE LAW OF DIVINE ORDER

When you flip a switch, you expect light. You recognize the switch, the light bulb, and the socket in which the bulb rests. When you want light, you probably give little thought to the wires in the wall that run down to the basement and out to the street. You are not concerned about the hundreds of poles along the streets and highways that are connected to a generator in a place you cannot see. Although these are the principal elements involved in your ability to have light, you are focused on the fact that the room is dark, the switch works, the bulb is good, and the bill is paid. You expect light to appear when you flip the switch. Nevertheless, other principles and forces are at work, whether or not you can see them or choose to acknowledge them. Life, love, beauty are all life principles you accept whether or not you can see or touch them. As a result of these often intangible principles, you expect and accept tangible results. What you may not recognize or understand is that what you receive in the tangible world is an outgrowth of what transpires in the intangible world. It is called the law of divine order.

Divine order is the natural flow and outgrowth of a series of tangible and intangible principles working in harmony. One season following another and daylight following darkness are examples of the universal principle of divine order. Other examples are conditions manifesting in response to a pattern of thinking, and actions being taken in response to the spoken word. As it operates in the spiritual world, the presence of divine order brings forth the good of the universe, the natural outgrowth of a natural course of events. As it operates in our lives, particularly when we are ignorant of the law, divine order brings into manifestation what we think, feel, and say with the greatest conviction.

Divine order makes us conscious of what we are thinking. When I hear people talk about being broke, stupid, tired, confused, or lonely, only to experience more of the same, I remind them that it is divine order. What you say and see and do, you become and do. When you talk about or act negatively toward other people, wishing them harm or treating them unfairly, you are probably unaware of the repercussions this will have in your own life. When you are treated unjustly, unfairly, or badly by someone else, under a completely different set of circumstances, you are outraged. You have no idea that your experience is the effect of your own thoughts and the operation of divine order. The elders in the family probably told you that everything you think, everything you do, everything you say will come back in the mirror of self, somehow, someway, someday. It is called divine order, and it works whether you recognize it or not.

SHIFT HAPPENS

Whatever you focus your mind on grows. No matter what you are doing, it is the concentrated energy of your thoughts that gives meaning to your experiences. It is difficult to try to explain to people that if you work two jobs with the consciousness that you don't have enough money, you will never have enough money. If you pinch and scrape to get money, trying to save, trying to make it, you will continue to pinch and scrape, never having enough to save or to make it. If you think you don't have time, you won't have time. If you think you can take care of it tomorrow, tomorrow will never come. The list is endless.

As you become more responsible in life, it is also important to establish and maintain balance. Life is about balance. Making clear, conscious choices that fill every moment of your life is a responsible thing to do. Taking full advantage of all opportunities available in all arenas is the way to create a balanced life. Most of us do not work because we want to; we work because we think we have to work for money. We want to be responsible, and we have been taught that the only way to get money is to work for it. In this society, until you learn how to make money work for you, that is true. Unfortunately for many people, work is all they do. To have balance in life, you must choose to do more than work. What about fun? You need fun to keep your mind off work. How about rest? Rest is more than sleeping in order to get ready for the next day of work. Rest is allowing the mind and body to surrender all activity. What about solitude? Taking a few moments away from the hectic pace of life can be very rewarding. It is called a mental-health break. Let us not forget the mind. Education. It helps to keep the gray matter upstairs from getting dusty. There is so much to life, and in order to feel that you are accomplishing anything at all, you must have balance.

Black men need balance. A strong, solid, and stable character needs balance. From where I sit, it appears that you are trying so hard to be responsible and have become so addicted to doing the right *thing*, in the right *way*, that you have fallen out of balance. Fighting and struggling to survive will throw you out of balance. In the process of struggling, there is no way goodness, abundance, and success can find you if you are always moving, doing something, and still not covering all your bases in life. The universe is an orderly system of activities and affairs. Things flow in and out. When your home, environment, and activities are not in order and balance, the universal flow of good things will move right past you without stopping. Order, as it relates to balance, means doing things on time, within the time you commit yourself to do them. It does not mean that you do the same thing all the time, in the same way. Black men need time to play—not to compete, but to play just for the fun of it. You also need time to learn, to relax, to study, and, of course, to pray. There is nothing in life more important than being a well-rounded, complete human being. The only way to achieve this is to balance the time and energy of your life.

As you begin to refocus your energy, major changes begin to take place. You find more time to do the things you never had time to do before. You have energy to spare, whereas without balance you may have been tired and worn out. The more activities you have to focus on, the less time you have to spend worrying about problems. There are twelve areas of life (discussed below) that require nurturing and attention in order for you to achieve balance. In each of these areas, you should have a short-term and a long-range goal. Do not overload yourself! An inch is a cinch. A yard is hard. If you have been ignoring any of these areas of your life, start by making a small commitment. Do a new thing every day, or every other day, until you have done it forty times. Forty is the number of the foundation. It takes at least forty repetitions of a thing before the shift takes place in the mind. Set your goals at small intervals: three months, six months, nine months, one year. Set two or three goals for each interval. Add one or two things at the beginning of each new interval until you have completed all your goals.

One of the major reasons plans fail is that we try to do too much at one time. It becomes so overwhelming we give up. Once you give up on doing what you planned to do, you have a reason to beat up on yourself; then you feel so bad you don't bother to make more plans. That is pure human drama! Start slow. Do a little at a time. Congratulate yourself when you complete a task or a series of events. Don't even talk about what you're doing—you never know when a "nega-holic" is lurking around waiting to cast a web of doubt over you. People will begin to notice the change in you. When they comment about how good you look, or how much better you are doing, you are the only one who needs to know why. In learning to assume responsibility and live in balance, it is important to honor the agreements you make with yourself. This is a major step toward building self-esteem. When you say you are going to do something, do it. If there is an emergency and you cannot fulfill your agreement, let yourself know. Make a new plan and stick to it. Remember, no one is more important to you than you. The ego is going to resist you and test you. Stick to the plan! Follow your goals! Keep your affairs in order. You are moving toward balance. The rewards will be great!

Vision

It is very important to have a vision for yourself, your life, and the world. Your vision is what you would like to realize as the optimum conditions of your life. Do not worry about how it will happen. See the end; the universe will take care of the details in divine time and divine order. If you have a vision for yourself in each of the twelve areas required for balance, you are sure to achieve balance quickly. Remember, you are part of a dynamic whole. In your vision, you might also want to include how your efforts will help to make the world a better place. My vision is to live in a world where people love and accept one another unconditionally. It begins with me loving and accepting everyone unconditionally.

Purpose

Your purpose is what you have come to life to do. It is doing what you love, what you are good at, to create your vision of the world. Everyone has a purpose. As my brother-friend Reverend Michael Beckwith says, "Your purpose gave birth to you." When you are on purpose, your life has meaning. You are making a valuable contribution by doing what you love. Having a job means you are "just over broke." Having a purpose means having a "life assignment." It is the difference between spending your life doing what you think you have to do and spending your life in meaningful activity. As you achieve greater balance in your life, your skills and interest will point you toward your purpose. My purpose is to revitalize spiritual consciousness through writing and teaching the world about the wealth of African culture.

Mission

You just have to do it. If you do not do it, you will not be able to do anything else. That is your mission. When you are on a mission, you are charged! You are determined! You are high on the energy of what you are doing. What are you doing to create your vision for your life and the world? That is your mission. How will you contribute to your growth and the evolution of the world? That is your mission. What is the burning desire in your soul that will not go away? It haunts you. It stalks you. It calls you into action anytime, anyplace. That is your mission. Without it, your life is not worth living. My mission is to use my gift of the ability to write and speak publicly to revitalize the traditions and spiritual heritage of African people.

To achieve balance in your life, you need a vision, mission, purpose, and plan of action for at least twelve months in the following twelve areas.

Spiritual Life

Activity in the area of your spiritual life should be designed to develop, strengthen, or deepen your relationship with the Creator, the spirit of your own head, and the spiritual energies of the universe. Prayer, meditation, reading spiritual material, going to church, temple, or mosque are the types of activities that will help to bring balance to your spiritual life. You can set a goal in this area even if you are not sure of how to accomplish it. For example, "to have a deeper understanding of God." You will then use this goal to create activities such as meditation, going to a spiritual class, and so on.

Your spiritual life requires your constant attention. Try to set goals that you can follow every day for a set period of time, adding more activities at specific intervals. If you are not sure what your spiritual goals are, set that as a goal: "to find out what my spiritual goals are." Spend at least ten minutes a day contemplating just that question. Since your spirit is always with you, the answer will be revealed fairly quickly.

Physical Life and Health

If the body is the temple, it will be rather difficult to accomplish the goals for your spiritual life without clear goals for your physical life. This is the category in which you want to set goals for anything that has to do with the physical body: weight loss, exercise, dental health, medical health, eye examinations, foot care, and so on. Massage and colon therapy would fall in this category. When was the last time you had your eyes checked? Your teeth examined? A pedicure? manicure? massage? If you are a male more than forty years old, have you had your annual colon examination? If you are sexually active, have you had an HIV test? What is your diet like? Is it time to surrender fried foods? beer? alcohol? cigarettes? sugar? chocolate?

There are so many things we need to do to keep our bodies healthy, doing just one a week would take us through half a year. In your planning, don't forget the corns, the cavities, the hair bumps, that ache in the left elbow, and that little bulge around the middle. You might want to begin with just fifteen minutes of daily stretching exercises. Now don't run out and join the health club, again, if you know you are not going to go. Ten sit-ups, ten push-ups, ten deep knee bends will not cost you a dime. If you have not been exercising at all, that is probably all you can do anyway. Make plans to give the temple a complete overhaul, and keep up a good maintenance schedule.

Personal Appearance

If you were asked to describe your style, what would you call it? Is your style reflected in the way you dress, or is it just an ambition you hope to achieve? It is important that you are happy with the way you look. Remember, you are God's representative. Do not be a tacky one! Is it time to change your eyeglass frames? Haven't you been wearing those sneakers long enough? Do you own a suit? Do you need one? How about that African garb you have been threatening to buy? Set goals for your wardrobe, hairstyle, shoes, work and play clothes. Make a commitment to buy yourself something every pay period or once a month. The quickest way to get the things you want is to create a vacuum. Give away or throw away everything that does not fit, is torn, or is out of style. Whatever you get rid of will be replaced by something better. Decide what you want to look like, and begin to take steps in that direction.

Career

Your ancestors did not look for jobs. They built institutions. In today's society, that would be synonymous with building a career. An acronym for *job* is *Just Over Broke*. A career is the continuous, successive course of one's life that enhances inherent talents, gifts, and abilities. Everything you have ever done in your life is a part of your career. The key is to learn how to make it pay off for you. Your career path should also encompass your vision, purpose, and mission. It is a direct line to creating the kind of reality you wish to experience in life. *See the end,* where you want to be, and let the universe take care of the details.

Where do you want to be at the end of this year? Next year? In five years? At the end of your physical life? A good way to establish your career path is to write your obituary. That's right! Write down the things you want to be said about you when you cross over. Be sure to include all the things you have done, contributed, and accomplished. Include those people who have supported and assisted you. Do not put an age or a date on it. Simply begin to live in a manner that will make what you have written a reality. Set your goals realistically. Begin, step by step, to live your obituary, taking into consideration all you have done and all you desire to do.

Education

You never stop learning. You are never too old to learn. It is important to maintain a steady and consistent momentum of learning if you want to achieve balance. Education is not limited to degrees and credentials. It may also include learning a new skill, enhancing those things you are already good at, or just reviewing what you already know. Not all learning takes place in a classroom. Reading is a way of learning. Talking is a way of learning. Doing is the best way to learn.

Have you been putting off going back to school? Don't let the money stop you. Check the weekly television guide. Public broadcasting stations offer many educational programs. If you are in a profession, do you have a mentor? Mentors are excellent teaching instruments.

Wherever you are in your professional and career life, having clear-cut goals to enhance your skills enables you to take the best and make it better, to take the fast and make it faster. The goal of continuing education is to achieve excellence in your chosen field or interest.

Hobbies/Fun Time

Fun is good for you. It is activity or nonactivity designed to make you laugh and feel good. No matter how old you are, you need a little fun in your life every day. What do you do just for the fun of it? Fun is not competitive. It has no specific goal for the end results. It is an opportunity to expand your mind while allowing it to relax. Fun keeps you young. Fun keeps you alive. Hobbies are great if you do not make them competitive. Hobbies include collecting things, researching things, exploring things, and participating in athletics. Not watching athletics; engaging in athletics. When making your plans and goals for the year or the rest of your life, be sure to include time to have a little fun.

Family Life

For many people, it is difficult to determine where we end and the family begins. It is important that you have good, strong family relationships; however, the focus must be on the quality of the relationships. It is not enough to *be* with your family. You must also be present and *do* with your family. By the way, family means *all of the family.* Have you been to the burial ground of those family members who have made their transition? If not, be sure to include regular, consistent visits. That is a form of ancestor worship. When setting goals for this area of your life, be sure to include cleaning up relationships with family members with whom you are at odds. Perhaps it is time to let bygones go. Since this is your life, your vision, you may have to forgive and forget. It will be good for *your* soul.

Families are the training ground for learning to interact with the rest of the world. If you cannot get along with your blood family, how do you expect to get along with your world family? Make plans to bury the past. Make the first telephone call. Write that long-overdue letter. Be willing to ask for forgiveness and give a little where it is needed. The blood that runs through you can be your poison or your lifeline.

That is what family is all about: keeping the bloodline flowing. While you're at it, figure out how you can spend quality time with your children daily, weekly, monthly. They really do need more from you than food, clothing, and shelter. And by all means, don't forget to take your wife, mate, significant other out on a date every now and then. Make it a special, quality event.

Personal Relationships

Personal relationships include friendships, loveships, business and social relationships. Who are your best friends? Have you been out together lately? Have you spoken to one another recently? Have you told your friends how you feel about them? It is important to keep your nurturing and supportive relationships alive and well. You might want to keep a supply of cards on hand. Thank-you cards. How-are-you cards. Just-thinking-about-you cards. When you cannot make contact in person, a card is quite sufficient.

Throughout your life, people have given you assistance, information, and guidance. When it comes in handy, let them know. It is also important for you to remember Grandma's instructions, "Flush!" Every now and then, take an inventory of your life. Figure out who is in your life and why. We often hang on to old, toxic, worn-out relationships that keep our lives cluttered and prevent new, more nurturing relationships from coming in. Do you have friends and acquaintances you do not want or need in your life? If you do, flush! Release them from your heart and mind. How do you flush people away? Write them a letter. Let them know you are moving on. It is not necessary to mail the letter; however, you must write it to be clear. When they call, do not take the calls. When you see them, be cordial but be busy. Do not be dishonest and make plans you have no desire or intention of keeping. If you believe the person can handle it, simply let him or her know, "Our relationship is no longer good for either of us and I choose to move on." Say it with love and in peace. Then do what Grandma told you to do after you had flushed. *Wash your hands!*

Earnings

It is never wise or self-motivating to accept a position based on what *they* want to pay you. It is always best to have an income goal. "Where the mind goes, the power flows." Consciously work to shift your beliefs from the idea that work and job-related activity are the only ways in which you can attract income. A useful way to think of money is as an acronym for *My Own Natural Energy Yield*. Whatever your energy is concerning money will determine how you attract money. It is equally important to remember that *God is your source and your supply*, not the job, not your friends, your family, the IRS, or the state lottery board.

The most helpful tools I discovered in building my own prosperity consciousness were *The Abundance Book*, by John Randolph Price, and *Think and Grow Rich*, by Dennis Kimbro. These are two comprehensive tools for learning and understanding the principles of money and earning. When setting goals in this area, do not forget to include giving, saving, and investing. If you believe there is a lack or scarcity of money, you will also believe you do not have enough money to do any of these things. This could be the very reason you find it difficult to maximize your earning potential. If you do not give to others, or save for the rainy days, or invest in your own future, you will not receive from the storehouse of universal abundance. Like attracts like, and money attracts more money. If you want a sound financial base, familiarize yourself with the spiritual laws of money and prosperity.

Home

Your home is like your teeth; if it is not solid, comfortable, well provided for, you cannot nurture the rest of your life. Are you happy in and with your home? Does it look the way you want it to look? How can you improve the appearance? condition? aesthetic appeal? Your home is not only your safe haven, it is a reflection of your consciousness. Whatever is going on in your mind will be reflected in the condition of your home. Are your closets cluttered? Is your basement or attic full of junk? Is your home furnished with things that are broken? Not working? That is a reflection of the state of relationships in your life. In setting your goals for home improvement, a good rule of thumb is, If it does not work, get rid of it! That is, of course, unless it is a family heirloom or something with sentimental value.

Are your floors clean? Are they in good repair? Floors represent the foundation of your character. Are there dust bunnies hanging out in the corners? To achieve balance and clarity in your life, you must have a solid, clean foundation. Your home and the conditions in which you live are a good place to start. A word of caution: as you clean and structure your home, a shift will occur in your consciousness. Things will look different, and people will look different. If this should happen, do not go into fear. There is nothing wrong with you. There is really nothing wrong with the other people around. However, when you clean up and clear out your environment, your mind also becomes clear. You may see things you have never seen before.

The word *environment* is an important concept for Black men to understand. *Environ-*, meaning "surrounding," and *-ment*, meaning "mind," translate to "whatever occupies your surroundings affects your mind." If your living environment is ill-equipped, it can lead to mental decay and the loss of innate knowledge. A traditional African spiritual teacher I spoke with recommended that the living environment for the single Black male be one that creates balance. He said, "Men do not need to be reminded they are men. They need images that uplift the feminine energy of womanhood and motherhood." You may want to consider including pictures and artifacts of the great African queens and African American mothers in your living environment.

Color is another important aspect to consider. The colors you use in your home can stimulate healthy vibrations and energy. White walls stimulate clarity and peace. Light blue walls stimulate healing. The home should also captivate the sense of smell. Vessels of perfumed water create a purified and balanced energy. Lavender, rose, myrrh, sandalwood, and amber are excellent fragrances for a man's home. If incense is used, it should not contain sawdust or gum arabic. The darker the incense is, the greater the degree of purity. Light or colored incense sticks contain large amounts of sawdust. It is important for Black men to focus your spiritual energy in your bedrooms. You might want to consider keeping a small altar somewhere in the room. Using images of great women and queens, along with candles, flowers, and aromatics, will help to enhance your spiritual energy even while you sleep. The spiritual energy created in the home helps to balance and purify the mind and emotions. With a limited amount of effort and the minimal cost of spiritualizing your home environment, you can enhance your spiritual consciousness.

Community

Traditionally, African culture is not centered on the *I* nature of the individual; instead, it focuses on *we* as a collective consciousness. Your community is an extension of your home. African people cannot live in a place and not be concerned with or involved in their immediately surrounding environment. It goes against everything our ancestors taught. It is not enough to know your neighbors. Who are the elected officials who represent you community? How long have they been in office? What is their position on crime? drugs? taxation? What are they doing to create change? improvement? Who is the captain of your community police department? How long has he been in office? How many trees are there on your block? Is there a garden? How many businesses are there in your community? What services do they provide for the community? From what location? What are you doing to ensure that the services are well provided? You can become so accustomed to having things done for you that you forget it is your responsibility to see and ensure that they are done.

Community means more than just knowing the name of the area in which you live. It is being active in all aspects of group survival in that area. Black men are being asked to be present in our communities. You are being asked to walk the streets, to protect the elders, women, and children. You are being asked to build and support businesses. You are being asked to hold the government accountable and demand the services needed for our collective protection and well-being. When men are present initiating thought into action, every block, in every neighborhood, will have a support group and an action group. There are far too many Black women, children, and elders who suffer and die alone because Black men are not present. Community from an African perspective is the energy created by people living and working together to ensure the survival of the people. What goals do you have to become more involved with your community?

Service

What you give, you get back—tenfold. That is what service is about. Service is giving and doing, expecting nothing in return. Service is more than volunteering your time, energy, and resources. Service is also anonymous giving: buying a bag of groceries and leaving it at a shelter;

paying the toll for the car behind you when you cross the bridge; leaving money to pay for a stranger's lunch in a restaurant; sending a money order without your name on it to someone you know is in need. Service is giving what you have in order to get what you need.

When I was growing up, my grandmother taught me about seed money and seed time. She told me, If you plant a seed, it must grow. Giving without expectation of return is like planting a seed. You are making a deposit in the universal bank of goodness. When you are in need, there will be something in your account to draw down. That is what service is: giving to and drawing from the universal bank. To bring yourself into balance, you must give. You must serve. Money, time, information, things you no longer have use of, are valuable to someone, somewhere at any time in the universe. When you make your plans and goals for balancing your life, be sure to include service. Without service, life is simply work.

DAILY MINIMUM REQUIREMENT

Make a commitment to spend at least fifteen minutes a day working on your vision, mission, and purpose statements. Write and rewrite until you have a concise statement for each that reflects your heart's desire. Once you have these three basic statements completed, begin working on each of the twelve areas. You will need a vision, a mission, and a purpose for each area and two clearly defined, attainable goals for a one-year period. Break the goals into time segments, such as three months, six months, nine months, and one year. These will be your progress markers. As you realize the fulfillment of a goal, don't forget to celebrate yourself and to thank Spirit.

Right Action

At first, I thought there was a party line, two conversations going on at once. Then reality hit me. It was my son's voice coming across the telephone line loud and clear. "It's your fault! You are the reason I am like this! Nothing I did was ever good enough for you! You ruined me and my life!" Like every mother, I wanted only the best for my son. The thought that I had given him anything less than the best was devastating. But now, it was out. He had said what he needed to say. I knew he felt better. I also knew that on this day, from his prison cell, my only son had begun to heal.

There is an old saying, "If we knew better, we would do better." I had my son when I was sixteen years old. His father chose to move on with his life. I had no choice. I decided to prove to the world that I was not just another teenage mother. I was going to raise my son and raise him right. My son would not be another inner-city Black male. He was going to be *somebody,* and I told him so every chance I got. I reminded him of what not to do, how not to be. I screened his friends, his calls, and his activities. I had to. I was a single mother. I had to stay on top of things—the house, the bills, work, my relationships, and, of course, my son.

My son was truly blessed. Not only did he have an energetic, aggressive mother, I was Afrocentric too. He got history. He got culture. He heard the stories of struggle and revolution. He was on a picket line at age seven. He marched in his first civil rights protest at age ten. He participated in boycotts and sat quietly in all the Pan-African meetings I attended. By age thirteen, he let it be known that all he really wanted to do was play football. I let him know that that was a total waste of time. Too risky, if you ask me. It was his dream. I stole that dream by sending him to an academic high school that did not have a football team. He never forgave me for that.

While I was making every attempt to run my son's life, mine was falling apart. A series of bad relationships, economic instability, emotional imbalance, and the usual drama of being a Black woman in America was the order of the day for me. I was a hypocrite. While I was telling my son stories of achieving the impossible dream, I was living a total nightmare. I forgot that children can see. I wanted my son to be more, do more, have more than I had as a child. What I did not realize was, he had the right to choose. My job was to nurture, support, and guide him, not choose for him. When I took away his right to choose for himself, I killed his spirit. I took away his power. A powerless person is an angry person. An angry person rebels as a way of acting out his anger. What I heard that day in my son's voice was seething anger. Rage. And it was all directed at me.

One of the most difficult tasks I faced as a woman was raising my son without his father. My fear that he would fail made it difficult for me to give him what he needed to succeed. He told me all he ever wanted and needed was my support. I gave him mandates and demands. He said he wanted me to trust him. I gave him responsibility and stayed on his back to make sure he did it the right way, my way. My son wanted freedom to fall, to grow, to make mistakes and learn from those mistakes. I gave him just enough rope to hang himself. When he did, I criticized him and chastised him. With a rapid-fire precision, he recounted incident after incident to demonstrate how my behavior had confused, belittled, and emotionally castrated him. My son wanted to be a man. I had absolutely no idea what that meant. He could not explain it to me, so we both cried. He in his prison cell, I at the kitchen table.

It is hard for male children to tell their mothers what they really feel. I imagine they do not want to hurt our feelings. They do not want to seem disrespectful. As mothers, when we are so consumed about their *doing it right*, we unintentionally make it hard for them to talk to us. It is hard for a frightened mother to allow her son to be who he really is, a person with thoughts, feelings, and dreams. When a mother is raising a man-child, she wants to protect him. She wants him to have the best. My son told me that what I called protection felt like oppression. What I thought was best for him had nothing to do with what he wanted for himself. I had to admit to him that I had been a fearful child who was beaten and frightened into submission. He felt I had done the same to him. When peer pressure forced him to prove his manhood, he had no idea what it was. He had to prove he was not afraid of anything, including me. That quest landed him in jail, and for the first time in a long while, my son was talking to me. As bad as I felt, I knew this was not the time to be emotional or defensive. My son was telling me exactly how he felt. I had to do more than listen. I had to hear him.

Had I really ruined his life? No. He admitted that his choices and decisions were his own. What I had given him and done for him was the best I could give and do. Did he know that I loved him more than life itself? Yes. But that was too much responsibility for a kid. Kids only want to know they are loved and feel they are loved. A few cookies now and then don't hurt, either. Children cannot handle the pressure of knowing that if they mess up, their mama is going to die. That is too much responsibility in the middle of puberty. I was a dramatic, bosom-clutching, always-on-the-verge-of-a-nervous-breakdown kind of mother, but was I too strict? No, he said. But my fears were not his fears. My fears smothered him and took away his freedom to choose. Did he blame me for what had happened to him? It was not about blame. It was about searching, growing, falling, and getting up again. What about his father? Did he think he would have done better with his father around? No. He had two parents. I was both of them. How could I help him now? Love him without any demands or expectations. Stop mothering him and be his friend. I agreed to try. He reminded me of something I had told him, "There is no *try*. There is only *do* or *don't do*." On that day, I stopped calling him "my son." His name is Damon. He is my granddaughter's father, my daughters' brother, my male offspring, and my friend.

Damon taught me a great deal about being a man that day; he taught me how much I did not know and would probably never know. My programming about men was that they were angry, domineering, selfish, confused, and dangerous. Those distorted perceptions became infused in my parenting skills.

My relationships with men up to that point had been far less than rewarding. I blamed them and put that in the mental potluck I was creating about Black men. My father, brother, husband, lovers, and son were not necessarily bad examples of who Black men are, but they were not the examples I wanted to continue using. I was now a priest, providing counseling and other services for men. I realized I had to go back to the drawing board. I had to find new information and new examples.

12

THE PRINCIPLES OF
SPIRITUAL MANHOOD

*When do we say No! to misguided
teenaged boys and young men who
disrespect their elders and whose
identity are multiple earrings, beep-
ers, starter jackets, pants low across
the cracks of their butts, their ini-
tials carved out on the backs of their
heads, untied sports shoes, four letter
words and faces that never smile in
public?*

      Haki Madhubuti, Claiming
Earth: Race, Rage, Rape, Redemption

According to the dictionary, principle is "a general or fun-damental rule or truth on which others are based." In my years of studying spiritual sciences, I have discovered that Spirit is the only principle or truth from which everything else flows. As a principle, Spirit provides guidance, structure, form, and boundaries. In this sense, boundaries are not synonymous with limitations or restrictions. Rather, spiritual boundaries are the parameters within which you act. One dictionary definition of God is "the creator and ruler of the universe, regarded as almighty." According to the Bible, "God is Spirit." Putting these definitions together, we can say that God is Spirit, the creator and ruler of the universe. In essence, I have discovered that the Spirit that is God is the principal truth that created and rules the universe.

As the creator and ruler, God knows no failure, fault, illness, lack, limitation, fear, doubt, greed, or hate. As a result, when you work through the principle of God, you will eliminate the presence of these restrictions from your life. Many attributes and demonstrations of God surround you every day, although you may not always recognize them. The sun is God. The wind is God. Fire and water are representations of God. Life and death represent God. Trees, grass, flowers, fish, birds, snakes, dogs, groundhogs are all expressions of God because they serve a purpose in the divine order of life. Diversity is God. Mercy is God. Justice is God. Truth is God. Love is God. These elements and attributes surround you in the beauty and mystery we call nature. If you want to know about God, study nature. There you will learn everything you need to know about attending to the details of our lives.

Please be clear that even with God surrounding and supporting you, this does not mean that you will not encounter difficulty in life. You will have good days. You will have bad days. Recognizing, understanding, and embracing spirituality does not mean your life will miraculously become a sanctuary of goodness and glory. To the contrary, your life will probably become very chaotic. Difficulty is the nature of true evolution. It is a reminder that with Spirit as the guiding principle of your life, you must know that you cannot fail. Failure is another tool of the ego. The ego will use every opportunity to point out that you are *not right* and *not good enough*. When you buy into this type of internal conflict, you will ultimately fail in your attempts to transform your life. Remember, thoughts cause effects, not God. God is the principle. It is up to you to activate the principle in your consciousness. By watching nature and understanding your own nature, you will find that the principles become clear.

YOU DON'T KNOW WHAT
YOU DON'T KNOW

My relationship with my father was distant and erratic. In watching him, I did not get much information about the truth of manhood. My brother was almost a carbon copy of my father. He provided very little useful information. The only other man I had in my life was my godfather. I began to watch him, study him, and listen to him very closely. I never told him what I was doing. I just did it. I began to notice how slowly and deliberately my godfather moved. He never rushed. He never seemed scattered or stressed out. "Everything happens when it is supposed to happen. Your job is to make sure you get to where it is happening in one piece." My godfather taught me about the principles of divine time and divine order. No matter how fast you move, you cannot change the timing and order of what will happen. My godfather also taught me about the importance of paying attention to details. Details have nothing to do with crossing t's or dotting i's. From a spiritual perspective, details pertain to the seen and the unseen. Bále taught me you must always take into consideration the forces at work on the metaphysical as well as the physical level. Invoke the ancestors, honor the energy of the natural elements, and always make sure that what is going on in your head and heart is consistent with what you are doing. If either your head or your heart tells you not to move, don't move.

As I continued to study my godfather, I began to explore the divinity of nature. That search took me into the study of the sciences of nature such as herbs, minerals and stones, astrology, and numerology. Through this search, I encountered several strong, spiritually centered Black men to love me. Most of them are mentioned on the Acknowledgments page of this work. In their own way, each of them silently taught me about manhood. I watched them work. I could talk to them about anything. I talked to them about the challenges I faced trying to define myself and the men around me. They never did the work for me. What they did was support me in reaching my own understanding. They assisted me in finding out where to look.

There were many times when these men took care of me, from supporting me financially to providing me with a place to live. They supported me in working things out and figuring them out while they protected me. They taught me about nonsexual love between a man and a woman. Three in particular—Ron Norwood, an herbalist and iridologist; Basil Farrington, a musician and astrologer; and Ralph Stevenson, a devoted student of life—helped me to transform my consciousness from that of an emotionally unbalanced woman into that of a consciously well-balanced being. I do not know if they realized what they were doing, but these men taught me how to live my truth and be exactly who I was. Like my godfather, each of these men affirmed me as a gifted, talented, and beautiful spirit, expressing as a Black woman. They were neither threatened by me nor afraid of me. I discovered not only that these men considered me their *sister*, but that I was a part of them, a part of their own consciousness. They understood my inherent nature as well as their own. We were able to blend those natures into relationships of wholeness.

It was about this time that I encountered the book entitled *A Course in Miracles.* The basic premise of *The Course* is that nothing exists in the world except you and God. Everything you see is either a reflection of you or a reflection of God. Every individual sees the world from his or her own internal frame of reference, determined by that individual's dominant thoughts, ideas, desires, and emotions. *The Course* teaches that "Projection makes perception." We perceive ourselves as lone, separate entities fighting against the world. We then project our ideas onto the world, and the world reflects back to us the very things we have created.

At first, the concept seemed completely absurd. However, taken in the context of what I had learned about nature and the mandates of Yoruba culture, and what I understood to be God's goal for human beings, it all began to make sense. God's goal for you is peace. You find peace by learning how to give love. When you are at peace, you can see, hear, think, and experience everything from a spiritual foundation. When you are not at peace, not moving from a foundation of love, you are in fear. The way to avoid fear is to live in order, balance, harmony, truth, and unconditional love. You must nurture yourself and others with patience, responsible action, compassionate response, disciplined activity, selfless service, and a willingness to learn. Using these principles as the guiding forces in your life causes your perception to shift. When it does, you will find inner peace and outward purpose. More important, you will find God.

PRINCIPLES STRUCTURE CHARACTER

The quest for spiritual transformation, enlightenment, and empowerment is also a character-building exercise. As you begin to incorporate and embrace spiritual principles, character traits such as discipline, commitment, and responsibility are also strengthened. As you begin to recognize and honor the operation of principles and natural law in your life, you become less sensitive to petty or insignificant matters. You are able to discern the truth underlying all external events and experiences. You begin to disconnect your internal emotional buttons. The principles for character development and spiritual growth are the same for both men and women. Yet, because of the differences in our nature and purpose, it may appear that we are doing different things. Remember, men act outwardly. What you believe manifests as behavior that will be visible to others. Women turn inward. A woman's beliefs are held in her emotional body and may not manifest as clearly in her behavior. While we can see what a man believes, the same is not always true for women. In order to transcend the restrictions and limitations you face in your own being and in the world, you must act upon the premise of spiritual principle. When you adhere to principle, your mind shifts into alignment with natural law. The result will be a renewed sense of *Self* empowered through self-determination with spiritual support.

The Principles of Spiritual Manhood presented below can provide you with a basic framework for the transformation of your consciousness. As your thought process and thought patterns shift, you develop a new perspective that will overcome the devastating effects of your previous social indoctrination. These principles are in no way exhaustive. They are meant to assist you in becoming conscious of the Self as the divine and noble expression of the Creator on earth.

1. DEVELOP A PERSONAL
RELATIONSHIP WITH GOD

In *Parenthesis in Eternity*, author Joel Goldsmith makes a remarkable point when he says, "Most of us do not pray to God. We pray to some concept of God. We pray to what we have been told God is or what we would like God to be." Most of us were taught that we need an intermediary between ourselves and God. When we think of going to God or praying to God, we think first of the intermediary. For some, this is the minister; for others, saints or bishops. It is easy to become confused and lose sight of the fact that it is communion with God that we seek.

God is your every breath. You must ask yourself, What does that mean? Also ask, What is my image of God? What are my concepts, beliefs, ideas about God? Do not ask what God can do *for* you or *to* you but who and what God is in your life. We are living in a time, some call it the Aquarian Age, the age of knowing, when people must *know* what it is they believe. Spiritual growth in this age no longer hinges upon believing what you have been told to believe. It is no longer enough to just *believe in* God. The energy of the universe is calling upon you to *know* what God is and to know how God works in your life and body. How does it feel when God is moving in your life? How do you make and maintain contact with God? Prayer, conscious breath, and meditation are helpful tools you can use; the more time you spend in introspection and quiet contemplation, the stronger will become your contact with and consciousness of the presence of God.

2. DEVELOP A RELATIONSHIP WITH THE SPIRIT OF YOUR OWN HEAD

Programming, indoctrination, education, and socialization have taught you to trust everyone and everything except yourself. There is a spirit, a life force, in your head that knows exactly what you have come into this life to do. You must learn how to hear the voice of your own soul. You must learn to trust and follow its guidance. Blessing your head on a daily basis is a good place to start; however, you must also carefully monitor your thoughts. Listen for negative self-talk: "I can't," "I don't know," "I'm stupid," "I'm broke." When those thoughts come into your mind, cancel them out. Tell yourself the truth, "I am a loved child of a powerful Father. All that the Father is, I am!" Examine everything you now believe about yourself. When others tell you things about yourself, do not be eager to believe everything they say. Examine it. Confess your responsibility and accountability. Keep the portions of information that you can use, and release what is not true about you. There is an ancient African parable that says, "You are not responsible if a bird lands on your head. You become responsible when the bird builds a nest in your hair."

3. HONOR YOUR BODY TEMPLE

Black men, take care of your body. The body needs light, fresh air, exercise, good nutrition, and rest. Learn how to eat, when to eat, and what to eat. Learn how to stop *doing*. Do not be afraid to admit it when you are tired. Make a commitment to engage in at least fifteen minutes of energetic exercise three to four times a week. Become conscious of the people with whom you are having intimate relations. Intercourse is the ultimate and divine act of creation. Whoever you have intercourse with and whatever energy you and your partner bring to the act will eventually be recreated in your life. Engaging in sexual encounters when there is dishonesty, fear, anger, or guilt in the consciousness will create situations of this kind in your life. To honor your body temple, you must be conscious of whom you are worshiping with and in whose temple you are worshiping.

It is also a wise choice to have a complete physical examination once a year. If you do not like doctors, you may want to consider a naturopathic practitioner, who treats for prevention rather than cure. Or an iridologist, who can analyze the condition of the iris of the eye to determine the overall condition of the organs and systems of the body. You can also incorporate other holistic health practices into your schedule on a regular basis. Reflexology, colon irrigation, massage therapy, and Reiki are all excellent ways to check in on and check up on your body.

4. LEARN TO RECOGNIZE AND LIVE BY NATURAL LAWS AND PRINCIPLES

There is a natural order to everything in God's universe. Things may not turn out the way you expect them to turn out, but they evolve the way they are divinely designed to evolve. Several books are listed in the bibliography that can help you familiarize yourself with the concepts of natural law and universal principles. Know these laws and principles. Learn to recognize how they operate in the world and when they are operating in your life. When you are on the right side of the law, you cannot go wrong.

5. FIND YOUR SPIRITUAL CENTER AND HONOR IT AT ALL TIMES

Centering means having your head and heart in alignment. When you are centered, your thoughts and words complement each other. It is an experience of internal and external balance. Your spiritual center is that place within your body or being upon which you can focus your energy to gain authentic, internal power. When you are centered, where you are and what you are doing becomes an enlightening, if not always pleasant, experience. Your solar plexus, approximately two inches above your navel, is your powerhouse. It is probably the first place you experience the stress of toxic emotions. Learn what it feels like to be centered. If you are in a place or around people and you begin to feel uncomfortable, check your center. Your spirit is your internal radar. You may be having a reaction to negative energy. You may be having a reaction to negative people. Whatever it is, if it throws you off-center, honor yourself enough to move on.

6. SPEAK WITH A CONSCIOUS TONGUE

Words are things that create conditions. Every time you open your mouth to speak, you release the energy force of your soul. Say only those things you truly wish to experience. Do not speak about what you do not want. Do not curse yourself or anyone else. Do not wish for another what you yourself would not want to live with. It goes back to the very thing your grandmother told you, "If you don't have something nice to say, don't say anything at all." This does not mean that you should not speak the truth. It means that when you speak, you must be fully conscious of what you are saying. In other words, speak from your center and your heart, not from your ego.

7. TELL THE TRUTH TO YOURSELF ABOUT YOURSELF

We all have something we are ashamed of or feel guilty about. Each of us has a clever method for disguising our "ugly ways." Undoubtedly, the day will come when you are forced to face the very thing you have tucked away. If you know what your weaknesses are, you will not be shocked when someone else tells you about them. It is a good practice to take yourself into account at the end of each day. Examine everything you have done and the motivations for your behavior. Tell yourself the truth about what you have done, what you are doing, and what you want to do. When you find that you have not lived up to your highest potential and greatest expectations, forgive yourself and others and make a commitment to improve yourself. You will discover that once you can deal honestly with yourself, those in your life will begin to live up to the same standard. The best part of telling yourself the truth about yourself is that once you do it and clean up your act, no one else has to know about it.

8. KNOW YOUR PURPOSE

What is the purpose of your life? What have you come here to do? Everyone has a purpose, a spiritual mission that he or she must fulfill before leaving this life. When you are not on purpose, things do not go well in your life. There always seems to be something you want but cannot get. Nothing will satisfy the urge of your soul except the fulfillment of your purpose. Many people believe that what they want to do may not be what God wants them to do. God wants you to be happy. If planting trees, painting pictures, or playing drums makes you happy, do it. The presence of God in you will guide you to make the right decisions and help you learn how to make your purpose pay off for you. A word of caution: never do anything *just* for the money. Do what you love because you love it. Find the thing you are good at and learn how to do it in a way that serves and brings joy to other people. When you can do the thing you love to serve and bring joy to others, you will be on purpose.

9. SEE THE GOOD IN EVERYONE AND EVERYTHING

In this life, we are always teaching and learning at the same time. There will be times when people come into your life and behave in a very unloving or ungodly manner. Usually, we take this very personally. When you are on the path of spiritual transformation, you can never be sure how your lessons will show up. In your interactions with others, always ask yourself, Am I teaching a lesson? Am I learning a lesson? Am I the object through which a lesson is being taught? Spirit will always respond. Once you understand the purpose of the experience, your encounters with even the most unpleasant people will become much more meaningful.

Supporting this theory, Dr. Johnnie Coleman, founder of Christ Universal Temple in Chicago, teaches, "Things don't just happen. They happen just." When we face disappointments, challenges, and obstacles, the first thing we ask is "Why me?" As Les Brown would say, "Why not you? Would you like to recommend that it happen to someone else?" Life is a series of lessons. No matter what shows up, there is a lesson to be learned. Why you? To increase your faith, strengthen your ability to endure, bring forth hidden talents and abilities. Why you? Because you need a little nudge now and then to keep you on track. Perhaps you have not been paying attention. Or maybe you have not been taking care of details. When unexpected, unpleasant events or people show up in your life, do not curse them; bless them and ask that what you need to know be revealed. It is your lesson. When you see your lesson, resist the urge to ignore it or make excuses for yourself. Remember, things always happen just as they should.

10. CONDUCT YOUR OWN INDEPENDENT INVESTIGATION OF TRUTH

God will meet you wherever you are. No one can tell you what is true, good, or right for you. Since we all have our own lessons to learn, we all grow at different rates and achieve different levels of understanding at various times. Things that did not make sense to you five years ago may be perfectly clear today. Things that make no sense today will become clear with the passage of time. Learn to examine everything. Learn to read the symbolic messages of life and nature. Investigate the events in your life by first turning within and then examining the external world. Spirit will bring you to as much clarity and understanding as you can handle right where you are. One small thing you may want to keep in mind is that the truth is consistent. It will not change with the passage of time. Investigate what you hear and what you want to know by identifying the consistencies.

11. LIVE IN BALANCE

Dr. Dennis Kimbro, author of *Think and Grow Rich: A Black Choice*, teaches that success is a six-pointed star: peace of mind, health and energy, loving relationships, financial freedom and independence, worthy goals and ideals, and a sense of meaning and purpose. The only way to achieve these six ideals is to pay attention to every aspect of your life. In chapter 11 we reviewed balance. You must accept nothing less than 100 percent for yourself in your life. Mediocrity is poison—half-doing, doing half, having half done, having under half done, doing for nothing, doing with nothing, getting nothing done—the kind of energy that eventually kills the spirit. If you are not in balance, you will not find peace, purpose, or satisfaction.

12. HONOR YOUR WORD BY DOING WHAT YOU SAY YOU WILL DO

Nothing more quickly undermines and erodes the sense of Self than not honoring what you say you will do. It is a vicious cycle. You say you are going to do something. You do not do it. Because you feel bad about not doing it, you lie about why you did not do it. Then you feel bad about lying. Whenever you see the person you disappointed and lied to, you embellish the story, going deeper into the explanation of why you did not do it in the first place. Then you feel bad about lying again. Why not honor your word?

If for some reason you change your mind, let the person know. Renegotiate your agreement. There are times when we make a commitment with very good intentions. When the time rolls around to fulfill the commitment, we may not feel like doing it. Tough! Do it anyway. Or we may think something else is more important. Wrong. Why did you make another commitment if you already had one? If you are unable to fulfill your commitment, tell the truth. Forgetting is never an acceptable excuse when this society chops down thousands of trees a year to make paper. Write it down! It is important for your self-esteem and balance in life to tell the truth and honor your word.

13. RELINQUISH THE NEED TO BE RIGHT

I once thought I could not write. I was wrong, however. Had I held on to believing I was right, you would not be holding this book in your hands. There is no right. There is no wrong. There just is. Everyone views life from where he or she is, which may not be where everyone else is, or anyone else is. That does not make them right or wrong. It does not make you right or wrong. As long as you hold on to the need to be right, you will never move from the place you are in, mentally, emotionally, or spiritually. But then again, you could be right. Maybe where you are is exactly where you want to be.

WALKING YOUR TALK

There is a African American spiritual that says, "It's time to get ready to put on the long white robe." In Yoruba culture, we are taught that the white robe is your character, your *Iwa* (pronounced E-wa). When you wear white, you must be very careful of what you do. If not, you will soil your white robe. Obatala is the keeper of the white robe. He represents the universal principles of knowledge, patience, wisdom, humility, service, and wealth. The symbols for some of these principles are the elephant, with its deliberate strength and stability; the snail, a slow-moving creature that always reaches its destination; the monkey, one of the most intelligent animals known, who is also devoted to the family; and the chameleon, who is able to adapt to any environment in which it is found but never loses its essence.

The white robe also makes you conscious of your environment and how you behave at all times. If you make a wrong move in the wrong direction, you will be seen. If you move carelessly or hastily, you run the risk of soiling your white robe. Black men are being called upon not to allow the ways of the world to continue to soil your white robe, your character. Using spiritual principles as the guiding forces in your life enables you to develop a strong character, woven in the traditions of those powerful men in your lineage who first discovered the existence of life principles. As you develop pride in your robe, you will find yourself growing closer to the peace and love of God within you.

Principles are of little or no value unless you put them into practice. It does not matter what you know if that information does not in some way make you a better person. In order to demonstrate your understanding of the knowledge you gain, you will be called upon to take action. Action is focused, which makes it very different from *doing*. Many of us get stuck in the action phase. A friend of mine calls it "analysis paralysis," the phenomenon of becoming so bogged down by what to do and how to do it that you do nothing. This too is a function of ego. When you decide to take charge of your own transformation, your ego is going to fight you. The ego realizes that if you get clear and discover your true connection to God, ego is out of a job. It will show up as your own resistance. You might convince yourself that you are comfortable with the way things are rather than admit to being afraid that a new way won't work. The need to know everything and the desire to be in control do not help matters either. For those who may face this challenge, the next steps are offered. These are stepping-stones, additional guidelines to assist you on the journey to greater insight and deeper understanding.

DAILY SPIRITUAL SCHEDULE

If you have been following the daily minimum requirement, you are now ready to begin a regular spiritual-life regime. By incorporating into your life all the principles and practices explored, you have the ingredients for a well-balanced spiritual diet. Offered here are two daily schedules: one for beginners, the other for more advanced practitioners. Feel free to change the starting time to meet your needs. You can also interchange the exercises given here with others you may know or are already practicing. If you read a particular sacred text, by all means incorporate that practice into the schedule. Do as little or as much as you are comfortable with. The soul is like a muscle. It must be exercised regularly to gain strength. The key is to do something consistently and persistently. It is called *commitment*.

Beginners' Morning Schedule

Step One—5:30 A.M. Immediately upon waking, walk to the nearest window and open it as wide as possible. (During the cold season, you can wear a robe or sweatshirt.)

Standing before the window, take seven to ten deep breaths as described in chapter 5.

Stand silently and allow your breath to return to normal again.

Step Two—5:35 A.M. Standing before your ancestral altar, recite the Ancestral Prayer and invoke the ancestors on your list. If you have chosen not to create an ancestral altar, move to the next step.

Perform the head-blessing ceremony outlined in chapter 4.

Step Three—5:45 A.M. Recite the Affirmation for Empowerment.

(*Note:* If you wish to read from the Bible, Koran, or other sacred text, do it immediately after you recite the Affirmation for Empowerment.)

Step Four—5:50 A.M. Sitting in a comfortable but firm straight-back chair or sitting cross-legged on the floor, do the Balancing Breath exercise outlined in chapter 5. Do four repetitions on each nostril.

Allow your breath to return to normal.

Next you will do two repetitions of the Meditative Breath exercise.

Allow your eyes to remain closed and begin your meditation.

Step Five—6:00 A.M. You may first want to pray silently for yourself and your family, using whatever words come to mind or a prayer from a sacred text. If you need support or guidance about a particular situation, ask for it now in prayer.

Another good way to begin meditation is to ask a question of a spiritual nature. For example, Who am I? What is my soul's purpose? How can I serve the universe better? Who or what is God? Or you may want to contemplate a spiritual principle such as peace, love, truth, honor, joy. In this case, mentally repeat the word or question as many times as you can until your mind starts to wander. Once it does, listen to your thoughts.

You may want to use music to help you keep track of time. Using a very soft instrumental selection or a selection that has particular meaning to you, allow it to play during your meditation. When it stops, allow yourself to slowly evolve from the meditative state. First, wiggle your fingers and toes. Next, slowly move your head from side to side. Slowly open your eyes and allow them to adjust to the light before you move.

Step Six—6:15 A.M. Select a principle from the Spiritual Transformation chart in chapter 2. Read the explanation and the keyword.

Copy the affirmation onto an index card that you will keep with you throughout the day.

Make a commitment to incorporate this principle into your daily activities. It is advisable to practice one principle for seven days before selecting another. Of course, you can work with two principles at once if you choose. A word of caution, though: Be gentle with yourself. Don't push yourself by attempting to do too much. That is the ego setting you up for defeat.

Repeat and contemplate the affirmation at regular intervals throughout the day, such as for three to five minutes once an hour or every other hour, before all meals, and so on.

If you want additional support, write the keyword down and keep it where you can see it. You can also look it up in the dictionary and incorporate the definition into your practice of the principle.

Throughout the day, live, breathe, and act out the principle. Become the embodiment of that word for the next seven days.

Step Seven—6:30 A.M. Begin and have a blessed day.

Beginners' Evening Schedule

(You will need a notebook and a pencil every evening.)

Step One—10:30 P.M. Standing before an open window, take seven to ten deep breaths.

Allow your breathing to return to normal.

Do four repetitions of the Balancing Breath on each nostril.

Allow your breathing to return to normal.

Step Two—10:40 P.M. Sitting in a quiet place, mentally recount the events of the day. What did you do? What did you eat? How did you incorporate the principle into your activities? When did you forget to incorporate or act upon the principle? Who was involved? What did you do? What did the other person or people say?

Step Three—10:45 P.M. Using only ten to fifteen words in a sentence, write down all the events in which you were able to practice the principle. Next, write down those occasions when you violated the principle, noting who was involved. Also note how close the event was to the time before or after you had eaten. Check your meal content for sugar, caffeine, white-flour products, and meat. You will begin to notice a pattern in several days. You may want to limit your intake of those products.

Step Four—10:50 P.M. Write the following Forgiveness Decree ten times for yourself and ten times for each of the people with whom you encountered difficulty during the day. If you do not have a name, use the word *everybody*.

I *Your Name* forgive myself for all violations of universal principle. I forgive myself totally and unconditionally.

I *Your Name* forgive *Name/everybody* totally and unconditionally. I now claim the truth as the presence in the midst of you.

Step Five—11:10 P.M. Spend five to ten minutes in silent prayer, self-affirmation, or contemplation of a spiritual principle.

You are now ready to retire for the day. A good friend of mine once told me that the key to a peaceful mind and good health is to go to bed the same day you woke up. Try it!

Advanced Morning Schedule

Follow steps one, two, and three of the Beginners' Schedule.

Step Four Do eight to twelve repetitions of the Balancing Breath, followed by two repetitions of the Pituitary Breath. Complete the breathing exercise with four repetitions of the Meditative Breath.

Step Five Begin your meditation by opening your eyes. Gently (do not force), raise your eyes into an upward position, as if you are trying to see your eyebrows.

Holding your eyes in this position, mentally affirm, "I Am!" If your eyes become strained, allow them to close while you continue the affirmation until your mind trails off. Ten minutes is usually enough time.

If you have prayer beads, use them to repeat the affirmation 108 times.

Follow steps six and seven from the Beginners' Schedule.

Follow all the steps of the Beginners' Schedule.

In exercising the Forgiveness Decree, you will write the decree twenty-one times rather than ten. Each week you will increase your writing by three (week 1, twenty-one repetitions; week 2, twenty-four repetitions; and so on) until you are writing each decree thirty-five times. When there are no other people involved, continue to write the decree for yourself.

It is recommended that beginners spend seven consecutive days with each principle. When you have completed all the principles, you can begin the Advanced Schedule.

Resist the urge to compete with yourself. Participate in these exercises because you want to, not because you have anything to prove. Remember, you cannot cheat Spirit. If you miss a day, you must begin the cycle over. And do not skip steps. Do what you are comfortable doing, but once you set the routine, complete the entire routine. Feel free to delete or add on whatever you have made a part of your life, such as physical exercise or fasting. Transformation is a process of growth. Growth takes time. What is more important than giving time to your own transformational growth process?

THERE IS STRENGTH IN NUMBERS

One of the most poignant memories of my childhood is of my father, his best friend, Mr. Rootman, and several of their acquaintances sitting in the living room on Sunday evenings hooting and hollering. Their conversations ranged from screaming-and-shouting matches to quiet, almost scared discussions to which no one else in the house was privy. Those men took care of one another. Whenever my father got arrested, Mr. Rootman or Mr. Johnny would call and make sure we had something to eat. Whenever my brother and I were around them, they loved and scolded us as they would their own children. I did not know it then, but those men had a support network.

Support groups are a necessary element on the spiritual journey. A sister-friend of mine calls them swap meets—coming together to swap ideas, information, challenges, money, and whatever else is needed to ensure the survival and evolution of every member of the group.

Women support one another naturally. They meet over coffee, on public transportation, and in offices around the country to talk about children, men, their challenges. Women are also more prone to pick up the telephone and call out for support.

Black men need to nurture and support one another if the entire community of Black men is to survive. You must hold one another up, pull one another up, and keep one another on "the good foot" in the areas of your life in which men are challenged. Men must talk to one another about parenting, about the women in their lives, about their fears and aspirations. Black men need to mother one another. That is, to teach, support, encourage, and love yourselves healthy.

Black male support groups should not be based on the traditional European psychosocial model, where people come together to discuss their problems and fix one another. Brothers who come together must do so based on the premise that there is nothing wrong with you. Your goal is to support one another in confronting the challenges you face in learning your individual and collective lessons as men, in order to evolve mentally, emotionally, and spiritually. You must come together to heal the effects of the miseducation, spiritual separation, and emotional battering you have experienced. In the sharing of experiences, ideas, and information, groups of Black men will be able to influence the entire community.

In order to heal, Black men must question every value, philosophy, and ideal they now hold to be true. You must be willing to challenge your own opinions and view your experiences from a spiritual rather than a logical perspective. This is a difficult task in confrontational or combative venues such as the workplace or an educational setting. In support groups, however, where Black men can come together to share, explore, and expand their collective and individual ideas without vying for leadership, comparing educational achievements, or competing for status, and without regard for economic holdings, the energy is bound to enlighten the members. When you can step out in the world knowing there are four, five, or ten other men you can call on to support and assist you unconditionally, you can move out of the anger of isolation into the strength of unity. A primary motivation for the gathering of Black men in supportive groups must be to explore, expand, and evolve your understanding and practice of unconditional love for yourselves, Black women, and the African American community as a whole.

BUILDING BLOCKS

There is nothing new under the sun. Everything that has been done, has been done. Your experiences are not new in the universe; they are new to you. You must trust in the fact that there is an answer for the experiences you face. Hundreds of thousands of ancestors have walked these same roads in another time and place. The insight those ancestors have is invaluable. You can tap into the power of these beings with communal ancestor worship. You can draw upon the power and wisdom of those who have walked the path before you by establishing a Board of Life Directors.

A Board of Life Directors is an altar, shrine, corner of the living room with pictures and artifacts of the powerful Black men and women who lived before you and paved a way for you. Nat Turner, the courageous soldier; Frederick Douglass, the powerful orator; Marcus Moziah Garvey, the statesman and organizer; Chaka Zulu, the battle strategist; Malcolm X, the disciplined and astute leader and teacher; Dr. Martin Luther King, Jr., the peacemaker. As well as your great-uncle Amos and others. These can all be influential energies, ready and available to guide and assist you.

If you should decide to establish a board, don't forget to include women. These queens, mothers, sisters, and friends bring forth a powerful healing energy. Queen Nzinga, Harriet Tubman, Sojourner Truth, Madam C. J. Walker, Ida B. Wells are examples of powerful women who made mighty contributions to the lives of all people. Each of these women lived by a specific set of principles in pursuit of her life's mission. The spiritual energy these woman offer is sure to be a welcome addition to your unfolding consciousness.

When you are faced with a challenge, sit before the board and ask yourself, What would Marcus Garvey do if he were confronted with this situation? What did Frederick Douglass say about this or a similar situation he faced? How did Harriet Tubman conduct herself when faced with a challenge? How did the Honorable Elijah Mohammed say one should behave when confronted by a situation like this? What battle strategy would Chaka Zulu use to confront this situation? Principles do not change. The manner in which the principles play out and are employed merely appears to be different. These people, whether they are your family or your communal ancestors, lived by principles and philosophies that have been tried and tested. That information is available to you because we are all a part of one spiritual divine mind.

There is no reason to reinvent the wheel. If the wheel exists, the principles for its development exist. They exist in spirit. Rather than running around or running away from difficulties, you can direct the events in your lives by learning from and receiving guidance from the masters—those who have already lived and learned. A Board of Life Directors need not be elaborate. It can be pictures on a poster board. You can meditate with the photographs and tap into the energy. It can be quotes written on index cards. There are power and wisdom in the written and spoken word. It can be an entire room filled with pictures, quotes, books, and other things you have gathered to remind you that somebody has been confronted with this situation before. If they knew what to do, you will know what to do. In honoring communal ancestors by incorporating into your life the principles they used to move through life, you can develop the greatest survival tool available to any living being: the value and insights of wisdom. With the wisdom of those who paved the way guiding you, you cannot fail.

Atonement

Dear Damon,

I have received your most recent letter and I was very glad to hear from you. I have not blocked your collect calls. I have not been paid for quite some time and I do not have a telephone. I am thankful for this time to *be still* and listen to my own thoughts. I recognize that you have grown a great deal and believe you have made great strides in your personal development, but it still feels to me that there are many things you do not understand. I am sure you have an idea that my financial situation is not the best it could be right now, yet you write asking me to do something for you. You and I both know the amount of money you have had, have wasted, and did not save for a rainy day. This is why I am so amazed that when you need, you have no qualms about asking me, no matter what my situation may be. I guess that is what sons believe mothers are for. It does not, however, make me feel good.

Every day, I pray for you. I pray for your enlightenment and your growth. I ask God to touch you right where you are and bring your heart and mind into alignment with his will for you. I pray that you will become one with God and the spirit of God within you. I know that prayer can get into places I cannot reach. I know that prayer can straighten out situations I do not understand. I guess I need to pray a little harder and a little longer for you.

I spent $22.00 to buy the book you asked me to buy. I spent another $2.90 to send it to you. I am not responsible if the corrections department loses the book. Now, with my telephone off, no money to pay the rent, you want me to pay to photocopy the book and send it to you. That will not happen. I have sent you more than $100.00 worth of books in the last month, more than enough for you to read for the next year. Read them over and over again. Each time you read them, you will discover something new. You may even discover how to get the $25.00 you need to submit your college application. The time has come for you to do for yourself. You must learn how to figure things out and make them work for you. You must pray and ask for guidance.

I am happy that you are studying with the brothers; however, being a Muslim, a Christian, or anything else means absolutely nothing if it does not help you find a better way to live. If your chosen faith does not open your mind to the great possibilities of life, it means absolutely nothing. I know that while you are in prison, reading helps you pass the time. The issue is, how is it going to help you when you get out if you are still thinking the same way, feeling the same way, acting the same way? You do not need God or Allah to keep you where you are. You want the Creative Force of the Higher Consciousness to move you to a new place in your mind and heart.

I was quite shocked to read in your letter "A divorce would crush me" and "I want for my daughter what I did not have, two parents." The fact of the matter is, you are already divorced. You do not live with your wife. You do not support your wife. You have broken your marriage vows by being unfaithful and not fulfilling your responsibilities as a husband: "To love, honor, and obey." The fact that your wife uses your name, if she does, and the fact that you exchanged vows do not mean a thing. Where is the honor? You have not honored her. She does not honor you, "in sickness and in health." Right now, you are in a state of "sickness"; where is your wife? "For richer for poorer"; aren't you poor in spirit and finances right now? Where is your wife? And where were you when she needed you? You cannot correct a wrong, Damon. You can learn a lesson, ask for forgiveness, and move on. You cannot build for your daughter what you did not have, because that may not be what she needs. You can give her what you have, with the best intentions and unconditional love. It will be up to her to accept or reject what you give her.

The truth of the matter is, you have always had two parents. I have always been your mother. Wayne has always been your father. You have always known where I was. You have always known who and where Wayne was. We may not have lived together, but you have *always* had a father. You had Grandpa. You had Charles. You had Ernest. You had Everard. They were not your biological fathers, but they were there for you when your father was not. You must accept your blessings however they come. You have always had a man in your life. Charles, as bad as he treated me, never let you children be without everything you needed. You had a home. You had food. God knows, you had clothes. While you were growing up, there was nothing you needed that you did not have. It was not until you were sixteen that things got bad for us. Think about it. What did you ever do without? You were eating shrimps for lunch when you were five years old. There was always a man to play with you, nurture you, and support you. A male presence was there for you at the worst of times. They treated you the same way they treated their own children; in some cases, you were treated better. It is unfortunate that when they left me, they also left you. I always asked them to speak to you. They chose not to.

Now if you are saying that you wanted "your father" in the house, that is a different issue. Knowing the kind of person your father is, tell me what difference would it have made for him to be in the house? He has proved himself to be irresponsible, emotionally unavailable, selfish, and undependable. These are things you have discovered about him. You said, "He is and always has been out for himself." Is that the kind of father you wanted present? Is that the kind of man you would want me to live with? Would you have wanted me to go through life with your father, knowing what you now know about him? Think about it. When you love people, you want them to be happy, even when their happiness means you must make a sacrifice.

Your father left me when I was three months pregnant with you. He demonstrated that he did not respect me as a woman or as the mother of his son. He is not to blame nor is he at fault. The truth is, Damon, I did not respect myself. I did not know who I was or what I had come into this life to do. I was a sick, frightened young girl, with no guidance. I was looking for love in the bed. I was using my vagina instead of my head. There is no reason I should have had sex with anyone when I was sixteen years old. Your father and I did not have a relationship. We were not even boyfriend and girlfriend. I was looking for a daddy. He had a hard-on. It is really that simple. Why you chose, in your spirit, to come through our bodies is part of God's plan for you. If you want to know why, ask God. I realize it is not easy to accept certain things about your mother, but you must remember, I have not always been your mother. I came into this life with my own issues, challenges, and obstacles to overcome. When you came into my life, I was knee-deep in a pile of crap. Unfortunately, you had to walk through it with me. God knew that it would someday pay off for both of us.

Things happen in our lives so that we can learn from them. The reason I have had so many relationships that did not work is because I have always tried to build for you what I did not have—a family. It did not work because we have to do what we do because we want to do it, not because we are trying to make up for something else. My lesson in life was to live with what was given to me, see the good in it, and strive to do better. I spent most of my life trying to find the father I did not have growing up. I did not realize it at the time; however, I learned my lesson, and now you must learn yours.

Old eyes can see much better than young eyes. As parents, we often see what our children are doing and we want something better for them. Unfortunately, we do not always know how to say what we see, so we say the wrong thing. I have told you from the very beginning that your relationship with your wife was not built on a stable foundation. It always appeared as if she was using you to escape the unstable relationship she had with her mother. Perhaps what I should have said was, "Damon, I know our family life has not been what you wanted or needed; however, you can make your own life what you want it to be. If you want the best, you do not have to settle for less than the best." In your eyes, your wife was/is the best for you, but what are you comparing her to? The environments to which you have been exposed have not been the best. The people you have known have not been the best. How can you evaluate what is good or bad if you have only experienced mediocre?

I see what you are doing and have done because my eyes are sixteen years older than yours. I am not saying that things will not work out for you and your wife; that I do not know. What I am saying is, at twenty-three years old, your eyes are still closed. When you have spent more than seventeen of those years in my house, looking at life through my eyes, and another almost three years in and out of prison, how many years have you really used your own eyes? And when you did use your eyes, what did you see? Quick ways to make money and break the law. Ways to make yourself feel important in violation of man's law and God's law. You are still blind to what life is really all about. The Bible says, "Eyes have not seen and ears have not heard what God has in store for those who love him." You are still blind to who you are and what God has in store for you.

If you think God made you to be "crushed" by a mere human woman, who comes from the same God you do, you cannot know God. How do you know why God brought you into this woman's life? Maybe you came to save her, to help her, to teach her a lesson. Now you want things to go the way you think they should go, not the way God planned. In the past, you were very good to your wife and her mother. Perhaps you were the tool God was using to help them out. When God's plan is fulfilled, you must move on to the next phase of the plan.

If you believe God brought your daughter onto this earth for "you" to take care of, you are not only blind, you are dumb. In *The Prophet* Kahlil Gibran wrote, "Your children are not your children. They are the sons and daughters of life searching for their own. They come through you but they are not from you. Although they are with you, they belong not to you." God has a divine plan for us all. Our job is to tap into the energy of God and bring ourselves into alignment with that plan. Sometimes things do not go the way we plan or the way we think they should go; that does not mean we are wrong or that God is wrong. It simply means we have to dig a little deeper, search a little harder to find the meaning, the lesson.

There are many things I wish I could have done for you and your sisters that I did not do. That is because I had my own blindness and sickness to heal. That does not mean I was wrong or bad. It simply means I had to work to get my eyes open. That did not happen for me until I stopped the *drama* of looking for a daddy, trying to *please Daddy* and make him proud of me. In all the time I spent doing that, I was trying to be who and what I was not. Not so long ago I stopped the drama and said, Okay, God, what am I supposed to be doing? At that point, my life totally fell apart.

You see, Damon, whatever is going on in your life comes from inside of you. Even my telephone being disconnected is an internal issue. All the negative thoughts and emotional garbage must be cleaned out before God can build a foundation inside us. When the stuff starts coming out, it looks like trouble; it looks like things are going bad; it looks like we are doing the wrong thing. Nothing could be farther from the truth. The truth is, when we go to God, he must tear us down in order to build us up. God cannot build upon our distorted ideas, foolish beliefs, miseducation, and misinformation. All of that must come out as conditions we live through, so that we can see what we have been thinking. When things go bad in our lives, we try to fix them because we don't realize God is fixing us. Until we see the bad stuff, we cannot make up our minds not to do the things that brought us to that point in the first place.

I am forty years old and I am just beginning to understand who I am and what God wants me to do. There are times when I doubt. That is when I pray. There are times when I am afraid. That is when I remember, "Fear not, for I am with you." There are times when I want to throw my hands up, go get a "real job" working for somebody else from nine to five, and say "Forget this crap!" Then I remember, "For everything, there is a season. A time to laugh and a time to cry." I have been crying for almost forty years. It is time for me to laugh. In order to laugh, I KNOW I must work through the crap, live with the bad, and have my eyes opened wide to the miracle of life called ME.

Right now, I want nothing more than a family, a home, and a man to love me, work with me, build with me, and share life with me. I do not want to raise any more children. I do not want to *suffer.* I do not want to be broke. I want to live my life to the fullest every day, enjoying every moment. I know that is about to happen. I also know, in the divine time and the divine way, it will happen. I am no longer willing to accept less than the best. I still make mistakes, but now when I do, my eyes are opened enough for me to say, Okay, that is a mistake, I cannot do that again. I catch myself in the process and change what I am doing.

You have always wanted to have your way. You have always wanted things to go the way you want them to go. When you get an idea in your head, you will not let it go. I remember how you would always say, "If it kills me, I will . . ." If you do not open your eyes soon, this thing with your wife and mother-in-law will kill you. It will kill your spirit. It will kill your mind. I know you have prayed and asked God to "show you." Well, I think he is showing you, but your eyes are closed. Your wife does not write, she does not send you money; her hair is more important than your coat. She makes absolutely no attempt to mend or heal your relationship. You continue to hold on and insist. Could it be that God is showing you who she really is? Could it be that you need to use your mother-in-law to excuse your wife for what she is doing? She married you without her mother's permission and against my advice. She knew you were selling drugs and stealing cars before her mother knew it. She knew that the two of you were not prepared and could not afford to have a baby. When she wanted you, she did exactly what her mother told her not to do. Now she is showing you she does not want you, and you want to blame her mother. Why? Because your eyes and ears are still closed. You are still blind and you are making yourself dumb.

After all that has happened between you and me, I am still here for you, doing what I can for you. That is my choice. I could have said to hell with you a long time ago. I did not because I am your mother, in good times and in bad, for richer for poorer. Parenting, like marriage, is *till death us do part*. That is what a relationship is about. You must take the good and the bad, do what you can, and pray for better. God is trying to tell you something, Damon. I think it would be wise for you to listen. I know it is not easy. I know you think you are right and it is not fair. I know you wish it was another way. Maybe one day it will be different; if God has it in the plan for you, it will be different. If you want so badly to be with the wrong person, imagine how wonderful it will be when the right person comes along. For right now, take your blinders off! Get off your knees! It is not a nine-to-five job. Prayer must begin in your heart. Remember, what you let go will come back to you if it is yours. And God never closes one door without opening another.

When I was pregnant with you, a very dear friend of mine offered to help me get an abortion. This was in 1970 when abortions were still illegal. I thought about it for a very long time, and I decided that was not what I wanted to do. Something inside of me knew, no matter what, I would make it and you would make it. When I looked in your little face, I knew I had made the right decision. You were a beautiful baby. You were never any trouble. You grew into a beautiful child who was not difficult to love or take care of. You are now a beautiful man. You are strong. You are healthy. You are a master! I used to be ashamed to say, "My son is in jail." I would lie about it and tell people you were away with your wife, who is in the navy. Now I want the world to know, because I know you are healing. As you heal, a part of me heals. When I think about it, I was in the prison of needing to be loved for almost forty years of my life. Now I know that I am love and that God loves me. I also know that God loves you, Damon, even when your wife isn't sure she does.

There are many types of jails, Damon. Some people are in the jail of their limited minds. Many people are in the jail of drinking alcohol, taking drugs, working a nine-to-five job they hate, or living in bad relationships. We are all doing some kind of time. The only difference is, some of us have keys to our cells and others do not. Nobody can imprison your mind but you. Nobody can imprison your spirit. My son was born of the Master and nobody makes a deal with the Master and loses!

I love you.

I support you.

I pray for your highest and your best.

13

STILL WATERS

The more spiritually enlightened you
become, the less politically depen-
dent you become.
    Minister Louis Farrakhan

Why would the average Black man want to open the can of spiritual worms? What do you stand to win? To lose? The answer to these questions hinges on your acceptance of the truth, which is that you are a spiritual being having a temporary physical experience. If you believe that, it stands to reason that your life, your existence, is governed by spiritual laws as well as physical laws. If you are a solid, upstanding citizen, doing all the things required of you, and your life is still not moving, going in the direction you would like, it may be that it is time for you to address your spiritual self. Even if your life is marvelous, wonderful, you may be searching for a deeper sense of peace, understanding, or purposefulness. In such cases, you too may be encouraged to look beyond the physical to the spiritual.

Black men are literally dying in the streets. Those of you who are not being shot are poisoning yourselves with drugs, foods, and alcohol. I see Black men dying in a hail of fear, confusion, hopelessness, and powerlessness. You must know it was not meant to be this way. You were born to be masters. You were born to have it all. You were born fully equipped with the grace of God and everything you need to make it through this life in one piece and in peace. What has happened to you? You, like the rest of the world, live in violation of the most sacred laws of nature, "Do unto others . . ." and "Seek ye first the kingdom . . ." You, like the rest of the world, have accepted the idea that human beings have the ultimate power over life and death. Even those of you who know that is not quite true cannot figure out why humankind has so much influence over the tides of your life. The answer is simple. Your spiritual memory has been shattered. You have forgotten you are a spirit. You are no longer at one with your Creator.

It is not easy to live in the physical world, tempted by physical lusts, and keep your mind focused on a higher consciousness of which you see no physical evidence. It is not a simple task to be among people who couldn't care less about your spirit, or God, or what that means. When you interact in the world, espousing spiritual concepts, people look at you as if you are crazy. They are attuned to the ways of the world. They always have a rational explanation for the things you try to explain from a spiritual perspective. The result is conflict. You may find yourself in conflict on your job, in your home, and in your relationships. It is not enough to know spiritual principles. You must know the law underlying the principles. It is not enough to breathe, pray, meditate, and rub crystals on your head. You must understand the metaphysical principles that dictate how and why such practices work. When you know the law, practice the law, trust in the law, it will work. It will create lasting and powerful changes in your mind and your life. Unfortunately, getting to the place of faithful, trusting patience is not an easy task.

What does a Black man who is at one with God and living according to spiritual law and principle look like? How is his life any better than yours? I think he looks like my godfather, a spiritually conscious man who knows he is an African for a spiritual purpose. He knows it from the core of his being and he lives his purpose. He does not ask for approval or acceptance. He does not have a need to defend himself or slander you. A spiritually conscious Black man has an air or an energy of blessed self-assurance and confidence. You can see it when you see him. He is not pushy or aggressive. He is not loud or aggressive. You probably do not see him often, out in the public, proclaiming his superiority. He is most probably humble, very quiet, slow-moving, and always willing and able to assist and support you.

A spiritually conscious Black man expressing the heritage of his ancestors and at one with his Creator is not stressed out. He is not frenzied about or frazzled by the ways of the world. He goes about his tasks, working, building, teaching, in a quiet but dignified manner. When he speaks to you, his words penetrate your being, and you know he is speaking his truth. He knows things. You don't know how he knows them, but he does. And when he speaks to you about the things he knows, it opens your mind to an entirely new level of thinking. A spiritually conscious Black man is still "one of the boys." He tells good jokes and laughs at your funny stories. When he is in the group, however, the energy is different; the conversation is directed, more meaningful. He is teaching and learning at the same time. He does not criticize you but is always able to offer you another way of looking at things. He may get hot under the collar and sometimes angry, but he is able to apologize and ask for forgiveness once he recognizes his mistakes.

A spiritually conscious Black man who is at one with his Creator and knows that he is an African stands on principle. He does not look for shortcuts or the easy way out. He is willing to do whatever is necessary, whenever necessary, to achieve his desired goal. The quality of his intent is always to achieve the best possible outcome for the good of all involved. He has personal goals, needs, and desires, but he is willing to put them aside, delay his own personal satisfaction, to ensure that whatever group he is in moves ahead collectively. A spiritually conscious African man may not be wealthy. He is certainly not flashy or fancy. He has exactly what he needs; he never worries about how he will get it; and more often than not, he has enough to share with you if you need it. He does not believe in lack, restriction, or limitation. He recognizes the universe as an abundant, benevolent, user-friendly environment to which he always has immediate access through a peaceful mind and stillness of heart. Through self-imposed periods of stillness, he is empowered with a sense of oneness with his Creator.

Who is this spiritually conscious African man? Where is he? He is you. Just look in the mirror and you will connect with the spark of divinity in your soul. So much has been done to you to take you off track. That is all in the past now. As of this day, at this very moment, you have all that is required to move beyond the past into the newness of now. There is nothing holding you back other than your unwillingness to accept and believe in yourself. It may not make much sense to you. Your ego will bring to mind all sorts of counterarguments, reasons to question and dismiss the fact that you are powerful. Don't fall prey to that old trick again! You can stay right where you are, doing exactly what you are doing, if that makes you happy. If it does not, if you want to do more, be more, have more, you will have to exercise your faith. You will have to trust yourself. You will have to trust in the presence of God in you. You will need to develop a consciousness of oneness with God and live in that place "twenty-four-seven."

People are not going to like it when you begin to change, when you surrender yourself to Spirit and become one with God. Even those who love and care about you will become frightened. They want you to stay the same because that is the way they know you. They have no idea what you are about to become, and they will be afraid of losing you. Do not worry about it. Those who are destined to be in your life will be there. They will love you, support and assist you through your metamorphosis. You are going to lose some people and some things. As you grow, those things that are no longer useful to you, no longer necessary for your highest and greatest good, will fall away. You will be tempted to hold on. Your ego will tell you that you are losing control. Tell your ego to SHUT UP! You do not need any more advice from the energy that has kept you where you do not want to be. Your ego is ever so willing to tell you what will not work; how often does it give you information that does work?

There are some questions that will come to mind as you begin or further your spiritual journey. *How do I know if I am doing it right?* That's your ego again, tempting you to doubt yourself. There is no one way, one formula, one standardized approach to spiritual enlightenment. As a matter of fact, the worst experience of your life may be the very thing that turns you on to a deeper understanding. If you have pure intent, make the effort to still your mind and ask the universe for guidance. In time, everything you need will come to you: the right teacher, the necessary information, and confidence in what you are doing. *How do I blend my cultural beliefs and my spiritual discipline?* Be careful not to invent things. There are a number of people who are self-proclaimed this, that, or the other in the name of being African. A wealth of information is available on the customs, cultures, and spiritual heritage of African people. You can research the particular culture that appeals to you. You can ask questions of those you know adhere to the principles of that culture. You can pray and ask the ancestors to take you where you should be. You do not have to make things up or follow others who have made them up.

What can I expect once I begin to live a more spiritually conscious life? Change. Everything will begin to change. How you feel, the way things look, how things sound will all change. Things that were once very important to you will no longer be that way. People you once thought were the cat's meow will not be able to get near your milk bowl. As you expand your consciousness, your understanding will evolve and everything around you will change. *As a Black man, are my spiritual practices different from those of other people?* Yes and no. Spirit is spirit. It will affect different people in different ways, based on who they are and their level of development. As a Black man, you are governed by the same spiritual laws and principles as the rest of the world. Because of your cellular ancestral memory, however, you will express your knowledge in a manner unlike other people. Keep in mind that no one is right, no one is wrong; everyone is uniquely divine.

In completing this work I realized two things. The first is that this work is absolutely necessary. The second is that this work is totally unnecessary. It is necessary because I have seen no concentrated effort, outside the church, to present Black men in America with the process required for spiritual evolution. Religion has failed you miserably in this area. Many things churches have been doing in blackface represent the very cultural bias that offends the ancestral energy moving through your veins. Somehow, many Black women have been able to see through this and break through the veils to reach the true essence of spirituality. The same is not true for Black men. You have been stuck in a religious and life process that promotes being in charge, being in control, being better than and getting more than somebody else. That is not the African way. The African way is evolution of the individual for the salvation of the whole group. The African way is flexible. It is designed to meet the needs of the individual *and* the group while working in harmony with the laws of nature.

Spirituality is not anything that you do; it is what you are. You are that by divine right. Not because you have a degree or because you run a church. Spirituality is not broken down into denominations, groups, sects, or cults. No one can ordain you to be a spiritual being. I believe there are many men who have been "called" to do the work of God. I do not believe, however, that they are all in the church. If God calls you to serve him, why do you need a degree, credentials? Did the people who are authorizing you to serve hear what God said to you when he called you? Some Black men have become trapped in the credentialization of the Holy Spirit. You use the Bible as a weapon. If you know what the Bible says, welcome to the club. If you do not, you are damned to hell. This line of thinking does not take into account the many ancient holy works that guided humanity for centuries before the Bible was written. It does not take into account the specialization of Spirit as evidenced in 1 Corinthians 12:4, "Now there are diversities of gifts, but the same Spirit." This line of thinking also frightens too many Black men who want to know and understand the nature of their own souls. For those Black men who do not embrace the text, the traditions, and the rituals of the orthodox religion, what do you do? Where do you go?

It is for that reason that a book like this is necessary. Something must be done to give those hundreds of thousands of Black men who are not in the church a place to be in their spiritual lives. There is a spiritual life beyond books and choirs and committees. There is a spiritual purpose underlying the experiences of Black men. No one book, one way, or one person has the answer. It is my hope that this work will inspire you to seek the truth of God for yourselves. I realize I have expressed some ideas that will offend some people. Hopefully, we will have the opportunity to discuss the different roads to God. If not, I am sure they will get over it. Others will determine that I have lost my mind. The truth is, I am in the process of finding my mind. For those who are vigilantly searching for the same light, you may find the spark you need to get on the path. For that I am grateful.

The reason this work is totally unnecessary is that you do not need anything to get to that place of God within yourself. A book will not take you there. No lecture, seminar, or workshop will open that door. That place is in your heart. When you find it, you will transcend every experience, every tidbit of information, every thought you have ever had. When you find God right in the center of your being, it will literally "blow your mind"! It is much like the song "You Are My Friend," sung by Patti LaBelle, "I've been looking around and You were here all the time." All you need to get to God is a sincere desire and the expectation that you *will* get there.

For some, the theories presented in this work will seem too easy. "If it ain't hard, it ain't Black." We have become so addicted to struggling, when the way is easy we are suspicious, and we do not want it. As simple as it sounds, the truth is, the moment your decide that you are a spiritual being and begin to conduct your affairs in a spiritual manner, you will have astounding spiritual experiences. To this, I can testify. Realizing that far too many Black men have absolutely no idea what it means to be spiritual, I have followed the guidance of my spirit to present this work. I trust it will assist and support you on your journey inward. When the door opens and the truth begins to pour forth from you into the world, I ask you to do one thing: thank God, who alone is wise. Do not give me the praise. All I did was show up.

Once again I must remind you that when you invite Spirit into your life, there will be good days and bad days. Remember to stay centered. There will be challenges, which will force you to stretch and reach beyond your comfort zone. Trust the presence of God in you to protect and guide you. There will be situations in which you feel that you simply do not know what to do. Turn to the Board of Life Directors; call upon the ancestors. You may experience periods of isolation, of being alone. This is a sacred aloneness. It is a time and opportunity for you to learn your sacred lessons, receive divine insight. Throughout your process, you must carefully monitor your thoughts and emotions. When you find yourself thinking, feeling, or behaving in a way you know is counterproductive, put yourself in check. Do a new thing.

As you begin to transform and grow, you will be called upon to share your information. Don't be afraid. Spirit will send to you those you are to teach and will send you to those who will teach you. Be conscious of setting attainable goals for your spiritual quest. To be the best you that you can be is quite enough. When you start getting into chasing money, being famous, showing other people who you are and what you can do, know that you are headed for trouble. Stay humble. Always be willing to grow. Practice surrender of everything you now know and want. As your spiritual quest intensifies, your needs and wants will change as you do. Know that you are guided. Know that you are protected. Know that you are loved. God is depending on you. So is the world.

Ache! Ache! Ache!

GLOSSARY

*If you made it through the past, then
you passed!*   *Sun* RA

The terms and principles in this glossary are presented from a spiritual or metaphysical (beyond the physical) frame of reference, and as explanations rather than definitions. In some cases, what is offered may seem to be in conflict with or opposition to the intellect, the rational mind, and the dictionary. For additional research and inquiry, please refer to the following texts:

The Metaphysical Bible Dictionary. Unity Village, MO: Unity Books, 1931.
Filmore, Charles. *The Revealing Word.* Unity Village, MO: Unity Books, 1959.
Holmes, Ernest. *The Dictionary of New Thought Terms.* Marina Del Rey, CA: DeVross & Co., 1942.

SPIRITUAL TERMS AND PRINCIPLES

Acceptance: To know from within the self that all is well, even when you do not see or understand how it will turn out.

Accountability: Considering all actions as creative causes for which you must answer to a higher authority.

Affirmation: A statement spoken and accepted as truth.

Aggression: Pushing, forcing, moving against the natural or visible flow.

Alignment: Being in one accord, in harmony and balance with the flow of divine energy. Cooperation with the tangible and intangible energy of life.

Anger: Control mechanism of the ego. The emotional reaction to not having your way, or not having people and events meet your expectations.

Atonement: To become one. Alignment with the divine within the self.

Awareness: Intuitive knowledge. Ability to recognize and harness the spirit of truth in action.

Balance: Having and making time, or spending energy and time attending to all areas and aspects of life.

Belief: A mental and emotional acceptance of an idea as truth.

Blame: Holding external forces accountable for inner or physical well-being.

Change: A shift or movement in the flow of life. The outgrowth of the natural course of events.

Character: The composite makeup of mental, emotional, and spiritual traits that form the nature of your being. Level of integrity. Basic essence of a person. What you psychologically and emotionally rely upon, stand upon, look to, hold on to within yourself.

Christ: A state of consciousness that is the principle of God within man. The divine state of living reached through a spiritualized consciousness. The perfect word or idea of God, which unfolds into true being and an awareness of eternal life.

Commitment: The alignment of thoughts and emotions focused upon a goal or desire. Willingness to pursue. Unwavering focus, giving all you have to offer in pursuit of a desired course of events.

Compassion: The ability to see error without condemnation. An open and understanding heart able to offer love, mercy, and truth.

Confidence: Trust in self or another and the ability of self or another to manifest truth as a reality.

Consciousness: The totality of ideas accumulated in the mind that affects the state of being. A composite framework of beliefs, thoughts, emotions, sensations, and knowledge that feeds the conscious and subconscious mind.

Courage: Freedom from fear. The ability to be, stand, in the presence of anxiety, danger, or opposition. Stepping beyond the boundaries where you are psychologically, emotionally, or physically safe, or with which you are familiar, comfortable, and secure. A test of character.

Discernment: The ability to lay hold of truth. To see beyond appearances to that which is obscure and hidden but divine.

Decree: To command with spiritual and emotional authority. Words charged with the power of faith and truth, which produce and increase with usage and time.

Ego: The small, tiny voice that allows us to believe that we are separate from God. As the foundation of fear, a synonym for ego is easing God out, which leads to the belief that *your* way is *the* way.

Evolution: The calling to a higher order. Development achieved by adherence to spiritual law. The unfolding of natural events according to the divinely ordained spiritual plan.

Freedom: A mental and emotional construct. The ability to know and live truth. The ability to choose. A state of being without thought of confinement, restraint, limitation, or oppression. Having a sense of inner well-being that manifests in the outer world.

God: The substance of life. The supreme energy of mind. The life, power, spirit, presence, activity of truth. The father/mother principle that creates and sustains all life.

Grace: The saving, redeeming, transforming power that comes to man from God. Goodwill and favor unto humanity from God as a sign of mercy that leads to regeneration.

Healing: Restoration to a natural state of being. A state of oneness with God. Belief in, openness to, receptivity of the presence of God as spirit.

Humility: Willingness to serve without expectation of reward or recognition. Making room for the Holy Spirit, God's spirit, to express through you. Acknowledging God as the giver and doer of all things.

Illumination: Divinely inspired understanding. The ability to see beyond all physical manifestations to the spiritual principle as an active presence.

Instinct: The voice of Spirit within your consciousness. The presence of the Holy Spirit withing your being, which guides and protects.

Meditation: To still the physical/conscious mind to all thought. Continuous, contemplative thought on truth. A steady effort of the mind to know and hear the voice of God from within the being. The act of "not doing" in order to expand the consciousness of the being.

Power: The energy of the Holy Spirit. The influence and authority of natural law and divine or universal principles in action. Inner strength leading to the ability to do or act.

Prayer: Communication with and consciousness of the divine presence within the being. The act of talking to God.

Principle: Truth in a universal sense as it pertains to God. The orderly working out of truth into expressions or manifestation. The underlying plan by which Spirit moves in expressing itself. The "I Am" presence within everything living. The formless source that gives birth to all.

Purpose: Actions that are in alignment with the will of God. The underlying cause that sustains life. Active pursuit of divine principle.

Reiki: A technique of laying on of hands that balances, revitalizes, and harmonizes the universal life force (*chi* or *ki*) that exists in all living things.

Spirituality: A state of thought directly linking the mind to the one creative cause of life. A state of consciousness that grows and unfolds through disciplined activity relating to spirit. The active awareness and acknowledgment of the presence of Spirit. (Spirit when capitalized is a name for God.)

Subconscious mind: The feminine aspect of mind. The mental recorder. Essence of being that is always active. The emotional/mental storehouse of all knowledge, experience, and perceptions.

Superconscious mind: The essence or presence of God within the being. The "I Am" principle of life. That which remains eternally connected to the divine.

Surrender: Psychological and emotional release. Acknowledgment of the power of spiritual activity. Obedience to spiritual principle, which evolves into an experience of peace and well-being. An act of acceptance.

Transformation: Change within the form, structure, condition, or nature of the being.

Transition: *See* change.

Truth: An aspect of God that is absolute and all-encompassing. The foundation of spiritual principle. That which is in accord with the divine principle of God as the creative source and cause. The immutable, everlasting word that is now, has been, will ever be eternally consistent.

Understanding: Comprehension of the truth and spiritual principle. Integration of intellectual and spiritual knowledge.

Wisdom: Intuitive knowing and spiritual intuition. The voice of God within the being as the source of understanding and action. The ability to act in accordance with knowledge and principle.

BIBLIOGRAPHY

Akbar, Na'im. 1984. *Chains and Images of Psychological Slavery.* Jersey City, NJ: New Mind Productions.

———. 1991. *Visions for Black Men.* Tallahassee, FL: Mind Productions and Assoc.

———. 1995. *Natural Psychology and Human Transformation.* Tallahassee, FL: Mind Productions and Assoc.

Alder, Vera Stanley. 1968. *The Finding of the Third Eye.* York Beach, ME: Samuel Weiser.

Chia, Mantak. 1988. *Taoist Secrets of Love: Cultivating Male Sexual Energy.* Huntington, NY: Healing Tao Books.

Chopra, Deepak. 1990. *Magical Mind, Magical Body* (tape series). New York: Random House. New York: HarperCollins.

Cook, Maurice. 1981. *Dark Robes, Dark Brothers.* Toronto: Marcus Books, Hilarion Series.

Cunningham, Donna, and Andrew Ramer. 1988. *Further Dimensions of Healing Addictions.* San Rafael, CA: Cassandra Press.

deLubicz, Schwaller R. A. 1949. *The Temple in Man: Sacred Architecture and the Perfect Man.* Rochester, VT: Inner Traditions International.

Dyer, Wayne D. 1990. *You'll See It When You Believe It: The Way to Your Personal Transformation.* New York: Avon Books.

———. 1992. *Real Magic: Creating Miracles in Your Life.* New York: HarperCollins.

Fatunmbi, Fa'lokun. 1991. *Iwa-Pele/Ifa Quest.* New York: Original Publications.

———. 1992. *Awo: Ifa and Theology of Orisha Divination.* New York: Original Publications.

Filmore, Charles. 1949. *The Atom Smashing Power of the Mind.* Unity Village, MO: Unity Books.

———. 1949. *The Science of Mind: Basic Teaching of Religious Science.* Unity Village, MO: Unity Books.

Foundation for Inner Peace. 1975. *A Course in Miracles.* Tiburon, CA.

Gaer, Joseph. 1963. *What the Great Religions Believe.* New York: Penguin Books USA.

Goldsmith, Joel. 1958. *Practicing the Presence: The Inspirational Guide to Regaining Meaning and a Sense of Purpose in Your Life.* New York: HarperCollins.

Heider, John. 1985. *The Tao of Power.* Atlanta: Humanics New Age.

Holliwell, Raymond. 1964. *Working with the Law.* Phoenix: School of Christian Philosophy.

Karenga, Maulana. 1984. *The Husia: Sacred Wisdom of Ancient Egypt.* Los Angeles: University of Sankore Press.

Kelder, Peter. 1985. *Ancient Secret of the Fountain of Youth.* Gig Harbor, WA: Harbor Press.

Kimbro, Dennis. 1992. *Think and Grow Rich: A Black Choice.* New York: Fawcett Books.

———. 1993. *Daily Motivations for African American Success.* New York: Fawcett Columbine.

Kinner, Willis. 1963. *The Thirty Day Mental Diet.* Marina Del Rey, CA: De-Vross & Co.

Madhabuti, Haki. 1991. *Black Men: Dangerous, Single, Obsolete.* Chicago: Third World Publishing.

———. 1994. *Claiming Earth: Race, Rage, Rape, Redemption, Blacks Seeking a Culture of Enlightened Empowerment.* Chicago: Third World Publishing.

Marciniak, Barbara. 1992. *Bringers of the Dawn: Teaching of the Pleidians.* Santa Fe: Bear & Co.

Mason, John. 1989. *Black Gods: Orisha Concepts in the New World.* Brooklyn, NY: Yoruba Theological Archministry.

Mbiti, John S. 1975. *Introduction to African Religion.* 2d ed. Portsmouth, NH: Heinemann Educational Books.

Millman, Dan. 1993. *The Life You Were Born to Live.* Tiburon, CA: H J Kramer.

Montapert, Alfred Armand. 1977. *The Supreme Philosophy of Man: The Laws of Life.* Los Angeles: Books of Value.

Moore, Thomas. 1992. *Care of the Soul: A Guide for Cultivating Depth and Sacredness in Everyday Life.* New York: HarperCollins.

Nobles, Wade. 1980. *African Psychology: Toward Its Reclamation, Reascension and Revitalization.* Oakland, CA: Black Family Institute.

Queen Afua. 1991. *Heal Thyself: Liberation Through Purification.* Brooklyn, NY: A&B Books.

Ramcharaka, Yogi. 1905. *The Science of Breath.* Chicago: Yogi Publication Society.

Three Initiates. 1912. *The Kybalion: Hermetic Philosophy.* Chicago: Yogi Publication Society.

Tyndale House. 1971. *The Living Bible: Paraphrased.* Wheaton, IL.

Vanzant, Iyanla. 1991. *Tapping the Power Within: A Path to Self-Empowerment for Black Women.* New York: Harlem Readers & Writers.

———. 1993. *Acts of Faith: Daily Meditations for People of Color.* New York: Simon & Schuster, Fireside Books.

———. 1994. *The Value in the Valley: A Black Woman's Guide Through Life's Dilemmas.* New York: Simon & Schuster.

Yogananda, Paramahansa. 1944. *The Law of Success.* Los Angeles: Self-Realization Fellowship.

We invite you

To become a member of

Inner Visions Spiritual Life Maintenance Network.

As a member you will receive information on:

Discounts on Inner Visions products, services, lectures, workshops, and retreats facilitated by Iyanla Vanzant and other Inner Visions staff members;

Access to Holistic and Spiritual practitioners nationwide;

Catalog of Inner Visions services and products;

Bimonthly activity update on activities and support groups in your area;

Access to the Inner Visions prayer line and support network.

Fill out and mail in your form today!

I would like to become a member of the Inner Visions Spiritual Life Maintenance Network:

Name _____

Mailing Address_____

City_____ State_____ ZIP_____

If you have a friend or family member who is incarcerated, you may enroll him/her in our prison ministry:

Name_____ ID #_____

Mailing Address_____

City_____ State_____ ZIP_____

Mail this form and all other inquiries to:

Inner Visions
Spiritual Life Maintenance
P.O. Box 3231
Silver Spring, MD 20918–0231

Don't Give Up Five Minutes Before the Miracle!